Films in the Classroom:
A Practical Guide

by

Hannah Elsas Miller

The Scarecrow Press, Inc.
Metuchen, N.J. & London
1979

Library of Congress Cataloging in Publication Data

Miller, Hannah Elsas, 1926-
Films in the classroom.

Filmography: p.
Includes bibliographies and index.
1. Filmstrips in education--Handbooks, manuals, etc. 2. Moving pictures in education--Handbooks, manuals, etc. 3. Television in education--Handbooks, manuals, etc. I. Title.
LB1043.8.M54 371.33'522 78-21941
ISBN 0-8108-1184-7

Manufactured in the United States of America

TABLE OF CONTENTS

Chapter 3: TYPES OF FILMS

Chapter 4: CHOOSING FILMS: PREVIEWING

Chapter 5: SECURING FILMS

Chapter 8: MAKING FILMS

APPENDIXES

ACKNOWLEDGMENTS

I would like to thank the following for the help they offered, whether directly or indirectly, in the writing of this book: Professor Dorothy Garey, Library Science Department, Southern Connecticut State College, New Haven; Leo Dratfield and Anne Schutzer for their help when I first began to review films; Lois Porro for her typing help; Marge Fischer and Barbara Arnold, librarians, for their suggestions; Joanna Foster and Richard Harmetz for checking some of the facts; and Kay Elsas Broughton for her invaluable editing help.

Last, but not least, many thanks to my husband and sons, who helped in many special ways and encouraged me to write this book.

H. E. M.

INTRODUCTION

This book is addressed to teachers and future teachers, librarians and future librarians, and to administrators and all those who select and buy films, and use them as part of their teaching. It is hoped that the book will be used in audiovisual courses in teachers' colleges and library schools, so that teachers and librarians will arrive on the job equipped to handle a multi-media approach to learning. The book is intended to help teachers integrate films and other non-print media into the curriculum, and to help those who use films feel more relaxed and competent in using and choosing hardware and software, and to feel free to venture into new ways of using them. Most of all it is hoped that the need for visual as well as verbal competency for students will be recognized by those in charge of the classroom and library, along with the need for using all the senses and many different approaches to teaching and reaching students.

The book discusses why and how to preview films, where and how to rent and buy them, and how to use films in many different, but active ways in the classroom. Sources of films, including free films, and the distributors of films, university film libraries, public libraries, state Education Department film collections, and periodicals and books that preview films are discussed. Examples of films are used throughout.

Although the book has information for the neophyte, it is hoped that those with some expertise will also find information they consider important. Film making, the use of video, and film study are not dealt with in any depth, since these topics have been covered by others better qualified in these areas. There are references given, however, to satisfy those interested in pursuing these specialties.

Studies have shown that there is a high correlation between training in the use of media and their use by class-

RED BALLOON, from Macmillan Films, Inc.

room teachers.[1*] We know that the availability of materials and teachers' awareness of it have a significant effect on the amount of utilization. In most schools there is a media dearth, and teachers find that when they want to use it, it is often not there. It appears that efforts must be made on the part of the administrators, librarians, and media specialists to involve teachers from all subject areas in selecting materials and communicating their availability. This communication must be a constant one. A "now-and-then" bulletin will not hold anyone's interest. Hoban found that the "attitude of teachers towards innovation, their skills in dealing with them and the persistence of established habits and thoughts and action, are often ignored."[2]

The need for in-service training programs on using media, as well as in the operation of the equipment on which it is shown, has been demonstrated. Some teachers feel guilty about using films, others feel threatened by the "intru-

*Footnotes to the Introduction begin on page xiv.

sion" of non-print media into their classroom. There are still teachers who have some fear about using the equipment, all of which clearly show that training is necessary.

More emphasis is needed in teachers education courses on the value of non-print media, and how to incorporate it in classroom instruction in areas where no other media will do as well. More help should be offered in colleges and universities on the "where," "how," "when," and "what" of media usage.

Administrators who are knowledgeable about the value of media and are supportive of teachers who use it are most helpful. Unfortunately, some teachers must teach in schools where administrators resist change and dampen the enthusiasm of those who would like to try newer methods. The converse is also true. Some administrators show greater interest in expanding the use of and experimenting with new materials than teachers, who are often satisfied with present ways of teaching.

In a survey in the English Journal in 1939, it was reported that over 200 schools were engaged in film education, and it was concluded that before many more years, practically every school in the country would be making or would have made its own film offerings. Were we to make such a survey today, this prediction would still apply. We must conclude therefore, that not enough advance has been made.

In the November 1971 issue of the English Journal, Ken Donelson Lasan's article "Reinventing the Wheel: 10 Questions About Teaching and Using Films Being Asked in the 70s That Were Answered in the 40s," quotes answers dating back to 1934. One question was: "If films are so worthwhile, why are so few schools using them?" Answer: "Vested interest, lethargy, ignorance and misunderstanding stand in the way."[3] This was so in 1934, 1971 and is largely so today. It is folly to think that present and future teachers will be able to meet these roadblocks and to knock them down without serious training!

Where media use has been given a chance, it has proven itself to be a valuable tool in teaching reading, writing, speaking and other subjects.[4] Unfortunately many teachers and librarians only see films as entertainment, often ignoring that every good film has a message that can be used to teach. The early "instructional," inexpensive, unsophisticated film that talked down to students has been displaced by multi-faceted, short films, but too many of the old variety of films are still cluttering library shelves and closets.

The time may come when we will have to guard against overexposure to certain films. Students can become desensitized to this means of distributing information. Re-showing the same film year-after-year, exposing the same students to the same film for too many years of their lives, will have adverse effects.

Children come to school exposed to daily options of television, radio, record players, tape recorders, photos, story and picture books, and the accumulated information gathered from these. Many of them will have to be taught to be stimulated by things like colored paper, ditto sheets, paste, and scissors, standard equipment most kindergarten and first graders are faced with. The length of time schools spend teaching reading can hardly be justified in terms of cost, effort, and results, especially not when compared with the instantaneous information they gather from non-print media. A visual approach to learning has been deeply ingrained, especially with pre-schoolers who grew up with "Sesame Street." Recognizing that children learn in a variety of ways, providing these ways by breathing new life into daily routines has just begun in many schools, and many educators and others are asking, is it happening fast enough?

After World War II, projection equipment was cumbersome and unreliable, as well as difficult to operate. This has changed. However, reliability of equipment is frequently still not high enough and logistical support is often not available.

Overcoming Some of the Obstacles to Using Media

Although many teachers are not anxious to try new methods of teaching, when introducing non-print media to a school there are various ways of helping to interest the more reluctant members of the staff.

1. Make the literature of media use available. Media & Methods is an excellent magazine to begin with (see Appendix B), and books like Good Looking, by David Sohn.[5]

2. Advertise the availability of workshops and courses

both in the system, and at nearby universities and colleges.

3. Advertise local film festivals sponsored by public libraries, universities and colleges that can be attended by teachers as well as students and their parents.

4. Use television selectively for film showings, and educational TV where appropriate.

5. Learn to face objections and arguments against the use of media. Convince those who oppose its use that what you are doing is "teaching," and worth the expense. Since media is considered a "frill" by many, catalog successes, and be ready to use this information.[6]

6. Invite administrators and others to come and watch films with your classes. Persuade rather than argue.

7. Share your equipment and films with other teachers. Combine classes to watch a film and plan ahead when using media to cut cost.

8. Try to get special scheduling, like that given some science laboratories, for film study courses, so that longer films can be screened in their entirety.

9. Learn to be a media advocate with those in charge of the budget. Members of the administration, Boards of Education and state legislators should be some of your targets.

What Films Will Not Do

Unfortunately there does not exist a medium which will cut through the confusion now prevalent in education. Films are NOT a magic formula. They will not reach those now "turned off" by education, unless teachers have skills and know the pros and cons of film usage and film study, and even then, not every student will like any given film. Some may not even want to see films. The highly structured human and physical environment of most schools may well work against the process of growth and development in some students. However, there have been changes in the patterns of communication as experienced by the young, regardless of their experience with formal education. These modes of communication now include expression, visual images, spoken and written words, sound images, gestures and facial expressions that may be foreign to their teacher. Not all students taking a film course are there because they like films. Some just need the credit.[7] Hugh Gilmore in his article "What Film Teaching Is Not"[8] states that it has been his experience that the demand for film courses and film talks must be created. Elementary school age students may be eager to try making films, but those of high school age are reluctant to do so. Once they do, film making can give them a better feeling about themselves and added confidence that carries over to other areas.

Even in schools where teachers and students are enthusiastic about films, there may be a shortage of funds and equipment. Teachers will need to find sources of free films, use television, find their own funding, read the literature for ideas, and learn to be creative with what supplies there are.

Conclusion

Multi-media education is basic because we live in a media environment. This includes radio, TV, newspapers, magazines, and communication satellites orbiting the earth. Peter Schillaci stated this very well when he said: "Our primary environment is now informational, and earth itself, cradled in communications becomes a media event."[9]

The commitment necessary to use media is a big one. Teachers will find themselves more involved than ever before, but also more satisfied. Demands will be made on their time and skills, and on their understanding of themselves and those they reach. Their reward must be the results of this teaching. The interest and motivation shown by students, and the awakening of new interests and new knowledge on the part of those being taught is enough for most of us.

FOOTNOTES

1. Webb, Harry. "Teacher Characteristics and Educational Film Utilization," Audiovisual Instruction, September 1964, p. 494.

2. Hoban, Charles. The State of the Art of Instructional Films. An ERIC paper 1971.

3. Donelson, Ken. "Reinventing the Wheel: 10 Questions About Teaching and Using Films Being Asked in the 70's That Were Answered in the 40's," English Journal, November 1971, p. 12.

4. Schillaci, Peter. "The Basics Backlash: A Threat to Media," Media & Methods, September 1976, pp. 20-21.

5. Sohn, David. Good Looking. Philadelphia: North American Publishing Co. (A Media & Methods Book), 1976.

6. Dannenbaum, Joan. "From Media Users to Media Advocates," Media & Methods, September 1976, pp. 24-28.

7. Schillaci, op. cit., p. 30.

8. Gilmore, Hugh. "What Film Teaching Is Not," from the book Good Looking by David Sohn, op. cit., p. 30.

9. Schillaci, op. cit., p. 58.

Chapter 1: NON-PRINT MEDIA EQUIPMENT

INTRODUCTION

The purpose of this chapter is to give the reader some guidelines on where to find information about hardware and software, what to look for in buying, as well as how to maintain it, once owned by you. Frequently the type and amount of equipment are limited by your budget. You, the teacher or librarian, may not even be consulted before equipment is purchased, however, you should know what is available even if you are only in charge of using and storing it. You should also be prepared to offer suggestions should you be consulted on the purchase of new hard- or software.

There are in-service courses in many school systems on media. If your system does not offer such a course, speak to your principal and/or supervisor about having someone knowledgeable come in to give a workshop, including information on equipment, or inquire at the nearest university or college. Every member of your staff should be comfortable with the equipment in your school or library, or the use of it will be limited. The more accessible it is, the more it will be used.

There need not be confusion about the many manufacturers and distributors of hardware and software, if teachers and librarians are prepared to know where to find information. There is much material available to those willing to invest a little time before buying. Distributors and manufacturers of equipment are only too ready to descend on you and smother you with brochures, demonstrations, samples and special "deals." There are several impartial evaluation periodicals you should consult long before even circling a number on an information card so often found conveniently placed in some journals. Film News, Media & Methods, Audiovisual Instruction are a few of those that have good coverage (see Appendixes B and C).

The Association for Educational Communication and Technology (AECT) at their 1974 convention had as its theme: "Educational technology has advanced more rapidly than its acceptance and use in the classroom. Can the media profession and/or AECT increase and encourage sophisticated use of classroom media throughout the educational community?"1* It was suggested that certain conditions must be created for this to take place:

1. Users of media must be involved in the selection and planning for use, and they must accept the need for improvement.

2. Adequate assistance in the area of personnel, equipment, materials and evaluation must be available.

3. Those using media must be willing to search for and accept new ways of using it.

4. Teacher training institutions must be held accountable to develop models of instructional development, and for disseminating media use. Too many teachers still consider non-print media a threat to their classroom role. Teacher training institutions have not done their job in this area.

5. Teachers must get away from comfortable and familiar ways if they prove ineffective for learners.

6. Perhaps most important, we must reduce the hassle involved in getting software and hardware into the classroom to use.

The rapid technological advances in both equipment and software have caused some anxiety among many users. More durability and reliability, and less sophisticated hardware should be encouraged by users. Equipment is being simplified every year, and the skills needed to operate the machines should be minimal. Students and teachers should become involved in the working of the equipment, as well as in making some of their own learning materials. Commercial producers must be responsible for testing their products in the field and making the results available. We must all work towards making this a reality.

---

*Footnotes to Chapter 1 begin on page 20.

HARDWARE

General Standards

1. Make no assumptions about the equipment. Try the machine where it is going to be used (e.g., carrels). Load, unload and operate it, to make sure it is simple to use.

2. Make sure the picture is the right size for your purpose.

3. Check for hazards such as surfaces that get too hot, sharp corners, electric shocks.

4. Check the convenience and accessibility of controls for loading, focusing, volume control and other adjustments. Is it necessary to move the machine to make adjustments?

5. Check noise! A noisy machine drowns out the soundtrack.

6. Check for sound reproduction.

7. Automation: Is ease of operation sacrificed to difficult maintenance and repair? (Some of the newer machines, although self-threading, are more complicated to repair). Check "how-to" fix stuck or broken tapes, films, etc. Compare the machine you are considering with simpler (and sometimes cheaper) versions.

8. Cartridge and Cassettes: Check for compatibility. Most will work only in the projector they are designed for, and are not interchangeable with other makes of machines. Many of them cannot be reversed, and must be played through. Often repairs, such as splicing, can only be done by the manufacturer.

9. Equipment only built for durability and economy may not give the best results. Compare! On the other hand inexpensive machines may become costly when they need frequent repair. You may have to make difficult decisions.

10. Check to make sure the equipment is instructionally effective, and that there will be maximum usage. Find

out who will want to use it and when. Is the machine one you will feel comfortable with, and which suits your purpose, as well as that of your class?

11. Check the closets in your school. There may be equipment in usable condition which has not seen the light of day for a long time. Have it carefully checked out by a local laboratory and put into running condition. (Many schools have their own aide or assistant in charge of maintenance.) If you can save money here, you will have more to spend on software.

12. Never purchase electronic equipment which does not have the UL seal of approval. (Underwriters' Laboratory tests the electrical safety of equipment.)

13. All electrical equipment must have a three-wire/three-prong plug grounded power cord.

14. Make sure you try the machine yourself. Don't watch the salesman do it. If the machine is not as simple as promised it will be abused.

15. Decide on the media you will be using. "Let the material determine the machines, because the materials do the teaching, not the machines."[2]

Screens

Even the experts cannot agree whether or not a screen is always necessary. Michael Eisler, who frequently wrote about equipment in Previews, said: "Screens are often not needed. Any light colored, smooth surface will do. For extremely bright areas special screens are available. But check for possible problems. Some give a poor picture when viewed from an angle. Others are easily damaged and hard to clean."[3] Jeanne and Robert Bendik, in their book Filming Works Like This, say: "Walls are to hold a building up; poster board is to draw on; a motion picture screen is to see motion pictures on."[4] They go on to mention the loss of brightness when not using a screen and in the case of an off-white wall, loss of color.

Most teachers have found that screens are not always necessary. As Eisler mentioned, screens may be easily damaged, and are hard to clean. For filmstrips and 8mm loops, many machines now have built-in screens. Homemade box screens for individualized study can be used by one or two students, and many schools have added carrels to their libraries or media centers. When using screens, even small tears when fixed with tape show up when a picture is projected over them.

Screens are often damaged during transportation, and their surface may be injured with frequent raising and lowering, dirty hands, dust or anything sticking to the surface. Standard equipment for future classrooms should include recessed electrically operated screens. If you are participating in the planning of a new facility, make sure this is included as both a money and time-saver.

When you are choosing a screen, your first consideration must be brightness of the image. Depending on the size of the room you will be using, different size screens are available. The width of the screen should be matched to the lens. The makers of screens have charts to show this. Too large or too small a screen may spoil the image for viewers. Screens measuring 50" or 60" are the standard ones sold for classroom use.

The Kodak Ektalite Screen is useful in areas where darkening is not practical or desirable. It gives good brightness for narrow angle viewing. A specially treated aluminum surface is used. Ask for a demonstration! (Write to Kodak for information.)

There are different types of screens available. The ribbed lenticular screen is made up of a series of tiny, cylindrical lenses, embossed on the screen itself. It has a washable surface, and is quite bright over a fairly broad angle of view.

The beaded screen reflects light in a narrow angle (about thirty degrees), and gives sharper and brighter pictures. It must be handled with care. The matte screen, with a relatively wide angle of view, is used in auditoria and theaters for it reflects light evenly in all directions, providing an adequate image from all angles. The price is about the same for all of these. If you do select a screen for your school choose a heavy, sturdy model designed for institutional use.

Projectors

The amount of money you have to spend is the one factor which will most influence what kind of projector you buy. Next you should think of the size of the films you will be showing. If funds are limited consider buying a used projector. The main criteria for buying any projector are: 1) Reliability; 2) Ease of operation; and 3) Safety. Check the machine to see if it runs smoothly (i.e., at a consistent speed) without making a racket, and whether it scratches the film or damages sprocket holes. Automatic threaders jam on bad splices or torn sprocket holes, and you must still watch for tearing, buckling and burning of films. Run a film through the machine to see if you can extract it without damaging it once it is threaded. Film damage is important, especially when you own the films, for it can become expensive to repair them.

Listen for squeaks and whistles, banging or clattering noises. Turn the machine on in a quiet room with the sound turned off. Watch for jerking motions. Run a new black leader through the projector. If any scratches show up, don't buy it. Check the gate. If there are rough spots these could scratch the film. All projectors can hold 2,000 feet of film, but not all can take the strain of running that length of film. If you plan to run lengthy reels, test the machine, also checking that the light source does not overheat. Check the efficiency of the fan by running the machine for ten minutes to make sure that enough heat is being lost from the bulb through the ventilation grill so as not to burn the film.

If the projector is to be used in different places with different dimensions, you can purchase lenses with different focal lengths. The image dimensions should be adequate for the size of the room where the film is shown. Check the projected image around the edges for sharpness. A fixed focal length lens has a better quality than a variable focal length. Different brightness of image can be achieved with the same 1,000 bulb. Always try to get a projector with the brightest image, and focus on the grain of the image projected.

Old Bell and Howell projectors of the 300 series are very sturdy, if you can find them. They last for years without much trouble, but must be well maintained to safeguard films. Make sure to check all the items suggested above, and get a guarantee if buying a used machine.

Consider how your students will treat the equipment. Plastic parts cannot take too much abuse, and it is worth looking for a rugged piece of equipment. Remember also that experiences with equipment may be different. Take your time, study what's available, read some critiques of equipment and determine whether the machine you are buying is right for your situation.

Maintenance

Projectors

Preventive maintenance is the key to low operational cost.

1. Twice-a-year check-ups are necessary to guarantee good running condition. Remember, if your own projector is not available, you will either not be able to show films or will have to pay to rent one.

2. A weekly cleaning can be done by the student crew members. Allow time for the bulb to cool after using the machine and always disconnect the power cord before cleaning.

3. Lenses should be cleaned with special silicone coated cloths or lens tissues. A soiled handkerchief or coarse cloth can scratch the lens.

4. Register new equipment with the dealer or manufacturer for protection against loss, theft and breakdown of parts.

5. Use a soft, damp, lint-free cloth to clean the gate to keep accumulations of particles from showing up on your screen or scratching the film.

6. Test lenses, lamps and tubes periodically. Do not leave fingerprints on any of them. Do not wait for a part to break down.

7. Move machines carefully, especially when the lamp filaments are hot (and fragile).

8. Have spare bulbs handy at all times.

9. As a rule, do not lubricate projectors and/or cameras, unless your instruction manual specifically tells you where, how and how often. Permanently lubricated machines can be harmed by being oiled. Incorrect application can be equally harmful.

10. Be sure everyone who handles equipment has been carefully instructed.

Films

1. Thread films carefully. Make sure the film fits properly into sprockets, teeth and guides.

2. Loss of loops puts a strain on the film, may cause torn sprocket holes, and eventual breakage. It is most important to repair torn sprocket holes and breaks early to prevent serious damage.

3. Watch the rewinding. Although automatic, you need to stay with it!

4. If you own the film, you must maintain it by doing the following regularly:

a) Inspect the film after each showing. Do not handle it other than by its edges. Do not wind it too tightly. Adjacent turns of the film can cause scratches by grinding against each other.

b) Do not expose film to liquid. Alcohol and water are harmful! If the film is dirty pass it between the folds of a lint-free cloth, moistened with carbon tetrachloride or some other good cleaning fluid. Check a manual before using any chemicals to see if they are safe to use.

c) Treat the film with silicone coating to help it slide easier through the projection gate.

d) Make sure that shipping cases used for storage are in good condition.

e) You can replace footage by ordering replacement footage from the distributor. (If the film is rented some distributors rate their films according to the number of splices. Less than seven is rated "good," seven to fifteen, "fair.")

f) You must use a splicer to repair films. There are two ways of doing this: with liquid cement, called a lap splice; or with mylar tape, called a butt splice. Breaks are located by using a hand operated cranking stand. (Eastman Kodak and other companies will send instructions on splicing.)

Video

Basic systems of camera, videotape, recorder, monitor, and microphone cost between $1500 and $2000. Prices go up quickly when you begin to add editing, slow motion, and solenoid function controls, and are worth the price only if you know you will use them.

Where to get a system depends on how much freedom you have to make a purchase. Local dealers with demonstrated services and repair capabilities are more important than the VTR brand name. All advertised brands can produce good quality programs when used properly. Ask other schools, police and fire departments, local industries, or anyone using a VTR system in your community about which dealer is service-oriented. Don't get stuck without a spare part. Rent a unit from a local dealer to check performance. If his own rentals work well, this is some proof of his servicing capabilities. For the sake of convenience, get one service contract to cover the whole system.

Criteria for Evaluating Equipment

Price, availability, durability, ease of operation, longevity, service and reliability all apply to video equipment as well as any other you buy. In addition the following criteria are recommended by Welby Smith:

Flexibility: Since there are no all-purpose VTR systems, you should know in advance what you plan to do with yours. You may not be able to foresee all of the capabilities and limitations of a particular system, so take your time in making a selection.

Capacity for expansion: Determine whether you can add additional components to the system without making major modifications, or having to throw out other components. Try to avoid obsolescence.

Appropriate level of performance: If your plans are limited, a simple monochrome, single camera VTR system will do. Electronic editing adds to the cost. Appraise both your audience and types of VTR productions planned for, before making a final decision on equipment. Smith advises using a monochromatic camera, which is cheaper and easier to use, but buying a color VTR. They function perfectly together.

VTR Formats

1. Quarter-inch VTR is good for documenting events that require retention for long periods of time. The lower cost of quarter-inch tape makes sense when instant replay of activities or events is needed. Smith mentions image degradation when editing and duplicating this tape.

2. Half-inch VTR is used in open-reel VTRs and in VTRs incorporating the tape in an enclosed package. It is adaptable to a wide variety of production and distribution situations.

The Electronic Industries Association of Japan (EIAJ) has standardized basic reel-to-reel, black and white VTRs since 1970, and some American manufacturers have adopted this format. No VTR manufactured prior to 1969 is compatible with those following EIAJ standards. Now all EIAJ VTRs are compatible in both black and white and color, except old Sony 5000s.[6] Bensinger mentions these features in his Petersen's Guide: Easy maintenance, simplicity, fair editing, highly portable, and use limited only by the imagination of the user. Sony and Panasonic manufacture half-inch VTRs, and their relative low cost makes them competitive with three-quarter inch U-Matic. Panasonic, Sanyo and Sony make cartridge machines. The Panasonic is a rugged, portable, easy to use machine. Sanyo half-inch videocassette has a supply and take-up reel in a plastic case that can be removed and replaced without rewinding, unlike the Panasonic. The Sanyo recorder is small, portable and very reliable. It is only available in monochrome.

3. Three-quarter inch U-Matic VTR is the most flexible total system. Commercial networks and many independent stations originate their broadcasts with these machines. The tape cost is higher as is the system, but if you can afford it, study the advantages carefully. Since you can mix the components of VTR systems such as Panasonic, Sanyo and Sony, do some comparison shopping.

In buying any system, the first consideration is always budget and staff. The expense of a system demands studying what is available as well as what you plan to do with it. This should be a long-term commitment.

Aydelotte mentions that many VTR users have supplemented their systems with additional lights, microphones and mixers to improve the quality of their productions.[7] Again price and quality are the two most important considerations.

When adding to your system figure out the power requirements to avoid blowing out a tube in the middle of a production. Most AC power outlets have definite voltage and power limitations.

Aydelotte recommends a dynamic microphone for small VTR systems. Portable VTRs usually have a microphone built into the camera. It is important to monitor the sound. Investing in a good pair of headphones to check the sound of the original recording is a good idea. Correcting audio problems later necessitates much extra and expensive equipment, therefore making a test recording to check if the system is working is worthwhile.

Care of Video Tapes

1. Keep VTR as clean as possible when using video tape.
2. Use the same size reel for supply and take-up.
3. Minimize hand contact with the recording part of the tape.
4. Do not wrinkle or bend tape.
5. Do not expose the tape to dust, moisture, heat or extreme cold.
6. Avoid high humidity.
7. Always keep tape sealed in the package when not in use.
8. Never stack tapes on top of each other. Store vertically at room temperature.
9. Cut off wrinkles that develop if tape jams on VTR.

SOFTWARE

The clumsiness of the standard 16mm projector, plus reels of film and take-up reels, plus screens of the past, hampered the use of films. Technological advances have made much of this easier, including the use of films with small groups, and for individual instruction. Film loops, cassettes and cartridges have changed the format of film use, introduced carrels into the library, and encouraged film making by schools and community groups.

At one time 16mm was the amateur film gauge. Today most projection outside motion picture theaters is 16mm. Newsreels, some documentaries, industrial films, and most experimental films are shot in 16mm. It is standardized so that the camera can be French made, the film manufactured in Japan, the lenses in Germany and copies of the film produced in the U.S. A 16mm projection is larger than 8mm, and sound reproduction is often of better quality.

Super 8

Compared to the standardization of 16mm there still seems to be much confusion on the 8mm scene. There has been a general changeover from standard 8mm to super 8mm film. There are an estimated 250,000 super 8 sound projectors in the U.S. By 1972-3 super 8 began to take over the market, with industry using it for sales promotions, personnel training and public relations, and schools for more individualized work.

If you have 8mm films, take care of your projector, since both are on the way out. The 8mm film, which is inexpensive, has been used for home movies, but to meet the needs of standard educational and commercial use it was redesigned by Eastman Kodak as the super 8 format. The size of each frame was increased by almost half, and the quality of the picture improved. Room was made for a sound track, but the width of the film remained the same. Announced in 1962, the actual super 8 film reached the market only in 1965. By 1972 the super 8 raw stock sale exceeded regular 8mm sales.

The super 8mm sound cartridges are more economical than 16mm, without sacrificing significantly the quality of sound and picture. Time and better equipment have brought down the difference between the two, but as of this writing super 8mm is still inferior to 16mm.

Super 8mm cartridges use rear-screening devices,

which make them ideal for screening by individual and small groups. Loading is simple, and they are convenient in schools where inspection of the film after showing is difficult or too expensive to maintain. Children can operate them easily, and if film making is going on in your school, super 8 cameras are easier to use, less bulky, more automated, less expensive, and the cost of processing half that of 16mm films.

Physically and emotionally handicapped children have been found to benefit from handling this smaller format. Cartridges eliminate the need for mechanical know-how on the part of the teacher, who needs simply to plug in the cartridge or cassette, and push the button. It is relatively simple to reduce 16mm to super 8 for projection, and this is being done increasingly, giving access to many of the older films used in film study courses. Local and classroom productions, both individual and in cinema classes, can be inexpensively done, and projected to groups.

There are several reasons why the super 8 market has not grown as quickly as anticipated. The lack of standardization is the main one. The selling price of super 8 prints in containers is also relatively high. The market is there to place prints in every classroom, but since many containers and projectors are not interchangeable, there is no basis for broad distribution. There are differences in the soundtrack, which can be optical or magnetic. The super 8 picture with a magnetic track cannot play on a super 8 optical sound projector, and vice versa. Until and unless a combination projector becomes standard, a decision must be made by producers and distributors whether magnetic or optical sound will be standard.

There is <u>no</u> compatibility in the super 8 cartridge cassette, clamshell projector. Some of the containers cost more than the film they hold, and are not interchangeable from one machine to another. Cassettes are reel-to-reel, in plug-in containers. Clamshells are reels in containers with automatic threading, open reel-to-reel come with, or without automatic threading.

It is possible sometimes to have a film changed from one type of cartridge to another, since most films themselves are interchangeable. You must send the film in the cartridge you do not want to a film laboratory, and ask them to re-cartridge it. (Check your classified telephone book under "Motion Picture Film Laboratories.") Call first to make sure they have the specific type of cartridge you need. You will have to give the name and model of the projector you are using, the length of the film, sound or silent, and whether the soundtrack is magnetic or optical. The expense of switching cartridges depends on your need for the film. It is certainly less expensive than buying a new projector or another film. DuKane and Honeywell make projectors which play both super 8 and standard 8mm films, and both optical and magnetic sound tracks. They are self-threading, but they are also more expensive than less versatile machines.

To generalize the mechanical aspect of super 8mm films, all of them will play on any super 8 projector, <u>providing</u> they are placed in the proper cartridge for that machine, and <u>providing</u> the soundtrack is of the same type as the one used in the projector.

The educational world has now had an opportunity to try all of these film formats. Unfortunately, no one has stepped forward to hasten the standardization in films we have found in audio tapes.

Filmstrips

Filmstrips have been around for fifty years. Their brevity and mediocrity before the 1960's may explain their exclusion from critical consideration before this. By 1966 the educational establishment bought $44 million of audio-visual material. Of this, $16 million went for filmstrips. By 1970 there was a 1000 percent increase in filmstrip sales.[9]

There are advantages in using filmstrips which we need to be aware of.

1. Presentation can be paced to the ability of the class. You can stop anytime for discussions if the class gets restless, or if you wish to use only part of a strip.

2. They can be used for individualized studying by one, or just a few students.

3. Since they can be stopped anytime, they are useful as reference material.

4. They are less expensive than films and the projector is easier to set up and operate.

5. They need relatively less room-darkening.

6. They usually show one idea, one subject or the relationship between different elements, rather than dealing with many topics. This may be particularly beneficial for slow learners, or those who find it difficult to concentrate.

7. Clarification of facts that can be done better by showing photographs or diagrams can be easily presented with filmstrips.

Check for the following before buying any filmstrips: 1) color is sometimes not as good as in films; 2) too few frames (the average is 45-50 frames per filmstrip); 3) lack of coordination between picture and script; 4) recordings that suffer from distortion; 5) coy narration, distorted story-lines, or background music and sound effects that may over-power the script; 6) distortions of the original drawings and stories; and 7) captions that are not clearly distinguishable. (Beware of reading captions to your class, lest you imply that your students lack the ability and intelligence to read themselves.)

Let the filmstrip speak for itself, and permit the students to react and ask questions, rather than imposing your opinions and ideas on them.

<u>Criteria for Choosing Filmstrips</u>

1. Authenticity: Extremely important in filmstrip "reproductions" of children's books, folk tales and legends and classical mythology.

2. Sound and action synchronization.

3. Accuracy of content.

4. Color.

5. Usefulness for age, grade and situation for which they are intended.

Ethel Heins in her article "Literature Bedeviled: A Searching Look at Filmstrips" (<u>The Horn Book Magazine</u>,

1974) gives an excellent critique of filmstrips that do not meet the standards teachers and librarians must expect from any media. When books are represented by a few indifferent drawings and when "the subtlety of characterization, the emotional power, the style, true wit and virtuosity of great writing" are eliminated certainly no child will be inspired to read the complete book. The author states that this might better be accomplished by reading the original story to children.

Sources of Filmstrips

Reproductions of picture books for preschoolers, for library story hours and for use by children before they have learned to read are done by several companies. Teaching Resource Films has made filmstrips from Curious George books and some of the Virginia Lee Burton favorites ("Maybelle the Cable Car" and "Katy and the Big Snow"). Other sources are Macmillan, Scribner/Miller-Brody and McGraw-Hill Films (8 Happy Lion stories). Lyceum Productions' filmstrips of Ann Atwood's photographic book series--Haiku: The Mood of Earth--are particularly beautiful and useful for geology, ecology and the study of Japanese poetry.

There is an ever growing sophistication and improvement in the available filmstrips. The number of strips, as well as the number of distributors has increased. New categories are added all the time. Previews, in its yearly round-up of the year's best, rates filmstrips for excellence in these areas: Authenticity and Accuracy; Scope and Content; Organization; Technical Qualities; Usefulness.[10] The following distributors were mentioned more than once on lists appearing over the past few years:

Aims, Box 1010, Hollywood, Cal. 90028
Audio Visual, Pleasantville, N.Y. 10570
Coronet, 65 East South Water Street, Chicago, Ill. 60601
Current Affairs Films, 24 Danbury Rd., Wilton, Ct. 06857
Educational Audio Visual, Pleasantville, N.Y. 10570
Education Dimension Group, Box 126, Stamford, Ct. 06904
Encyclopaedia Britannica Educational Corp., 425 North Michigan Ave., Chicago, Ill. 60611
Films Inc., 1144 Wilmette Ave., Wilmette, Ill. 60091

Guidance Assn., Pleasantville, N.Y. 10570
Learning Resources, Division of Educational Development Corp., 202 Lake Miriam Dr., Lakeland, Fla. 33803
Macmillan Publishing Co., 34 McQueston Pkway, Mt. Vernon, N.Y. 10550
McGraw-Hill Films, 1221 Ave. of the Americas, New York, N.Y. 10020
Miller-Brody Productions, 342 Madison Ave., New York, N.Y. 10017
New York Times Films, 229 West 43 St., New York, N.Y. 10036
Prentice-Hall Media, 150 White Plains Rd., Tarrytown, N.Y. 10591
Random House, 201 East 50 St., New York, N.Y. 10022
Schloat Productions, 150 White Plains Rd., Tarrytown, N.Y. 10591
Scholastic Book Service, 904 Sylvan Ave., Englewood Cliffs, N.J. 07632
Scott Education Division, 104 Lower Westfield Rd., Holyoke, Mass. 01040
Teaching Resources Films, 2 Kisco Plaza, Mt. Kisco, N.Y. 10549
Time/Life Education, Box 834, Radio City P. O., New York, N.Y. 10010
Warren Schloat Productions, Pleasantville, N.Y. 10570
Weston Woods, Weston, Ct. 06880

Slides

Slides are 35mm transparencies that are easy to make and use. The bulk of those that are commercially produced deal with art and art history. Slides came into being in 1930, but, unfortunately, there have been few evaluative studies done on slides and slide use. They are an inexpensive media to store and handle, and can be made by students. They make the same impact on the viewer as filmstrips. Many schools have found slide making a most worthwhile activity, relatively simple and inexpensive, and the slides can be used over and over.

Sources of Slides

Metropolitan Museum of Art, New York City--The History of Art Slide Library, 1970.

The Audiovisual Marketplace, New York City, R. R. Bowker, bi-annual (lists sources).

Rufsold, Margaret and Carolyn Guss. Guide to Educational Media, Chicago, ALA, 1971 (lists sources).

Lanier, Vincent (compiler). Slides and Filmstrips on Art, National Art Educational Assn., 1201 16th St., N.W., Washington, D.C. 20036

Lennex, Tom. "Slide Acquisition: A Media Librarian's Problem," Previews, Nov. 1972.

Index to Educational Slides (3rd. ed. 1977) National Information Center for Educational Media (NICEM) Los Angeles, Cal. $42.50. Contains 28,000 annotated entries, plus subject index and list of distributors.

The many programs of the Center for Humanities, 2 Holland Ave., White Plains, N.Y. 10603 and other slide set producers. Eastman Kodak has many pamphlets on slide production. Write for 1977 Index to Kodak Information, Rochester, N.Y. 14650.

Records, Tapes and Cassettes

Records deserve more than a brief mention, for they have been used longer than any other non-print media. It is well known that high school students use radio and records more than any other media. Using rock music to start discussions on contemporary topics in school should follow easily from this. David Linton in his article "Rock and the Media"[11] mentions Frank Zappa's song "Overnight Sensation" by the Mothers of Invention as a good starter for a discussion on the effects of television. Cat Stevens' "Father and Son," the story of a relationship between this particular father and son should be excellent for family relations. Many songs about losing lovers also lend themselves to family relations classes. James Taylor's "Don't Let Me Be Lonely Tonight," and his "Fire and Rain" are just two of these, along with Simon and Garfunkel's "Bye Bye Love." The latter singers' "So Long Frank Lloyd Wright" might do very well as background music for a class in architecture.

Caedmon has several records of authors reading their own works of fiction for use by English classes: A. B.

Guthrie, Jr. "The Big Sky"; Joseph Heller "Catch 22"; Dylan Thomas "Adventures in the Skin Trade"; and J. R. R. Tolkien "The Hobbit," to mention just a few. (See Joseph Mersand's article "Sound Recordings of Fiction and Drama.")[12] Classes in theater arts and acting can gain much by listening to such records as "The Art of Ruth Draper" (Spoken Arts); Julie Harris reading "The Tempest" and "A Midsummer Night's Dream" (Caedmon). The short stories of Edgar Allan Poe (Spoken Arts) lend themselves to aural presentations. Caedmon also has two albums of Poe's stories.

Music classes have always been exposed to recorded music. With recordings getting technically better all the time, it might be interesting to compare the technical qualities of early recordings of voice and instruments with more recent ones. Exposing students to all kinds of music in school is to be highly recommended, but a wise teacher will not try to convert a student's musical taste.

Sources of Records, Tapes and Cassettes

Annual Index to Popular Music Record Reviews, Metuchen, N.J.: Scarecrow Press, 1973- .

Audio-Magazine. See Appendix C.

Black Box, a cassette, tape and poetry magazine, information clearing house and distribution center for 20th-century poetry available on tape. For copies of their catalog write: Black Box, P. O. Box 4174, Washington, D.C. 20015

Caedmon Records, 505 8th Ave., New York, N.Y. 10019

High Fidelity and High Fidelity/Musical America. See Appendix C.

The Library of Congress Catalog of Music and Phonorecords. Includes musical scores intended for performances, and sound phonorecords, both musical and non-musical. Nonmusical recordings cover all subject fields currently received by the Library of Congress and other American libraries participating in its cooperative program. From Library of Congress, Washington, D.C. 20541

Pastime Products, Inc., P. O. Box 35721, Houston, Tex.

77035. Original radio programs on cassettes.

Schwann Record and Tape Guides. 130 East 59 St., New York, N.Y. 10022. These are the oldest and most used catalogs. Issued monthly, the Record Guide ($1.60) contains over 45,000 stereo and quad records and tapes, both popular and classical. The Supplementary record guide is issued semi-annually ($1.50) and lists many records not found in the monthly listings. Included are popular and jazz over two years old, spoken, educational, humorous and mono and electronically reproduced stereo classical records. There is also a Children's Record Guide ($.50) and Basic Record of Jazz ($.50). The arrangement is alphabetical by composer, with works listed alphabetically by title. The guides are available at many of the larger record shops.

Spoken Arts, 310 North Ave., New Rochelle, N.Y. 10801

Tudor, Dean and Andrew Armitage, "The Best Popular Records of 1975," Previews, May 1976, pp. 10-15. Lists "Soul," "Blues," "Popular-Mood," "Rock," "Country," "Humor," and "Folk."

FOOTNOTES

1. Previews editorial. "On the Agenda, Forecasts of Issues at the AECT Convention," Previews, March 1974, p. 5.

2. Eisler, Michael. "One-on-One AV: The Users," Previews, December 1973, p. 13.

3. Eisler, Michael, op. cit., p. 12.

4. Bendik, Jeanne and Robert. Filming Works Like This. New York: McGraw-Hill Book Co., 1970, p. 83.

5. Smith, Welby. "VTR Update: Runnin' Hard Through the Video Looking Glass," Media & Methods, October 1976, pp. 17-19.

6. Bensinger, Charles and the editors of Photography Magazine. Petersen's Guide to Video Tape Recording, p. 49.

7. Aydelotte, Mark. "Lights and Mikes," Media & Methods, October 1976, p. 25.

8. Bensinger, op. cit., p. 28.

9. French, Janet. "Filmstrips," School Library Journal, March 15, 1970, p. 1162.

10. Previews. Annual listing (usually in May issue) of the best filmstrips of the year, arranged according to subject headings.

11. Linton, David. "Rock and the Media," Media & Methods, October 1976, pp. 56-9.

12. Mersand, Joseph. "Sound Recordings of Fiction and Drama," Media & Methods, March 1976, pp. 44-48.

SOURCES OF INFORMATION

Periodicals

American Film. American Film Institute, J. F. Kennedy Building for the Performing Arts, Washington, D.C. 20566

Audiovisual Instruction. 2901 Byrdhill Rd., Richmond, Va. 23205 (see Appendix C, p. 211).

Eric the Read. Clearinghouse on Information and Resources, School of Education, Center for Research and Development in Teaching, Syracuse University, Syracuse, N.Y. 13210

Film News. 250 West 57 Street, New York, N.Y. 10019. Regular column, "What's New in Equipment" (see Appendix B, p. 206).

Media & Methods. 134 North 13 Street, Philadelphia, Pa. 19107 (see Appendix B, p. 207).

Fast Forward. Newsletter of Association of AV Technicians (AAVT), Box 19268, Denver, Col. 80209

Books, Pamphlets and Organizations

AECT. Educational Technology. Definition & Glossary of Terms. Vol. I. AECT Publication Sales, Dept. A7, 1126 16th St., N.W., Washington, D.C. 20035. $21.95.

American Society for Training and Development (ASTD). Selecting and Developing Media. A practical approach to selecting and using instructional media. Includes video and computers. Order from ASTD Order Dept., P. O. Box 5307, Madison, Wis. 53705. Published by Van Nostrand Reinhold. $14.50.

Association of American Publishers (AAP). Explaining the New Copyright Law--A Guide to Legitimate Photocopying of Copyrighted Materials. AAP, 1707 L St., N.W., Washington, D.C. 20036. $1.00.

Association of A/V Technicians. Elsa C. Kaiser, Executive Manager, AAVT, Box 19268, Denver, Colo. National organization of A/V technicians in schools, industry. Publishes: 1) Newsletter, FAST FORWARD (a monthly) with shop tips, industry news, modifications, etc.; 2) With EPIE, Annotated Directory of Parts and Services for Audiovisual Equipment. $12 to members, $22 to non-members; 3) Repair Parts Directory. Identifies parts sources on over 700 brands of A/V equipment.

Audio-Visual Market Place: A Multi-Media Guide. New York: R. R. Bowker Co. Annual, expensive manual. Contains much useful information on products, distributors, equipment, etc.

Bensinger, Charles and the editors of Photography Magazine. Petersen's Guide to Video Tape Recording. Petersen Publishing Co., 8490 Sunset Blvd., Los Angeles, Cal. 90069. Answers to "What Is Video." Information on hardware and software. A complete guide. (1973) $3.95.

Education Products Information Exchange (EPIE). 495 Riverside Dr., New York, N.Y. 10027. Publishes: 1) EPIE Reports (9 times/year). Covers specific instructional products, materials and methods; 2) EPIEGRAM. A twice-a-month bulletin (past issues covered 8mm motion picture projectors, overhead projectors, etc.).

Gottesman, Ronald and Harry Goduld. Guidebook to Film. New York: Holt, Rinehart & Winston, Inc., 1972. A guide to books on equipment, festivals, film schools, books and periodicals, etc.

Kuhns, William and Thomas Giardino. Behind the Camera. Burton, Ohio: Geo. A. Pflaum, 1970. Detailed analysis of equipment, what to look for, what to buy.

Library of Congress Catalog: Motion Pictures and Filmstrips. Library of Congress, Card Division, Bldg. 159, Navy Yard Annex, Washington, D.C. 20541. Issued quarterly with annual cumulation. All motion pictures and filmstrips of educational and instructional value released in the U.S. and Canada, and cataloged by L.C. printed cards. Free.

Linton, Dolores and David. Practical Guide to Classroom Media. Dayton, Ohio: Pflaum/Standard, 1971. Practical advice on selecting equipment.

National Audiovisual Association (NAVA). Audiovisual Equipment and Directory. Annual. NAVA, 3150 Spring St., Fairfax, Va. 22030.

Parlato, Salvatore and Dolores. The Audiovisual Advisor. 1967. Market Station, Box 25, Buffalo, N.Y. 14302. A pamphlet with much of the information needed to start a media program.

Pincus, Edward. Guide to Filmmaking. New York: New American Library, Inc. Signet Book. Henry Regenary Co., 1969. Used by teachers and students as a textbook in classes of cinematography, this is often the one book recommended if there are budget limitations. A production manual, with explanations about choosing the best camera, etc. Does not include information on video.

REFERENCES

Brown, Mary. "Video and Cable," Sightlines Service Suplement on Equipment, January/February 1973, pp. 12-15.

Barshop, Ronald. "Focus on Filmstrip Projectors," Previews, December 1973, pp. 5-8.

Eisler, Michael. "Criteria for Choosing Hardware," Previews, December 1973.

Eisler, Michael. "8mm Muddle: Things Are More Standard Than They Seem," Previews, September 1972, pp. 5-7.

Eisler, Michael. "A Primer of Projectuals," Previews, October 1971, pp. 8-9.

Fransecky, Roger and James Lied. "Creative Use for Your Magic Lantern," Media & Methods, January 1976, pp. 40-41.

French, Janet. "Filmstrips," School Library Journal, March 15, 1970, pp. 1162-6.

Hoelel, Gisela. "Projection," University Film Study Center, Newsletter Supplement, vol. 3, no. 3.

Kuehn, Neal. "What About Super8 in Education?" Film News, September 1973, pp. 36-7.

Lennox, Tom. "Slide Acquisition: A Media Librarian's Problem," Previews, November 1972.

Levering, Philip. "The Best Supplement to 16mm-8mm Sound Cartridges," Film Library Quarterly, Fall 1972, pp. 40-41.

Martin, Arthur. "Getting Hooked on Cable TV," Previews, March 1973.

Parlato, Salvatore. "Projection," Newsletter Supplement, University Film Study Center, Box 275, Cambridge, Mass.

Parlato, Salvatore and Dolores. Audiovisual Advisor. The Audiovisual Advisor, Box 25, Market Station, Buffalo, N.Y. 14203 (rev. ed. 1967).

Rosenberg, Kenyon C. "The Selection of Audiovisual Equipment: A Few Basics," Previews, January 1975, pp. 7-14.

Rosenberg, Kenyon C. "Tape Recorders: Open Reel vs. Cassettes," Previews, October 1972.

Tieman, Philip. "Standards for Educational Equipment," Sightlines, March/April 1972, pp. 16-17.

Filmstrips

Eastman Kodak. Sources of Motion Pictures and Filmstrips (Pamphlet S-9). From Eastman Kodak Motion Picture and A/V Markets Division, Rochester, N.Y. 14650

Heins, Ethel. "Literature Bedeviled: A Searching Look at Filmstrips," Horn Book Magazine, 1974 (write to Horn Book for copy). A critique of filmstrips, good and bad, with examples.

Guide to Government-Loan Films. Serina Press, 70 Kennedy St., Alexandria, Va. 22305. 1974. Section on filmstrips and slides.

Patterson, Adele (comp.). "Filmstrips to Flip Over," Media & Methods, pp. 28-30. Annotated by subject headings.

Patterson, Adele (comp.). "First Class Filmstrips," Media & Methods, April 1977, pp. 41-56, 63+. Annotated lists of Literature, Language Arts, Humanities, Social Studies.

Spirt, Diane, "Best of the Year Filmstrips and Slides Roundup," Previews, April 1976, p. 10.

Slides

Bohr, Joel. "Say It with Pictures--A Creative Photography Workshop," Media & Methods, January 1977, p. 55.

Eastman Kodak has several slide programs on photography and printing; dates of programs range from 1971-1978. Send for "Your Programs from Kodak, 1978." A/V Library Distributor, Eastman Kodak, Rochester, N.Y. 14650

Eckhardt, Ned. "The Learning Potential of Picture Taking," Media & Methods, January 1977, pp. 48-55. Includes a list of resources.

King, Warren. "Winning Student Photographers," Media & Methods, January 1977, pp. 56-61.

Weseman, Robert. "A No-Camera Slide Show," Media & Methods, January 1977, pp. 63-64. "How-to-make."

Video Equipment

Bensinger, Charles and the editors of Photography Magazine. Petersen's Guide to Video Tape Recording. Petersen Publishing Co., 8490 Sunset Blvd., Los Angeles, Cal. 90069, 1973. $3.95. A complete guide to video use. Answers what it is, how it works, hardware and software needs. Each section lists and compares systems.

Gilliom, Bonnie Cherp and Ann Zimmer. ITV: Promise into Practice. Educational Media Center, Ohio Dept. of Education, 518 South Wall St., Columbus, Ohio 43215 (Attention G. R. Bowers) 1972. $6.85 (Xerox hard cover). The bulk of this book discusses the pragmatic use of ITV. Programming and studio production techniques, as well as hardware requirements are discussed. Includes an evaluation of teaching with television.

Mattingly, Grayson and Welby Smith. Introducing the Single-Camera VTR System: A Layman's Guide to Videtotape Recording. New York: Charles Scribner's Sons, 1971, 1973. $8.95. This simple, but comprehensive book is an excellent guide to using a VTR system. From discussions of why one would use such a system, to detailed analysis of the camera, video-cassette recorders, technical standards, production standards, the Port-a-Pac, and a glossary this is one of the few books on the topic for student use.

McAdam, Robert J. and Charles Vento. Portable Video Tape Recorder. A Guide for Teachers. National Education Assn. 1201 16th St., N.W., Washington, D.C. 20036, 1969. $2.00. Utilizing PVYT, operation of the equipment, and difference in available equipment are the basis of this book.

Moore, Frank J. A Guide to the Use of Closed Circuit Television (CCTV). Center for Effecting Education Change, Fairfax County Schools, Bailey Crossroads, Va., 1970. $3.35 (Xerox hard copy). Tells what a

CCTV system consists of, what it can be used for, and projects. Includes a short bibliography.

Potect, Howard G. Tom Swift and His Electric English Teacher. Dayton, Ohio: Pflaum Publishing, 1974. An oversize catalog which "tells you how to use media to teach English that will grab your students and make them learn." A different, if cluttered, approach to finding information for teachers and students who do not relate to the traditional. Includes video.

Videofreex. The Spaghetti City Video Manual. A Guide to Use, Repair and Maintain. New York: Praeger Publishers, 1973. $7.95. This is a manual for people who want to be more self-sufficient with video hardware. It is divided into 4 sections: Theory, Systems, Maintenance, and Not So Basic Maintenance. It contains the only bibliography we have found on understanding the basic video equipment, and learning to work with it.

Chapter 2: FILM TECHNIQUES

INTRODUCTION

In the opinion of one film maker, a film has failed if the viewer is conscious of technique while watching it. Others, especially those of us who teach with films, feel the enjoyment of a film can be heightened if we know what to look for. To film teachers and those experienced in film making techniques, camera work and photography are important ingredients in judging films. We all know a film can be unpleasant to sit through because the soundtrack or the film techniques are bad. Students can learn about the combination of sight and sound so vital to any movie. Classroom teachers and librarians often begin using films without expertise in this area, but they soon find that even without formal training, the more films they watch and use, the easier the choosing of them becomes. Visuals, such as photography and color, sound, editing, etc., will quickly become evident when one watches many films.

Films depend on rhythm, tempo, pace, lighting, color, music, symbols, etc. to communicate what the writer and director want their audience to see and feel. The following guidelines may help you when you are first starting out, but do not use them more than necessary. If your students ask questions requiring more technical knowledge than you possess, confess your ignorance, and suggest research on the topic. Make your own list of criteria, let your class help you, and above all be open to new ideas.

When teaching films, as in a course devoted to just films, rather than using them as part of the curriculum, technical components should be identified and analyzed, and there is more need for a structured approach. (See books like Need Johnny Read? by Frederick Goldman and Linda R.

Burnett for details.)[1]*

CRITERIA FOR TECHNICAL QUALITIES

Here are some criteria for technical qualities, including some suggested by the American Library Association.

1. Visual aspects of camera work, composition and framing, color, focus, exposure, special effects, as well as expressive contrasts (lighting), should be effectively used to convey moods, build up excitement, show action, and generally hold the interest of the audience. Ask these questions:

a) Are visuals, other than photographs (e.g. paintings, illustrations, maps, charts, etc.) well reproduced and effectively used?

b) Are titles, captions, and explanations readable and of suitable length? Are they in proper position? When sub-titles are used they can create difficult situations if children watching have a great span in reading ability and speed of reading. If given a choice, avoid films with sub-titles, except for foreign language films, where you must have them.

2. Just as important is originality of style. Not everything original is necessarily good, but certainly a freshness of viewpoint, or an inventive and creative approach to an old topic is sometimes not only refreshing, but of great help in reaching students.

3. The acting must be believable and convincing. This visually oriented generation is well trained in this aspect of films from the hours of TV and movie watching they have done. Films used in classrooms must be able to match the acting students have been exposed to before they even come to school.

A powerful performance often causes the viewer to identify with the character of the film. In most of today's films, acting is only one of several talents that combine to produce what we see. The effect of any performance depends on the collaboration of the director, the cameraman,

*Footnotes to Chapter 2 begin on page 34.

sound and lighting technicians and the editor. Film acting is an exacting art. Try to apply these criteria:[2]

a) Does the acting ring true to the characterization?

b) Does it relate reasonably to the other performances and characterizations?

c) Is it appropriate to the narrative, the theme, and the director's over-all conception?

4. Editing: In 1928 the Russian pioneer film maker V. I. Pudovkin said, "The foundation of film is editing." This is still true today. Editing controls continuity, pacing, and rhythm which are important in holding the interest of the viewer. Length of sequences, method of cutting (transitions), choice of cuts and clips, should be so well done that the viewer is not aware of any of this having taken place.

Often many different segments of film are used to make one movie by editing them together. The assembling and splicing of hundreds, and sometimes thousands of pieces of film, is a slow and very difficult process. By editing, emphasis can be placed on certain parts of the action. Effective continuity can manipulate time (i.e. showing passages of time, flash-backs, etc.). Editing sound and music means the soundtrack, including music, sound effects, and dialogue, must be matched to the visual print to give added dimensions. It is here the viewer must know what the director is trying to accomplish. Should voices be heard above the music or traffic sounds? Is the director experimenting with sounds and editing? Establish what the film maker is trying to do before judging his editing, for all of us react in different ways, depending on our background, experiences, mood, tastes, values, etc.

Color vs. Black and White

Theorists have tried to tackle the problem with only confused results. Nevertheless, here are a few guidelines. Color is usually preferred if given a choice, but sometimes when the photography is so good, or the subject a solemn and somber one, black and white may be chosen, or at least color is not missed. Where newsreel footage, or still photography is used, there is often no choice, especially if the film is an old one. When showing news events, the events are more important than the photography, although color can contribute to the mood. Most of us would definitely miss color in an animated film. Remember, color film is not as expressive as black and white, and the use of shadows and contrasts is limited.

The starkness of black and white can sometimes be used to make a point. If the film is only available in black and white, make sure the photography makes up for lack of color. With young film makers, the topic and what they have to say may be the most important reason for the film; therefore, lack of color (to save money) should not be considered a detriment. If you have decided on color, check the clarity of the colors used, and make sure they are natural. Old films do not necessarily preserve their original color, and there is nothing more embarrassing than presenting a travelogue or nature film with washed-out colors. Color costs more than black and white, therefore, when previewing the film, try to imagine it in black and white. You can get two films for the price of one if you order black and white.

Sometimes color filters are used to create certain moods. These filters may denote the coming of a storm or show poverty. Make sure the use of filters is not overdone. Sometimes it is difficult to even follow a story or the content of the script because of the overwhelming use of warm (red, orange, yellow) or cold (blue, green) filters.

Photography

Even the neophyte can see if a picture is in focus, if the image is clear or blurred (befitting the intended style), if close-ups are used when necessary, and in the case of films that are used as part of the curriculum, if there is enough repetition to make this a learning experience. Technical procedures used in films must help rather than confuse. Ask yourself, "Is the film worth watching without the soundtrack?" "Does it foster appreciation of beauty, form, shape, color, etc. ?" Apply the criteria given earlier.

Timeliness

Timeliness is another vital ingredient. One of the dangers of buying live-action films is that they become dated, not only in subject matter, but hair styles, clothes, language, props, musical backgrounds, attitudes and values. If the message of the film is important and well presented, changing styles can be explained before viewing the film, and need not necessarily make the film obsolete.

A five-year limit is probably a good general guide to apply, and many commercial catalogs now give the date of production. Don't forget the action of students in a film, if there are any. If they are too stiff and formal the audience may get distracted. Out-dated equipment, such as cars, planes and trains may cause the same reaction.

When showing films on developing or "third world" countries, and this is especially important in documentaries, be aware of racism and "colonial" attitudes. These are definitely undesirable and untimely, and demonstrate that values and viewpoints can become as outdated as hairstyles. Words like "native," "primitive," etc. are offensive to many people, as are references in demeaning language to people of foreign origins and backgrounds.

Sex stereotyping may be present in many older films. In an article in the Wilson Library Bulletin[3] we mentioned that most child heroes shown in past films were male. Certainly lawyers, doctors, statesmen, musicians, etc. are even today usually pictured as males. While we cannot always avoid such stereotyping when using older films, we can, and must be aware of it, and discuss it openly with our students.

Sound

Some of the same criteria apply to sound, which adds so much to the enjoyment of films. The choice of vocabulary and voices, a part of sound, should be taken into consideration when choosing films. Voices and narration must be clear and easy to understand, with good voice quality, diction, and timing. The vocabulary must be appropriate to the age and background of the viewer, and the generation watching the film. Condescending mannerisms and style on the part of the narrator are deadly bores to be avoided. Opinions in the narration may not always be objective or timely, and must be guarded against. Children's voices, although appealing to young and old alike, are often difficult to understand, especially in films that demonstrate skills.

Films using dialect should be previewed for clarity and ease in understanding, as well as appropriateness of use. A non-narrative format eliminates many of the problems mentioned here. All ages can watch this type of film on their own level, since no vocabulary is involved.

Music

Films have never been "silent" for there was music to accompany even the earliest ones. Mood music, at first no longer than two or three minutes, was eventually expanded to relate not only to mood, but to the pace and action of the scenes it accompanied.[4] Both the narrative and dramatic structure of film is strengthened by musical accompaniment.

In 1927 the film THE JAZZ SINGER, starring Al Jolson, had a final sound sequence added, which helped tremendously in making it a success. Despite its obvious necessity, music should not intrude, and it has been said that "The best film music is that which is not heard."[5] There were exceptions to this. Back in 1928 and 1929 Darius Milhaud, Dmitri Shostakovich and Sergei Prokofiev were writing music for European movies. In 1936 Virgil Thompson wrote music for some documentaries. Also in the 30's, American movies featured the music of Vincent Youmans (FLYING DOWN TO RIO), Irving Berlin (TOP HAT), Jerome Kern (SWING TIME), George Gershwin (SHALL WE DANCE), and Richard Rodgers (MISSISSIPPI).

Aaron Copland who composed the scores for OUR TOWN, THE RED PONY, OF MICE AND MEN, and THE NORTH STAR and the English composers Ralph Vaughan Williams and Sir William Walton, who wrote for the movies in the 40's, were equally outstanding. More recently there were ELVIRA MADIGAN with the romantic music of Mozart's Piano Concerto No. 21, THE GRADUATE with the songs of Simon and Garfunkel, the music of Elmer Bernstein in TO KILL A MOCKINGBIRD and THE MAGNIFICENT SEVEN, the music of Scott Joplin in THE STING, and Burt Bacharach, Jr.'s "Raindrops Keep Falling on My Head" from BUTCH CASSIDY AND THE SUNDANCE KID.

When you find that there is too much sound, whether music or other, cut it out entirely rather than permit it to spoil a film you wish to use with students. Atmosphere can be conveyed by silence, rustling leaves, howling winds, heavy breathing, waves breaking on the sand, the singing of birds, children's laughter, people eating, the sound of animals, the sound of the human heart, etc. Sound and/or music can be used to suggest humor, a person's attitude towards a given situation, or set the stage for a coming event. It is most important for students to realize this when watching a film.

James Limbacher in his book Using Films sums up this topic very well. "Technique for its own sake soon bores the general public. Choose a film which is able to evoke a response.... If a film leaves the audience exactly where it found them, it hardly qualifies as a good film."[7]

FOOTNOTES

1. Goldman, Frederick, and Linda Burnett. Need Johnny Read? Dayton, Ohio: Pflaum/Standard, 1971, p. 211.

2. Goldman, op. cit., p. 191.

3. Miller, Hannah. "Why Children's Films Aren't Rated R," Wilson Library Bulletin, October 1971, pp. 183-4.

4. Goldman, op. cit., p. 191.

5. Kolodin, Irving. "Sounds for the Silver Screen," Saturday Review, November 12, 1977, pp. 44-46.

6. Goldman, op. cit., p. 195.

7. Limbacher, James. Using Films: A Handbook for the Program Planner. New York: Educational Film Library Assoc., Inc., 1967.

REFERENCES

Anderson, David and Gary Wilburn. Visualize. Dayton, Ohio: Pflaum/Standard, 1971.

Bobker, Lee R. Elements of Film. New York: Harcourt, Brace and World, 1969.

Bowden, Liz-Anne, ed. *The Oxford Companion to Film.* Oxford University Press, 1976. Lists of films, list of major motion picture companies, discussions of movement, genres, the work of major theorists, critics, etc.

Feyen, Sharon and Don Wigal, eds. *Screen Experience: An Approach to Film.* Published for the National Curriculum Commission of The Journalism Education Association by Pflaum, Dayton, Ohio, 1969 (rev. ed., 1975).

Films Inc. "American Film Genre Program." Each genre unit contains extracts from two films. Accompanied by cassette lecture tapes and study guide. From Films Inc. (send for catalog), 1144 Wilmette Ave., Wilmette, Ill. 60091

Goldman, Frederick and Linda R. Burnett, *Need Johnny Read?* Dayton, Ohio: Pflaum/Standard, 1971.

Hampton, Benjamin, *History of the American Film Industry from Its Beginnings to 1931.* Dover Publ., 1970.

Huss, Roy and Norman Silverstein. *The Film Experience: Elements of Motion Picture Art.* New York: Harper & Row, 1968.

Janus Films. "The Art of Film." Covers screenwriting, the camera, the editing.

Janus Films. "Image, Music and Sound and the Director." Each film 22 min. Uses excerpts from feature length films. Send for catalog: Janus Films, 745 5th Ave., New York, N.Y. 10020

Kuhns, William and Thomas Giardino. *Behind the Camera.* Dayton, Ohio: Pflaum, 1970.

Limbacher, James L., ed. *Film Music: From Violins to Video.* Metuchen, N.J.: Scarecrow, 1974. $18.50.

Madsen, Roy Paul. *The Impact of Film: How Ideas Are Communicated Through Cinema and Television.* New York: Macmillan, 1973.

Robinson, David. *The History of World Cinema.* New York: Stein & Day, 1973. A comprehensive, general history of international cinema. Overview of films and film makers from before 1895-1972.

Ryan, Steve. "Teaching Film," Audiovisual Instruction, September 1977, pp. 38-39. A program in film education.

Sadoul, Georges. Dictionary of Films. Translated, edited and updated by Peter Morris. University of California Press, 1972. Credits, synopses, dates and critical comments about key films.

Sklar, Robert. Movie-Made America: A Social History of American Movies. New York: Random House, 1975.

Spottiswoode, Raymond. Film and Its Technique: A Grammar of Film. University of California Press, 1969. This maker of documentaries analyzes all the steps of production. Includes annotated bibliography.

Chapter 3: TYPES OF FILMS

DEFINITIONS

Much is made of the terms used to describe films, such as theatrical and non-theatrical, classroom or instructional, art films, avant-garde, etc. Put as simply as possible, a commercial film is any film which is for sale. In other words, any film other than free promotional films put out by non-profit organizations, corporations, or government agencies, is a commercial film. Theatrical releases are, for the most part, those 35mm Hollywood-type films one sees in movie theaters. These may include documentaries, and often short films, which can be shown as 35mm in movie houses, but reduced to 16mm to be shown in schools and libraries. Non-theatrical releases are almost always 16mm, which are difficult to blow up to 35mm without losing some clarity in the process. A course in film study will use standard genres to teach students to evaluate films by studying acting, editing, etc., as well as types of films. Here we will attempt to classify films as they are used in the classroom and library. Later in the chapter we will digress to themes and topics in keeping with "a practical" approach to film use and in order to give as many samples as possible.

Feature Films

Many full length features, such as THE DIARY OF ANNE FRANK (113 min., New Yorker Films), begin as 35mm and are then reduced to 16mm, to be sold or rented to schools, libraries and other community groups. Feature films are usually fifty minutes or longer and resemble plays and novels since they have a plot. Film extracts are short episodes from feature films. The Learning Corporation of America series "Searching for Values" includes 15 to 17 minute edited versions of such films as THE SWIMMER, TO SIR WITH LOVE, ON THE WATERFRONT, etc. "Great Themes of Literature," from the same distributor, includes specially edited versions of TAMING OF THE SHREW, starring Elizabeth Taylor and Richard Burton, Roman Polanski's MACBETH, and Paul Scofield in A MAN FOR ALL SEASONS, all in 28 minute versions, now sold and rented as non-theatrical, 16mm films. Films can be and are released as 16mm and 35mm at the same time.

Short Films

These can be used for many purposes and have finally been discovered by schools. Libraries have been showing 16mm short films for some years. They range from documentaries to animated and "children's" films. They may be experimental and/or avant-garde since short films are less expensive to produce than features, and are not subject to the commercial pressures of the marketplace.

Instructional Films

An instructional film is one that is used to teach or instruct, but hopefully will also educate. They can be sound or silent, 16mm or 8mm, or super 8mm used in instructional settings. By definition instruction, and/or teaching is the "giving of knowledge," education "draws forth" that which is already there. It is easy to see how a film can do both. The information in a film both teaches and draws forth a response, if the film is well made (see Non-Narrative Films, p. 49). In fact, classroom or instructional films of the past did not fulfill their promise of teaching, since many were dull, and poorly made. Many of them had poor photography and "saccharine narration."[1*] If any film can do the job, it must be the newer, more creative and less pedantic films that can and do instruct and educate. In a sense the viewer learns something from every film he or she sees, even if it's only how not to make a bad film.

Children's Films

Children's films is a misnomer. Any film made

---

*Footnotes to Chapter 3 begin on page 71.

Two scenes from PADDLE TO THE SEA, a National Film Board of Canada production.

exclusively for children (with very few exceptions) makes us suspect the producer of passing on inferior products. While some films are made from children's picture books, if well made there is no reason why adults cannot enjoy them also. Films can be seen on many levels, and whatever information and enjoyment a young person gets from watching a film (on the level they can understand) is enough reason to show the film, if it is a good one. Most distributors listing this category in their catalogs will also include the same films under other headings.

Art Films

The term art film is a confusing one. Again, it may have lost its original meaning, but to us it is a film about art. If a producer or distributor has such a category in his catalog, read the description carefully and find out what he means by it for the meaning depends on who is using the term.

Film as Art, to distinguish, includes classics as well as experimental and avant-garde films, which tomorrow may no longer retain that classification, but are there for the moment. The Educational Film Library Association at its annual Film Festivals has a separate category for these films, and they are shown at a separate showing, outside the regular schedule.

Documentaries

Documentaries are factual and visual presentations about actual topics or persons. Cinéma vérité is the photographing of an actual event without previous planning of the shots. Parts of newsreels fall into this category.

NEW APPROACHES

Stereotype definitions of the kinds of films available for schools are still in use, but most film makers have become aware of the need for a film which is less pedantic than "classroom films" used to be. In the past, lack of communication between schools and producers left the field wide open to inexpensive presentations of curriculum materials, made for a limited, and often financially unrewarding market. This has changed. Producers have begun to contact classroom teachers, the market has opened up with some government support, and greater interest in media has brought teachers and librarians to the job with more awareness of the young people of today and their tastes. Foreign short films have been introduced to libraries and classrooms thus creating a demand for well-made, multi-usage films.

One expatriate, Gene Deitch, is making films in Czechoslovakia because he found there was no place to make and market films in the U.S. He calls himself a "cultural refugee." In 1970 he wrote in an article in Film Library Quarterly that the market in America had not been for children's films at all, but only for films designed to sell things to parents, or to amuse the broadest possible cross-section of film audiences. He feels that a market has finally developed, and new possibilities and approaches are being discovered.[2]

There is no question that until 1940 films for schools avoided being "entertaining," but today even "classroom" films are using a lighter, more creative approach both in content and in their soundtracks. Lectures are omitted for the most part, with limited narration alternating with music, natural sounds, and the voices of the actors. "Think Metric," a new series of three films distributed by Arthur Barr, each nine minutes long, is a good example of this approach. MEASURE LENGTH, MEASURE WEIGHT, and MEASURE VOLUME all deal seriously with these topics, but children discuss in their own language what they are doing, and the pedantic narrator is gone from the scene. The photography is excellent, the changing scenery interesting enough to hold the eye of the viewer, and the soundtrack is up-to-date. There are many other examples of such films to be found in the catalogs of the distributors mentioned in this book (see Appendix F).

If you are asked to choose a film, the basic question you want to ask is simple: Is this a good film, and is it right for my students and my particular needs? Other questions might be: Will anyone watch it, and who? Subject matter can be treated in many ways, and you must consider which approach will work best with a particular group. Sometimes you will want a factual presentation, sometimes you just want to explore a new curriculum area with your class. At other times you need a "starter," a film to stimulate thinking and to start a discussion. Problem solving can be "kicked off" with a good film, as can other creative efforts.

Factual Films

For factual presentations there undoubtedly are entire areas where films can do a better job of teaching than textbooks. This is particularly true in the sciences and can be said as well of some of the arts and crafts films. Authenticity in presenting the subject, simplicity of explanations, and timeliness are the keys here.

Two of the most comprehensive and popular arts and crafts series are "Rediscovery: Art Media Series" and "At Your Fingertips" from Paramount. There are 13 films in the first series: CLAY, CRAYONS, COLLAGE, ENAMELING, PAPER CONSTRUCTION, POSTERS, PAPER MACHE, PRINTS, PUPPETS, SILKSCREEN, WATERCOLOR, STITCHERY, and WEAVING. "At Your Fingertips" is made up of six films: GRASSES, BOXES, PLAY CLAY, SUGAR AND SPICE, CYLINDER, and FLOATS. There are many excellent films in this subject area from other distributors, such as CONQUEST OF LIGHT (11 min., color, Pyramid) which shows how crystal is made, but the Paramount series are popular enough to be shown for entertainment as well as for learning. Two outstanding films from Chrystal Productions' CREATING WITH CERAMICS and CREATING WITH WATERCOLOR, will make any class want to start working in those media.

To mention a few examples of science films which fall into this category is probably unfair to all the other excellent films that there are, but here is a small selection to start you off. PASSION VINE BUTTERFLY (10 min., color, Aims) presents comprehensive close-ups of the life-cycle of this butterfly. The film is excellent as a generic example. THE UNSEEN WORLD (parts 1, 2, 3, 15-17 min., color, McGraw-Hill Films) goes from microscope to underwater camera to the telescope to bring the complexity of the universe to the viewer. THE WORLD OF DARKNESS (25 min., color, National Geographic) concerns the adaptation of different animals to the dark. It made its premier on television. BIRTH AND DEATH OF A STAR (30 min., color, producer American Institute of Physics, distributor Time-Life Films) uses animation and telescopic photography to portray the life-cycle of a star. THE SCIENCE SCREEN

REPORT, a series of nine twenty-minute films, each containing segments on research in science, medicine, technology and engineering, is distributed by Sterling Educational Films. The fields covered are biology, physics, chemistry, ecology, earth science, astronomy, meteorology, oceanography, education, and animal behavior. The four segments in each film can cover any four of these subject areas, and of course they can be shown together or separately. The films are produced in close association with the National Science Teachers Association, and there are nine films each year, produced one each month, September through May. Teachers' Guides are included with the films, and they are made to show the relevance of the current research being done in those fields. In some parts of the country, commercial sponsors have made the program available to the schools free of charge. Not all the films are appropriate for all levels, and each teacher will have to preview to see how the films and the work of the class match. Ward's MLA distributes "The Inhabitants of the Earth" series, produced by BioMedia Associates. This series of eleven films covers 27 major classes of protists and animal life forms. Stuart Finley, Inc. distributes a ten-film series "The Science of Energy." One of the films in this series, SOLAR GENERATION (21 min., color, 1976), is an excellent film for high school students and covers the topic of solar energy as well as any film we have seen.

Information Films

An information film must present facts, but it should be done in such a way that the audience will remember them. The film must be interesting enough so that the viewer will want to pay attention in order not to miss anything. Generally children have become used to factual presentations in classroom films, however, lectures and pedantic narration on films are no more attractive on film than when coming from a teacher standing in front of a class. A story which more subtly presents facts about a country, occasion, or situation may leave a lasting impression, but it is important to make sure the information is accurate and the point of view not misleading. This last item calls for objectivity when previewing, as well as when discussing a film.

A good example of stories which teach is the Learning Corporation of America's "Many Americans" series. There are eight films, each one about a young member of a

GERONIMO JONES, from Learning Corporation of America

minority group in this country. The point of reference in all of these appeals to children from a variety of backgrounds. GERONIMO JONES (21 min.) is about an Indian boy and his grandfather; FELIPA--NORTH OF THE BORDER (17 min.) with a girl heroine, is about a Chicana (Mexican-American) and her attempt to help her adult uncle; MIGUEL--UP FROM PUERTO RICO (15 min.) is perhaps the most appealing of the series, about a boy and his family who now live in a big city ghetto; SIU MEI WONG--WHO SHALL I BE? (18 min.) about a Chinese-American girl who must attend a Chinese private school every afternoon after attending a public school in the morning; TODD--GROWING UP IN APPALACHIA (13 min.) which deals with hunger and poverty in that region and the dilemma one boy faces when he finds food stamps he needs and wants but which are needed even more by the person who lost them; WILLIAM--FROM GEORGIA TO HARLEM (16 min.) is about a farm boy in a big city and how his values help him to prove himself; LEE SUZUKI--

FELIPA: NORTH OF THE BORDER, from Learning Corporation of America

HOME IN HAWAII (19 min.) about a young boy growing up in Hawaii; and MATTHEW ALIUK--ESKIMO IN TWO WORLDS (18 min.) about an Eskimo boy in a big city who decides to help his adult uncle who cannot adjust to life away from his hunting village. Compare these with "Come Over to My House" a series of 9 films from Xerox, featuring American children from different backgrounds.

The traditional film about foreign countries tells the viewer what to look for and how to see it, much in the style of a product of a tourist office, or the local Chamber of Commerce. Even films about the U.S. put out by state Chambers of Commerce have this fault. This lecture-type film rarely holds the attention of audiences. Fortunately, some of the more recent films about other countries are using more imaginative approaches by showing progress as well as problems and by permitting people in the film to tell their own story. PEOPLE OF VENICE (16 min., color, Churchill) is about a working-class family living in that

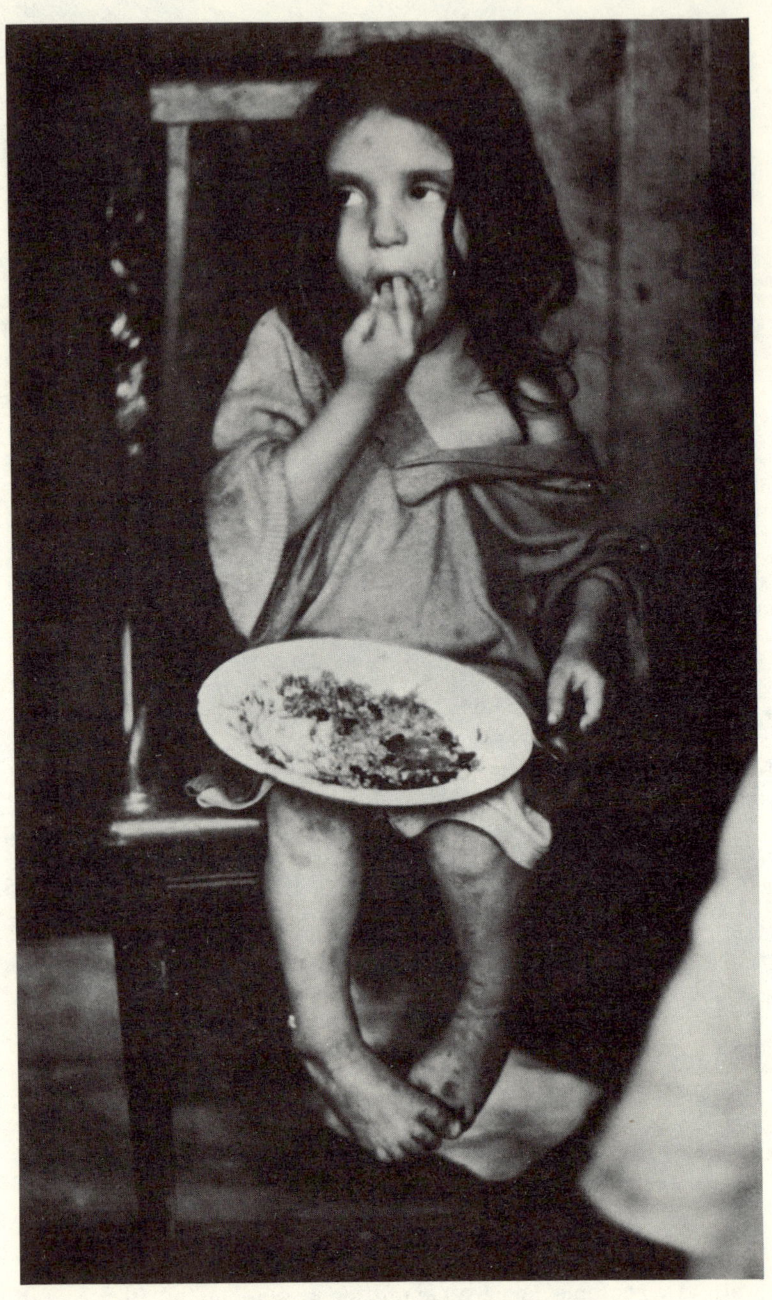

FLAVIO, from Films Inc.

THE RED BICYCLE, from Learning Corporation of America

JUGGERNAUT, from Learning Corporation of America

historic city. FLAVIO (12 min., b/w, Films Inc.) is a social documentary about an impoverished family of eleven, living in a hut in the poorest section of Rio de Janeiro. THE RED BICYCLE and THE TWO WORLDS OF MUSEMBE (13 min., color, LCA) from the "African Odyssey" series contrast the old and the new in fast-changing Africa.

There are films that describe particular events, such as JUGGERNAUT: A FILM OF INDIA (28 min., color, producer NFBC, distributor LCA) which emphasizes the contrasts between the old and the new, as the viewer follows a seventy-ton atomic reactor on its journey 700 miles across India; and THE LIVING ARTS OF JAPAN (30 min., color, free rental only, Consulate of Japan). These are rare, non-story films which fascinate children of all ages and can be seen many times. A properly prepared class will react more creatively to this type of film, will become curious about the country they have seen on film, and will remember more. There is no question but that more is demanded from the teacher as well, since the class needs more preparation, but the results make the effort worthwhile.

Leo Dratfield, formerly of Contemporary Films, now with Films Incorporated, was quoted in <u>Film News</u>: "Film is basically a visual medium and it is beginning to be better understood that it should be absorbed through the eyes and the mind, not the ears."[3] Much of this newer interest in non-didactic, nonverbal films is due to the introduction of films from Europe which had to be made with little or no narration for the international market. Leo Dratfield and Anne Schutzer of Contemporary Films were among the first to bring these to the attention of American audiences. They introduced them first to libraries and through them to schools. Some of the films made by Robert Churchill of Churchill Films and Julien Bryan of the International Film Foundation fall into this category. These pioneers, working right here in the U.S., have made a great contribution to film use in schools and libraries.

The National Film Board of Canada has made important contributions in this area. Their excellent products are distributed by many American companies. The Canadian Consulates are marvelous sources of some of their products, with the added attraction that they loan some of their films free of charge. (See other references to NFBC, and <u>Educator's Guide to Free Films</u>, Appendix E.)

Non-Narrative Films

Non-narrative films are those that communicate pictorially. There is no dialogue, or voice-over narration, and the only sounds are music to set the mood, and other noises for realism and special effects. The spoken word is

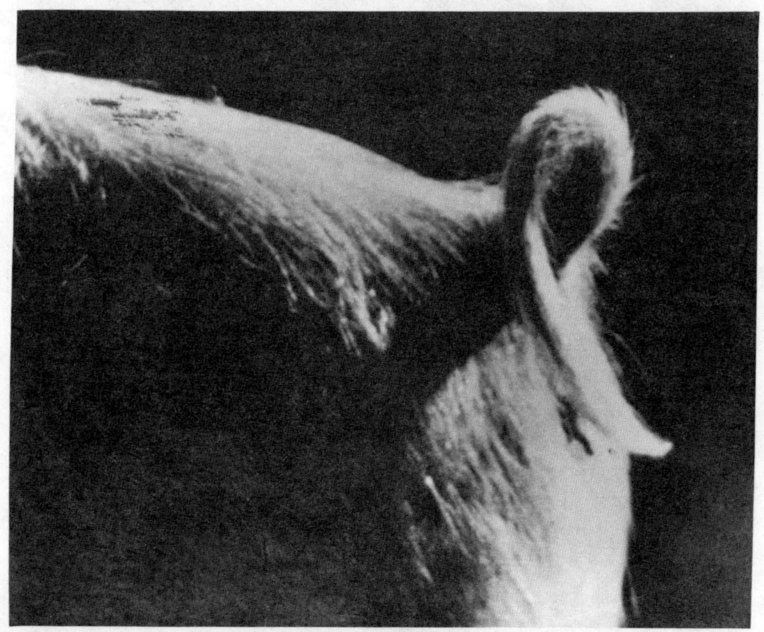

PIGS, from Churchill Films

rarely used. Examples of this type of film are PIGS (11 min., color) and COWS (11 min., color) both produced by Ed Schuman and distributed by Churchill Films, and films made by Julien Bryan and his International Film Foundation in the United States, as well as the many non-narrative films made abroad. These were the first bridge between children's films and adult films. Without words age levels disappear, and the viewer thus becomes the interpreter of what is seen. Showing non-narrative films gives students a chance to interpret and discuss their own reactions, to ask questions and initiate projects. For these reasons, non-narrative films should be chosen whenever possible.

Non-narrative films automatically weed out talkathons,

"Mountain People of Central Asia," a series from the International Film Foundation.

talking lectures, syrupy narration, and slanted and inaccurate narrations. Age levels are forgotten, which is good, for so often films made for children talk down to them or over their heads. Language barriers are eliminated, and the twenty million hard of hearing people in the United States can profit. The film without words has much going for it, but we must remember it is not a cure-all, is not suitable for all topics, and, as mentioned previously, calls for much preparation on the part of the teacher.

Other films made by Julien Bryan of the I. F. F. which use this approach are the series "Mountain People of Central Asia," and "African Village Life," as well as the "How We Live" series. These films were made with great care, beautifully photographed and executed, and have proven timeless because they do not use narration, because costumes of other nations are timeless to the Western eye, and because of their excellence. Julien Bryan believed "that children like to be left alone to make their own discoveries," and he thought that "it is exciting to make new short films which raise questions instead of answering them and which involve children."[4] The films show people from undeveloped countries in a natural way so we can admire their customs and beliefs with none of the "colonialism" sometimes shown.

Many non-narrative films are recommended for language arts in the lower grades, as well as guidance lessons and human relations. Just a few examples of nonverbal films for language arts (see p. 236 for longer list): SEE'N TELL (12 titles, 8-10 min., color, Films Inc.) stars animals, birds and insects with only natural environmental sounds and background music. Films encouraging the young to use their imagination, such as A KITE STORY (15 min., color, Churchill), THE LITTLE AIRPLANE THAT GREW (9 min., color, LCA), THUNDERSTORM (6 min., color, Churchill), SWIMMY (6 min., color, animation, Connecticut Films), A VISIT FROM SPACE (10 min., color, McGraw-Hill) are also fun to watch, making the learning experience pleasant and one the children tend to remember longer.

Some years ago Sightlines, the EFLA publication about films, published a "Best of Best" list, as chosen by their readers. The three children's films which made the list were WHITE MANE (30 min., b/w, Macmillan), THE RED BALLOON (34 min., color, Macmillan) and THE GOLDEN FISH (30 min., color, Macmillan). Edmond Sechan, the director of THE GOLDEN FISH, photographer of THE

Two scenes from "African Village Life," a series from the International Film Foundation.

"Mountain People of Central Asia," a series from the International Film Foundation.

RED BALLOON, and writer and director of THE STRING BEAN (Le Haricot) (17 min., b/w with color, McGraw-Hill) obviously believes in non-narrative films, for all of these were made in this format.

Films made by the great puppet-master Jiri Trnka, such as THE HAND (19 min., color, McGraw-Hill), again are non-narrative for they need no words to convey their message.

SUNDAY FATHER (11 min., color, Films Inc.) stars Dustin Hoffman as a divorced father who takes his young daughter on a once-a-week Sunday outing. With just a guitar and voice soundtrack, the feeling of sadness at a lack of communication and not knowing each other is portrayed.

Yet another area where non-narrative films are excellent is sports. Where there is enough action and the pacing and editing are well done, words are superfluous. Three films from Pyramid for sports enthusiasts of all ages are SKI WHIZ (6 min., color), one of Arthur Miller's zaniest ski films, TURNED ON (7 min., color), which shows some "way out" individual sports and SOLO (15 mins.,

SKI WHIZ, from Pyramid Films

color) about mountain climbing. In all three the action is strongly supported by excellent photography and music. "Breathtaking" is a good word to describe ABYSS (17 min., color, Phoenix) which tells of an attempt to climb the West Peak of Lavaredo in the Dolomites. It includes a 140 ft. fall of the climber and the hand-over-hand climb up a rope that saved his life.

Films Too Good for Words by Salvatore Parlato (Bowker) lists more than 1,000 films without words.

Open-Ended Films

Many films used for guidance and human relations are open-ended. These are films that offer both sides of an issue, or only the issue, with no answers or solutions. The audience becomes an active participant, discussions flow more naturally, and everyone becomes involved. Resolving the dilemma can take the form of discussions, writing, or role-playing. This technique can also be used for language arts.

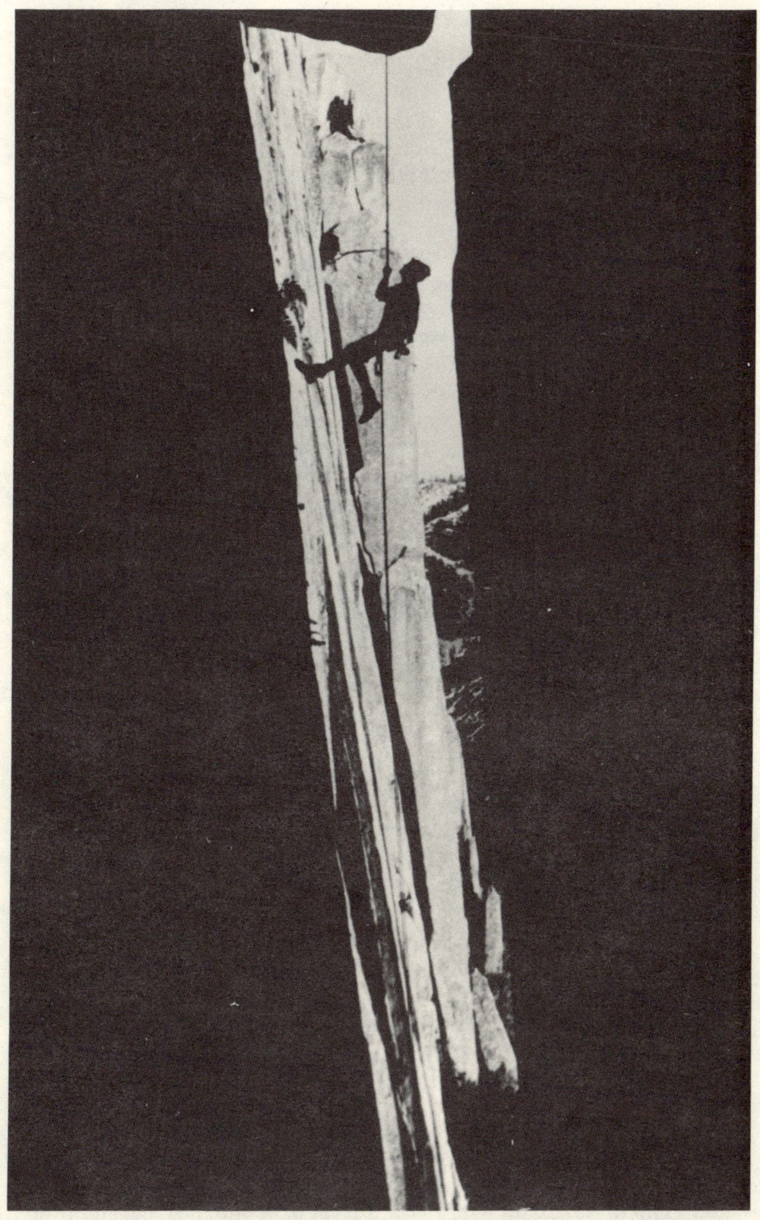

SOLO, from Pyramid Films

Human relations films which are open-ended really serve to "spark" discussions. A film on early childhood education, GUIDING BEHAVIOR (20 min., color, Churchill), shows several nursery school situations, with solutions left to the viewer. Churchill Films has produced open-ended films for grades four to seven to be used for guidance lessons. All of them are adapted from the book Role Playing for Social Values by Fannie and George Shaftel. PAPER DRIVE, TRICK OR TREAT, and THE CLUBHOUSE BOAT (15 min., color) are for the older grades, and THE BIKE and LOST PUPPY (14 min., color) for grades K-three. Another series, "The Searching Years," also from Churchill Films, is for older students. All of the films in the series were photographed at actual meetings of teen-agers and are realistic in that the conversations and confrontations that take place happened just as they appear in the films. It is important that teachers preview these films to give themselves some time to reflect on their own reactions before watching them with groups of teenagers, and getting involved in group discussions. (More about discussions in Chapter 5.) Some of the themes of these series are family relations, dating, marriage and differences. Sex stereotyping, racism, sexual relations, and drug use are some of the topics touched on by the young people in their discussions. You, the discussion leader, must be able to be objective in leading discussions following these films or be honest enough to get someone else to do so.

One of the best open-ended films is THE BILL OF RIGHTS IN ACTION: WOMEN'S RIGHTS (22 min., color, BFA). A girl asks admission to a boy's swimming team, and the ensuing argument reaches the courts. Each side presents its case, and there the film ends.

Iconographic Films

Then there are those films which are essentially shots of the pages of a book, sometimes with some animation added. Though these cannot replace films about real subject matter, they are sometimes useful in bringing together young audiences and books. The word iconographic means creating motion by moving the camera over the pages of the book, and almost all of this type of film is made of photographs taken of pages of picture books. Weston Woods, the best-known producer of iconographic films and the first to use the technique, has been reproducing award

THE HIDEOUT, from Churchill Films

THE BIKE, from Churchill Films

winning picture books for many years. WHISTLE FOR WILLIE (6 min., color), A LETTER TO AMY (7 min., color) and THE SNOWY DAY (6 min., color) are all from books by Ezra Jack Keats. Some of their more recent films such as PATRICK from the book by Quenton Blake (7 min., color, animated) and CHANGES, CHANGES from the book by Pat Hutchins (6 min., color, animated) have been directed by Gene Deitch and have been winning awards consistently. Many of the products of Weston Woods come in films, filmstrips, super 8 films, records, and in combinations of these. Although Weston Woods products have proven to be valuable in libraries and classrooms for exposing young children to books, many librarians in the past bought these films, to the exclusion of all others, because of the security of knowing the book first. Here again is an argument for previewing films, for then one becomes familiar with the subject matter of the films, and need not avoid new areas.

Another series using some iconographic techniques, mixed with live action shots of popular actors reading the

CHANGES, CHANGES, from Weston Woods

stories, is the "Reading Incentive Series," made up of 20 films, six to ten minutes long, which were produced by the Communications Laboratory of the Bank Street College of Education, and is distributed by McGraw-Hill Films. Many of them are read by male actors (e.g., Harry Belafonte and James Garner) and are a welcome addition to the classroom of the very young, for they are so little exposed to men during their school day. JOHN TABOR'S RIDE is read by Eli Wallach and, as the camera goes from the reader to the pages of the book to scenes of sea and shore, the actor's voice changes to represent the characters of this suspenseful story. THE THINKING BOOK, read by Sidney Poitier, in a whispery reading, enables the viewer to identify with the child in the story. Bill Cosby reads RICH CAT POOR CAT, a book of subtle social significance, as we are shown the witty illustrations. One advantage of this technique is that, like real animation, the films do not become dated as quickly as live action, although sometimes the music may.

BOOMSVILLE, from Learning Corporation of America

Animated Films

Most of the films mentioned in this chapter have been live-action films, involving photographs of people, places and things. What about animation? Must all animated films be "cartoons," and must all cartoons be silly? Absolutely not! Many kinds of art work and different types of presentations are available in animation, all of them very different from the "Tom and Jerry" cartoons with their mindless violence.

Richard Rauh, past chairman of ASIFA-East, the local branch of the International Filmmakers Association, defines animation as "the illusion of motion created by man's manipulation of images and pictures from frame to frame."[5] He feels the following points should be taken into consideration when evaluating animated films:

1. How well does the film come to a point? Is the overall sense of timing good? (American films are better at this than European ones, which tend to belabor the point.)

2. Animated films can make a statement quickly. It is a powerful medium, more easily controlled than live-action. Does the particular film you are considering do this?

3. Is the design right, or is it too cluttered?

4. Could the film be done better in live-action?

5. Check the technique, this includes direction, color, motion and characters.

According to Gene Deitch, with animation a "generalized and timeless kind of communication is achieved that live-action cannot match.... Drawings are always better for symbolic messages. Live-action must be handled more carefully to avoid dating."[6]

Animated films can be wonderfully entertaining, but often carry a message as a secondary feature, or, in some cases, convey a serious idea with a light touch. Many of the European short films mentioned previously are done in animation, which for the international market has obvious advantages. The National Film Board of Canada (NFBC) has done an excellent job at this. Topics, such as pollution

ARROW TO THE SUN, from Texture Films

and ecology, have been dealt with in such tongue-in-cheek animated films as BOOMSVILLE (11 min., color, LCA); THE RISE AND FALL OF THE GREAT LAKES (17 min., color, Pyramid); WHAT ON EARTH (9 min., color, McGraw-Hill) which gives a Martian-eye view of the world in which the automobile is the earth's true inhabitant and SECOND CHANCE: SEA (11 min., color, Pyramid, 1976) by Faith Hubley.

Films with a peace theme for children such as MORE (3 min., color, Macmillan), which is a satirical look at man's insatiable craving for material goods, TOYS (7 min., color, producer NFBC, distributor McGraw-Hill), FLOWER STORM (12 min., color, Paramount), and THE FLUTTERBY (9 min., color, Paramount), make a strong contribution to the classroom.

PUNCINELLA (11 min., color, Connecticut Films) is a beautifully choreographed animation by the Italian team of Emanuele Luzzati and Giulio Gianni, as are FREDERICK and SWIMMY, distributed by the same company. For the student of animation there are many different styles used in PUNCINELLA, an Academy Award nominee, and for the student of the social scene there is also a message. From these same two artists come two other films, excellent for their introduction to the music of Rossini, but primarily for fun, THE THIEVING MAGPIE (10 min., color, Universal Education and Visual Arts) and THE ITALIAN IN ALGIERS (10 min., color, Texture).

Other award-winning animated films of interest are THE DOODLE FILM (11 min., L. C. A.), THE OWL WHO MARRIED A GOOSE (7 min., color, producer NFBC, distributor Stephen Bosustow) in sand animation, and CLOSED MONDAYS (8 min., color, Pyramid).

Using his own style of animation, Gerald McDermett has made films which tell folktales from around the world, and add a light touch to the social studies class. Texture Films distributes ANANSI THE SPIDER (10 min., color) an African tale, THE MAGIC TREE (10 min., color) from the Congo, and ARROW TO THE SUN (10 min., color) from The Aconia Pueblo of New Mexico.

SIM Productions, a subsidiary of Weston Woods, combines animation and non-narrative films. Among them are THE GIANTS (11 min., color), a protest against violence, and MR. KOUMAL, a series of six, 1 to 2½ minute

THE OWL WHO MARRIED A GOOSE, prod. by the National Film Board of Canada; dist. by Stephen Bosustow.

reels about a universal "fall guy." These films tend to be excellent discussion starters.

FRANK FILMS (9 min., color, Pyramid), the 1974 Academy Award winner, has won just about every award offered today. It is an autobiographical film with a double soundtrack, and an unbelievable richness of technical proficiency. It is a superb design made up of thousands of cut-outs from magazine illustrations, used in a constantly changing collage. It must be seen many times to be fully appreciated on both a visual and aural level. There are many uses of this film from entertainment to discussions of choosing careers, forces affecting our times, and the impact of visual as opposed to the spoken or written.

Faith Hubley and her husband John, who died in 1976, are two film makers who have raised animation to a new art. Some of their work has appeared on "Sesame Street" and "Electric Company" of television fame, and they have made many films with social messages which have many uses. A WINDY DAY (9 min., color, Films Inc.) and CHILDREN OF THE SUN (10 min., color, UNICEF) were both made for UNICEF and have both a peace message and a special charm which appeal to children and adults in this message about the work of UNICEF (done in a most untradi-

THE GIANTS, from Weston Woods

tional way). URBANISSIMO (6 min., color, Films Inc.) is a clever and provocative film about cities and their environmental problems. This film was created for Expo '67 in Montreal, Canada. THE HAT (18 min., color, McGraw-Hill) is about a hat, the border between two hostile countries and our global future, and THE CRUISE (8 min., color, producer NFBC, distributor Eccentric Circle), is set on board a cruise ship, symbolic of our democratic system of government. One antisocial passenger begins to violate the rules, resulting in the gradual breakdown of the established pattern. Some of their earlier films, including MOONBIRD (10 min., color), are now distributed by Films Inc. EVERYBODY RIDES THE CAROUSEL (3 reels, approximately 21 min. each, color, Pyramid) describes the "eight rides" of psychoanalyst Erik H. Erikson's theory of personal development. Using animation and a minimum of music and appropriate human voices, short vignettes are used to capture each stage with unbelievable insight into human behavior and the use of animation.

Straight animation is often used to demonstrate the workings of engines, the formation of underground gases, etc. Phillip Stapp's SYMMETRY was made for the Brooklyn Polytechnic Institute under a grant from the National Science Foundation and uses animation to demonstrate principles of symmetry, balance, and position. Although a film for physics classes, the patterns themselves are enjoyable to watch.

Phillip Stapp has done much of the animation for Julien Bryan of the International Film Foundation, as did Richard Rauh at one time. Limited animation is used in their films about the history of countries to condense long periods of time. The technique is used in such films as POLAND (27 min., color), ISRAEL (31 min., color) and TROPICAL AFRICA (30 min., color). All have live photography to show the country today, but use animation to introduce the history of the country.

Norman McLaren has been working with the NFBC for many years. Given the freedom this organization can achieve, he has been finding novel and unexpected film forms. FIDDLE-DE-DEE (4 min., color, International Film Bureau) is painted directly on film, LOOPS (3 min., color, Pyramid) has a soundtrack drawn by hand, and live-

---

On opposite page: EVERYBODY RIDES THE CAROUSEL, from Pyramid Films.

A CHAIRY TALE, from the National Film Board of Canada

THE LIGHT FANTASTICK, from the National Film Board of Canada

action pixillation, which was introduced in NEIGHBORS (9 min., color, International Film Bureau) and is used as well in A CHAIRY TALE (10 min., b/w, NFBC). These are but a few samples of the innovative techniques used by Norman McLaren which have helped other film makers be more creative. THE LIGHT FANTASTICK (58 min., color, NFBC) emphasizes the work of McLaren, but mentions other "schools" of animation.

It has been said that animation, when used alone, is usually less successful in presenting information to older groups, but informational types of films which are completely animated are relatively rare because of the expense. There is no doubt that for younger children still immersed in their television cartoon watching a great amount of information can be learned from animated films. Our own feelings are that reactions vary from group to group (regardless of age), from film to film, and most important, from teacher to teacher. Again, previewing the film, taking one's own attitude into account, will help enormously in deciding what kind of film will best serve to meet one's objectives and goals.

Animation requires artistic talent, technical skill and the ability to see problems and foibles from a special point of view. Fuzzy thinking is as out-of-place as fuzzy drawing. It is potentially an international language, and is being used as such more and more. We in the U.S. are fortunate to have the use of animated films from many lands.

Films for Literature and Language Arts

When using films for literature and language arts more specific guidelines are needed. The following questions are helpful in judging films to be used:

1. Are the characterizations and the setting authentic?

2. Does the film extend the students' world beyond their immediate environment?

3. Is the student's imagination prodeed?

4. Are the voices of the film accurate for the ethnic background of the story?

In the case of language arts, add to these the possibilities for vocabulary growth, story telling and the fostering of children's drama and art.

An interesting way of introducing children to books is to show them a film about the author. MR. SHEPHARD AND MR. MILNE (91 min., color, Weston Woods) relies on a mixture of shots of the original locale and those taken from pages of their books. The narration by Christopher Robin Milne, the now grown-up boy of A. A. Milne's Winnie the Pooh series, adds another dimension to this excellent and delightful film. Weston Woods produced a series of films about author-illustrators of some of the picture books they have filmed (see Iconographic Films, p. 56). EZRA JACK KEATS (17 min., color), JAMES DAUGHERTY (19 min., color), MAURICE SENDAK (14 min., color) and ROBERT McCLOSKEY (18 min., color) are each featured in a film that shows them at work, talking about their books, and pages of some of their books. GENE DEITCH--THE PICTURE BOOK ANIMATED (25 min., color) is more about the art of animating a book than the book itself. It is fascinating to watch how carefully Deitch puts the components of the film/book together, how he tries to be authentic wherever possible, and how the soundtrack is "composed." In CREATING A CHILDREN'S BOOK (12 min., color, ACI)

Above: MR. SHEPHARD AND MR. MILNE, from Weston Woods. On opposite page: THE LIGHT FANTASTICK, from the National Film Board of Canada.

"Jolly Roger" Bradfield shows how he creates his books. ALAN GARNER, AUTHOR (11 min., color, Connecticut Films) gives the viewer insights into his writings, which combine fantasy and realism, and shows the actual settings for some of his books. In LEON GARFIELD (8 min., color), also from Connecticut Films, the author of many adventure stories tells how he accomplished some of the historic research for his books.

CONCLUSION

The number and quality of good films made for school and library use has greatly increased. According to Harmetz, the question now is "how soon will it be before these films can find their way into American movie theaters?"[7] Many of them have been shown in schools and libraries. Some have found their way to the television screen, and a few are being shown at special Saturday morning and matinee shows. The University of Southern California cinema department, the oldest and most active such department at the university level, started a course in January 1975 called "Children's Entertainment Cinema" taught on the graduate level by Richard Harmetz, of the Los Angeles Center of Films for Children.[8] This is probably the first such course being taught anywhere in the U.S., and it is limited to children's entertainment films.

Children are not passive viewers by nature, and it would be wrong to ignore their urge to participate. They know what they like and are not afraid to express their views audibly.[9] Films made for children and young adults must be the best, for they have learned to expect and demand nothing less.

When using a film marked "children's film" a guiding rule is "No film for children should be unacceptable to adults." Young children don't mind being children but they resent any suggestions that they are inferior just because they happen to be children, therefore never play down to them! If a young audience doesn't like an adult film it's because they don't understand the subject matter, because it's too long and complicated for them, or because there is too much dialogue.

While we are interested in the use of "children's films" in classrooms and libraries for their more creative approach to teaching, obviously most of the films listed above do not fall into this category. Many different approaches can produce excellent films that can teach anything from science to values. The role of the teacher becomes a different one when using films and therefore many teachers find their accepted roles threatened. The right film often can explain visually what cannot be done in any other way, and that is where the strength of using films lies.

FOOTNOTES

1. Sohn, David. Good Looking. Philadelphia: North American Publishing Company, 1976, p. 75.

2. Deitch, Gene. "An American in Prague," Film Library Quarterly, Fall 1969, p. 20.

3. Film News, December 1972, p. 19.

4. Bryan, Julien. International Film Foundation Catalog. Introduction, 1972-73.

5. Rauh, Richard, in a conversation with the author, June 1974.

6. Deitch, Gene, in a letter to the author.

7. Harmetz, Richard. "Coming Soon: More Films for Children," Los Angeles Times, November 8, 1974.

8. Harmetz, Richard, in a letter to the author, November 1974.

9. Children's Film Foundation Ltd., "Saturday Morning Cinema," 1967, pp. 6-8, 44.

REFERENCES

Books

Cowie, Peter (ed.). A Concise History of the Cinema. New York: A. S. Barnes, 1971.

Feyen, Sharon and Wigal, Don (eds.). Screen Experience:

An Approach to Film. Dayton, Ohio: Pflaum Publishers, 1969, rev. ed., 1975.

Friedlander, Madeline. Leading Film Discussions. New York: League of Women Voters, 817 Broadway, New York, N.Y. 10023, 1972. $1.50.

Kuhns, William and Carr, John. Movies in America: Teaching in the Dark. Dayton, Ohio: Pflaum/Standard, 1973.

Lacey, Richard. Seeing with Feeling: Films in the Classroom. Philadelphia: W. B. Saunders Co., 1972.

McLaughlin, Frank (ed.). The Mediate Teacher: Seminal Essays on Creative Teaching. Philadelphia: North American Publishing Company, 1975. (Section 2).

Parlato, Salvatore and Dolores. The Audio-Visual Advisor. Buffalo, N.Y., 1967. Box 25, Market Station, Buffalo 14203. $1.50.

Parlato, Salvatore J., Jr. Films Too Good for Words. New York: R. R. Bowker Co., 1973.

Rehrauer, George. The Film User's Handbook. New York: R. R. Bowker Co., 1975.

Schillaci, Anthony and Culkin, John (ed.). Films Deliver--Teaching Creatively with Films. New York: Citation Press, 1970.

Sohn, David. Film Study and the English Teacher. Indiana University Audio-Visual Center, 1968.

Weston Woods. SIM Presents Adventures in Education Through Non-Verbal Films. Weston, Conn.: Weston Woods (special catalog), 1973.

Periodicals

Eppel, Ron. "Animation Alive and Well," Media & Methods, April 1977, pp. 42-46.

French, Janet. "The State of the Art of A/V Reviewing, with Special Emphasis on Filmstrips," Library Journal, March 15, 1970, pp. 1162-7.

Greiner, Charles F. "Film Study Hang Ups," from Good Looking, David Sohn, ed. Philadelphia: North American Publishing Co., 1976.

Journal of the University Film Association (Temple University, Philadelphia, Pa.), vol. 29, no. 3, Summer 1977. Article on teaching film.

Kuhn, William. "The Instructional Film Is Dead," from Good Looking, David Sohn, ed. Philadelphia: North American Publishing Co., 1976, p. 27.

Lembo, Diana. "Notes from a Semi-Darkened Room," Library Journal, Feb. 15, 1970, pp. 737-9.

Lohmann, Karl B., Jr. "Are You Sure That Film's Worth Showing?" K-Eight, November 1973, p. 40, 53.

Miller, Hannah. "Films for Your Class: How to Pick the Best," Teacher, September 1972, pp. 127-8.

Parlato, Salvatore J. "Films for Your Class: A Guide to Programming Non-Verbal Films," Previews, February 1973, pp. 3-11.

Porte, Marha. "Fundamentals of Evaluation: Judging Films, a Complex of Many Elements," Film Library Quarterly, Fall 1972, p. 37.

Previews, "Evaluation," LJ/SLJ Previews, February 1973, p. 3.

Quinsberry, Nancy L., Terry Shepherd and Winonia Williams. "Criteria for the Selection of Records, Filmstrips and Films for Young Children," Audiovisual Instruction, April 1973, p. 36.

Rice, Susan. "What You See Is What You Get," Media & Methods, October 1973, p. 11.

Spencer, Alan. "Film Selection--A Cooperative Effort," Previews, January 1974, pp. 22-3.

Chapter 4: CHOOSING FILMS: PREVIEWING

WHY PREVIEW?

Is there one best way to choose a film? We recently came across a book on film study with two blank pages following the heading "Standards for Judging Good Films." That probably is a good starting point, since all of us bring our own experience, viewpoint, mood at the time of screening, criteria and values, to the film experience. Add to that the physical environment (e.g., companions, time of day, conditions of the projector and screen, etc.), the make-up of the class, background, sophistication, social awareness, tolerance of avant-gardism, religion and ethnic origin, and the interaction of the group at any given moment, and you have enough ingredients to make anyone hesitate in choosing the "one best film" for any group!

There is no excuse for not previewing a film before showing it to one's class, just as teachers would not use a book before reading it. Unfortunately, the eagerness to show a film leads teachers into making the mistake of not screening before showing. This may well ruin the effective use of films with that particular class, at least for some time to come. Here are some of the precautions one observes in previewing:

1. Make sure the correct film is on the reel. Just imagine your class ready for a film on the metric system, but when the lights go out, and the picture appears on the screen, there is a picture about a boy and his bike. A good teacher can, of course, rescue the situation and make the most of a mistake, but you can forget about the metric system for that day. (If you are substituting in a class and this happens, hope the film you are showing will hold the attention of the group and keep going. To try to stop the film will probably create chaos.)

2. Check the physical condition of the film. Frequent breaks spoil a screening and, unless your projectionist or you know how to splice a film and have the tools at hand, this means the end of the showing for that period.

3. The soundtrack should be clear and easily understood, and there should be no extraneous noises. If the class cannot hear or understand the narration, they will disrupt the showing with constant questions and comments.

4. Timeliness, although not usually as vital an ingredient as some others, should be checked. (See Chapter 2, p. 28.) If the film is an old one, but deemed essential, some explanation may help to prepare the class for "old-fashioned" hair styles, clothing, vintage cars and airplanes, etc., before viewing the film.

5. Vocabulary and sophistication of speech pattern of the actors should be on a level that the class can handle. Shakespeare may not be for your class in the original, depending on their background and exposure, and why spoil a film by showing it to a group that is not ready for it? Accents may be hard to understand or may offend, so check these as well.

6. The point of view or treatment of the subject matter may not be one you want to stress. Catalog descriptions are written to sell films and may be misleading. Even if the description is a good one for the film, reading about it and seeing it are very different experiences.

7. You've chosen a nature film or travelogue, but when you start showing the film, the color is washed out. It turns out to be an old film, but the catalog did not mention the year the film was released. It is better for your disappointment to be a private one.

8. Make sure the film has been rewound correctly. Sometimes films are not checked carefully enough and arrive backward on the reel, inside out, etc. It may take hours to straighten out a mess like that, especially without the proper tools.

Why take a chance? Preview, check and make sure conditions are the best you can make them. If the film is wrong for your group, perhaps there is time to look for another one. A quick check of your town's media center or public library may find a substitute film or filmstrip. If not, it is far better to do without for that particular lesson.

WHO SHOULD PREVIEW?

You have decided that you want to use films and have done your homework. You think you know how to use films, how to integrate them into the curriculum and the kind of films you will want to use. If you are about to order a film just for your class why not involve them in choosing the film? You can make a real learning situation by appointing a committee to check the catalogs, choose a film, and write for it. However, using a film just once with one group is an expensive way of utilizing films, unless the film is a free one. Certainly, when buying a film for your school, this is obviously not the best way of going about it.

In many schools the classroom teachers often show films that have been chosen by someone far removed from the teaching situation. Schools may belong to a film circuit in which they have no voice in the choice of films. The power to purchase a film should never be given to one person or even to a group that does not include representatives of those who will use the film. Film selection must be a cooperative effort, and there is no reason to exclude school classes, neighborhood young adults, college students, and even one's own children. The opinions of young people are valuable, and they are as critical in their evaluations as adults, and often more candid. We need to see our students' world through their own eyes, just as we need to listen and hear what they are saying, not what we think they are saying. If we really want to work with young people, we need to watch "their" programs on television, "their" movies, and listen to "their" music. Certainly they are the only ones who can let us know which films will "turn them on," and their reactions are not always predictable.

The perfectly delightful film PEOPLE SOUP (15 min., color, LCA), which has entertained adults for some years, is not always chosen by young audiences, yet is shown frequently by adults who choose it because they think "kids will love it." This regrettable situation may be understandable, but it points out that too few adults really attend to the reaction of students.

Another interesting example of this occurred at the

1974 Children's Film Festival at Gijon, Spain. All the adults there seemed to agree that children want to see justice done and that they identify with children and animals in the films they like. There was agreement as well, "that elementary-age children are repelled by bloody scenes and by the death of any character they have come to identify with."[1*] However, when it came to giving awards, the children gave first place to a Mexican film, THE ENCHANTED ISLAND, which is the retelling of Defoe's Robinson Crusoe, with a 10-year-old Friday as a religious son of a cannibal chief. While the children's jury could identify with this 10-year-old Friday, the festival chairman was attacked by the adults for allowing this "tasteless and violent film to be screened."[2]

Choose the best films you can get when previewing with reluctant fellow teachers. Include one or two students or young people from the community who "just happened to be there." This will indicate student interest in films, and if the young people are articulate and knowledgeable, so much the better.

Even should you feel no one else is interested, make an effort to involve a few other teachers. If your principal has given you a free hand, try not to assume the entire burden. Check with the school librarian, other schools, the local library, etc., before making a final choice of films to buy or rent.

Unless teachers in many subject areas are involved and exposed to what's available, film usage and film programs will be less successful. In studies on film usage, the importance of communication among librarians, administrators, audiovisual coordinators, and the classroom teacher has been shown. The most important communication is that everyone's ideas and comments are needed and wanted in formulating programs and ordering films.

Since there are a number of good reviewing journals (see Appendix B), teachers and librarians pressed for time often use reviews of others in selecting films. Reviews reflect one person's viewpoint, and film selection therefore should never be based on only one review. Remember the interrelation of the nature of the film and the individual personality of the reviewer. A film may meet the highest

---

*Footnotes to Chapter 4 begin on page 81.

artistic and technical standards, but the subject matter may not appeal to the viewer. Sometimes the wrong emphasis may repel the viewer. The same film can be praised and torn apart by different critics. Response to film is very personal and unique (although viewing is usually a group process), and since you are the one who will use the film, preview it yourself, even if you know the person who wrote the review and have agreed with his or her opinions in the past. If you can find several reviewers you can rely on, good!

A screening committee made up of teachers from different backgrounds and subject areas, as well as media people, will also involve many more of them in using any one film. Films can often be used in more than one classroom situation and subject area, thus saving money, and this is but one advantage of using screening committees from diverse areas of the school. Even if you feel no one in your school knows about films, invite them to help choose. The exposure to films will help teach them, and your invitation will make them more eager to use the films they have previewed with you.

WHEN AND WHERE TO PREVIEW

Lack of time is no excuse to delegate one person to rent or buy for an entire school or library, or even for the entire school system. No one disputes the many demands on a teacher's time during the day, and the lack of funds to send them to conventions and film festivals. There are, however, in-service courses and workshops within a school system that can be devoted to films, and in some schools lunch hours and free periods may be utilized to preview. If there are several films to be previewed by a group, try to have them arrive at the same time, and have a film previewing hour once a month.

At the Friends School in Wilmington, Delaware, the media committee puts announcements such as the following in the teachers' mailboxes: "HANGMAN will be in school on Monday for preview."[3]

The teachers' lunchroom, the art room, the local library, someone's home after school, any place is good for previewing. You do need a projector, but any white wall will do as a screen. If the room can be darkened, so much the better. If you are using someone's home, if you can meet in the evening, you need not worry about drapes, etc., to darken the room. For a formal showing "atmosphere" can make a big difference (see Chapter 6).

We realize that for some teachers the idea of previewing a film at home or at the local library after school hours may be a novel one, but we are just beginning to realize previewing a film is as much a part of lesson planning and preparation as reading a book or an article, and there certainly are no set places for that.

Not enough schools use teachers' and PTA meetings for previewing films, or better yet, showing them. In systems where films on alcohol, venereal diseases, and sex education are just being introduced, parents are sometimes offered the opportunity to see the film first. We would like to think teachers might like to preview films on universally accepted topics with parents as well, in order to get input from the community on subjects other than controversial ones. Teachers who want to preview films seem to find the time and place somehow. It is the reluctant user who may have to be led to a special place at a special time to preview.

PROBLEMS WHICH CAN BE PREVENTED BY PREVIEWING

Always preview to avoid: 1) Having the wrong film on the reel; 2) Having the film wound backward; 3) Having a damaged film; 4) Having a poor sound track. This will 5) assure that the film is right for your class; and 6) assure that you have time to prepare for showing the film.

Some films need no introduction. Others accomplish more when properly introduced. Non-narrative films may need more preparation than more traditionally narrated ones, although the message of the film often may be more effectively transmitted in this type of film.

Controversial topics, new subjects, and especially sensitive areas may require previewing groups representing different points of view, not only among the faculty, but among the parents as well. Again, the teacher must consider the many ingredients that determine the make-up of a class or school, and must be aware of these at all times.

SOME AUDIENCE CRITERIA TO USE

When previewing a new film, consider the following aspects about your intended audience.

1. Its background, including religions and ethnic origins.

2. Its sophistication, which can vary from class to class and school to school in the same town. There will be tremendous differences between urban and suburban schools.

3. Mood at the time of screening. This can change with the time of day, season, weather, day of the week, closeness to school vacation, etc.

4. Preparation of class for the screening. Is the class prepared to see a film, or was this a last-minute substitution for something else? Is the class prepared to absorb the material presented in this film? Do they know something about the topic? Is there a framework in which to place the information in the film?

5. Preparation of the teacher for the screening: Have you previewed the film? Can you tell your class something about the background of the film? Do you know whether it is non-narrative, open-ended, in color or b/w, up-to-date, etc.? Is there someone to operate the projector so that you are free to discuss the film or initiate whatever activity you plan after showing the film?

6. If the film deals with values, new or controversial areas, have you checked it for objectivity? Have you prepared your class if a point of view is expressed by the director of the film? Are they ready for the topic?

7. Make sure you have checked the film, room, projector, etc., to have everything necessary ready and in working order to make this screening experience a positive one (see Chapter 6).

8. Remember many films have cross-disciplinary appeal and use. It is wise, therefore, to screen with a committee from many subject areas to see if a film is useful in subjects other than your own. This saves money and means you can rent more films.

FOOTNOTES

1. Harmetz, Richard. "Coming Soon: More Films for Children," Los Angeles Times, November 8, 1974.

2. Harmetz, op. cit.

3. Mallery, David. "Films in the Life of the School," National Association of Independent Schools, 1968, p. 14.

REFERENCES

There are many evaluation aides available. Appendixes A, B, and C are devoted to periodicals and organizations offering previewing help. Among the most widely used journals are The Booklist, Previews, Sightlines, Film News, and Media & Methods.)

Miller, Hannah. "Films for Your Class: How to Pick the Best," Teacher, September 1972, pp. 127-8.

Rice, Susan. "What You See Is What You Get," Media & Methods, October 1973, p. 11.

Spencer, Alan. "Film Selection--A Cooperative Effort," Previews, January 1974, pp. 22-3.

Chapter 5: SECURING THE FILM

INTRODUCTION

You and your committee have decided on the type of film you want to use. You may even have previewed some of them at your local library or at the town's media center. But how do you get the films into your school? All the facts you need to know about borrowing, renting or buying films are readily available, if you know where to look. Public libraries and university libraries issue catalogs that are free or cost very little. The distributors listed in this book (Appendix F) will send free catalogs on request. Many offer new ones every year and issue supplements during the year. Once your name is placed on their mailing list, you automatically get these from the larger companies. The catalogs include notations as to color or b/w, price, running time, recommendations for use, release date (not all catalogs list this, but it is important), and often quotes from favorable reviews. In general, distributors' previewing policies assume you intend to purchase the film in question. Previewing for rental would amount to free rental and would mean loss of revenue.

It is important to check different distributors, for the price for either rental or purchase may vary for the same film. For example, some of the NFBC (National Film Board of Canada) films can be borrowed free of charge from the Canadian Consulates which are situated in many parts of the U.S. They can be rented from Pyramid Films, in California, and from many other commercial distributors. Most university film libraries (see Appendix F) charge less for rentals than commercial companies. Since the borrower always pays the return postage, the geographic location of the distributor can make a difference. This is just as important to remember for films you have gotten from the state education department, a library circuit, organizations which distribute films, members of a co-op, university libraries and commercial companies who rent films.

POSTAL RATES

With current postal rates, it is important to know about "fourth class library rate." Here is the statement from the Post Office manual covering this special rate. You can save a lot of money by remembering to mark your films and other non-print media "Library Rate." The bill was passed in 1953 during the Eisenhower administration to permit special low rates for educational materials.

> The following specific items when sent to or from schools, colleges, universities, public libraries, museums and herbaria and to and from nonprofit religious, educational, scientific, philanthropic, agricultural, labor, veterans, or fraternal organizations or associations, may be mailed at the library rate:
>
> (1) 16-millimeter or narrower width films; filmstrips; transparencies; slides, microfilms, all of which must be positive prints in final form for viewing.
>
> (2) Sound recordings.
>
> (3) Museum materials, specimens, collections, teaching aids, printed matter, and interpretive materials intended to inform and to further the educational work and interests of museums and herbaria.
>
> (4) Scientific or mathematical kits, instruments, or other devices.
>
> (5) Catalogs of the materials (1), (2), (3) and (4) having 24 or more pages, at least 22 of which are printed, and guides or scripts prepared solely for use with such materials.

DISTRIBUTORS' RULES

Once you have sent for several films, you will learn which distributors, university film libraries, public libraries, etc., are reliable and which send their films out on time and in good condition. If you are renting a feature film, you must sign a contract. Read it carefully and learn the rules. All catalogs have rules for rental and purchase, as well as preview policies, stated on the first few pages. Always read these!

MAKING ARRANGEMENTS TO PREVIEW

When previewing many films, films for the whole school year, or films for a film unit, order as many as possible at one time. Try sharing films with other departments. This helps the budget, and most films have cross-disciplinary value. You may want to phone the distributors and juggle your dates and film titles with their open dates. Don't forget school holidays! Phoning whenever possible is a wise investment, since letters take a long time. Call one or two days before your show date if your films have not yet arrived. This will still give the distributor time to rush a film to you, or you can try to get a substitute. Mariann Pezzella Winnick, in her Films for Early Childhood, stated rather dramatically the problems of ordering films when she said: "The suspense of receipt or non-receipt of each film ran very much like the Perils of Pauline from week to week and film can to film can."

Send the films back as soon as you have seen them. This is not only a courtesy to the next user, but some companies charge for extra days if you are renting. Specify the number of days if you are renting the film. Most rentals of short films are between $10 and $15 per day. Feature films can cost up to $200. Prices depend on running time, whether b/w or color, animated or live-action, as well as the policy of the rental agency. University film centers have special rates or weekly terms. Indiana University, University of Michigan, Michigan State and the University of Illinois are among those with large collections (see Appendix F for a more complete list). Richard Maynard, in his article "Quality Films at Bargain Prices" (Scholastic Teacher, October 1973, pp. 30-2), gives a list of ten feature films whose rental rates range from $25 to $37.50 when used in classrooms.

Try not to create a sense of obligation to any one distributor or producer by previewing too many of their films. Offers of a bonus should be guarded against, for accepting such inducements will paralyze a genuine evaluation effort. Whoever does the purchasing should be willing to shop around. Too often equipment and materials are bought from a salesman who is a friend of the principal or teacher, which does not necessarily make his products the best purchase.

If you are thinking of using films, make sure you have also considered filmstrips, 8mm and super 8mm films and videocassettes if your school owns monitors. These are cheaper. Some of the newer filmstrip viewers resemble television sets, which make them very appealing to children.

ADVANTAGES OF BUYING FILMS

Once you have decided on the media you want to use, or you have decided on films if your budget allows, consider the advantages of purchasing films. The most important consideration is easy access. The accessibility of books cannot be equalled until the films we use become part of the school library or city-wide media center. If you own the films, programming becomes less of a problem, and the films can be used many times, making in-depth studies possible. Once you have established good maintenance procedures--for ownership makes damage to the prints your responsibility--the prints will remain in good condition longer, for they will be used less than rental prints.

Owning films can actually save money. A film that rents at $10, if used ten times, can pay for the purchase of a $100 print. Thereafter it can be used more frequently and the cost of each use is reduced. Of course, care and maintenance for the film is more expensive than for books, but the advantages far outweigh the disadvantages, and many school libraries and media centers have begun to purchase at least a skeleton stock of films. Films are expensive because of royalties, high production costs and overhead, and profit to producers and distributors. Try to measure instruction cost per pupil to help explain film prices. Many school districts have gotten together to purchase films and pay an annual fee for this service.[1*]

Make sure you have checked with your administrator, your P.T.A., and last but not least, the budget, before starting an in-depth film program. Use student lobbies by showing them films owned by your school or town, the

*Footnotes to Chapter 5 begin on page 89.

public library or any of the free sources mentioned in Appendix E. Again, don't underestimate the power of students. To get faculty support, show the best films available to the staff, and make sure to ask their opinions and give them the sources of films you have found to be good.

When renting films, the more students who are shown the film, the less expensive the showing becomes. Try to arrange to have several classes use a film while it is at your school.

RAISING MONEY

Some innovative ideas for raising money to purchase or rent films can come from students and teachers. One Chicago high school has lunchtime film programs showing feature films and shorts. For the lunchtime program, feature action films can be shown in 20-minute sections, both to maintain interest and to bring forth the crowds. Evening programs for parents and the community, perhaps on a subscription basis, can also be profitable. There are many benefits to this kind of program, aside from raising money. Teachers and students have a chance to work together outside the classroom. Different segments of the student body can be brought together during a school-sponsored activity. It gives students an opportunity to become more discriminating in what they see both on television and in movies. Last, but not least, films during the lunch hour may help to control some of the more boisterous elements of the student body.

FREE FILMS

Appendix E contains an entire section on sources of free films. One of the best sources of free films is your public library, however they may limit lending to schools. Educator's Guide to Free Films (Educator's Progress Service, Randolph, Wis. 53956) is an excellent source. There is also an Educator's Guide to Free Filmstrips available. James Limbacher's book Using Films contains a list of free films, as does J. A. Kislia's Let's See It Again. These include your county or state educational dept. film libraries; local, state and federal government agencies; public relations departments of local businesses and industries (e.g., Bell Telephone, Eastman Kodak, American Cancer Society, life insurance companies); Modern Talking Picture Services; Association Films tourist offices and consulates. There is no central office in the U.S. which lists films other than the Library of Congress Catalogue of Motion Pictures and Filmstrips. (Library of Congress, Washington, D.C. 20540). This is an annual listing of films and filmstrips for which L.C. cards were issued. The list is alphabetical by title and includes the name of the distributor and year of release.

FEDERAL FUNDS

The Elementary and Secondary Education Act (ESEA) was first passed in 1965, and has been extended as it expires, sometimes from year to year. On September 24, 1977, a one-year extension of the existing but expiring education programs, which are advance funded, was signed by President Carter. This included ESEA Title IV-B school libraries and learning resources. Hearings on a five-year extension were still going on in the U.S. Senate as of this writing.

The Library Service and Construction Act (LSCA) was first passed in 1964. The latest extension, S 602, was signed by the President on October 5, 1977, and extends it for five more years. It provides a set-aside for urban libraries when funding for Title I library services exceeds $60 million. It caters to the needs of libraries in densely populated areas and isolated rural areas.

Under the Education Amendments of 1974, Public Law 93-380, the old ESEA Title II (Instructional Materials) merged with NDEA Title III (equipment and minor remodeling), and with the guidance, counseling and testing portion of ESEA Title III. Together, this is the new Title IV, or Elementary and Secondary Education Act, now under debate. The new ESEA Title IV-B (programs, libraries and learning resources) distributes federal funds to districts and states according to the ratio of school age children (5-17) in each state, to the number of school age children in all the states.

Each state then allocates funds to local Education Agencies (LEA) according to public and private school enrollment. Substantial funds may be distributed to areas having the greatest number of children, whose educational requirements are more than the average-cost-per-students;

to poverty areas where tax money for education is limited; and to areas where the local taxes are higher than state average, but per pupil expenditures are still below the average.

Title IV-B requires that the LEAs decide where the money should go. They may use funds to purchase library learning resources and instructional materials; to administer programs of testing, counseling and guidance; and to expand counseling and guidance services. This has created competition for Title IV-B dollars.

How to Fight for Title IV Dollars[2]

1. Get to know your Title IV district coordinator.

2. Get support from other districts, other staff members, parents, administrators and students.

3. Make well prepared presentations of current and future needs.

4. Know the time-table for funding, and get there in time!

5. Meet the "maintenance of effort" requirement. That is, that your school is spending at least as much of their own funds this year as last.

6. Document what the new acquisitions will accomplish for students.

7. Show that acquisitions are cost-effective.

8. On the state level there must be a State Advisory Council to LEA. Media advocates must work for full representation by library and media specialists on this council.

9. If your state is one of those that limits funds for instructional materials to textbooks, let the legislators know that you want that law changed.

10. "Power to the People" means that congress and the state legislatures and local school boards are accountable to the people they serve. Make yourself heard.

If you are serious about using non-print media in your school, be sure to get all the available information on Federal Funding. It may be up to you to be innovative, creative and persevering in looking for funds both within the system and outside it. For further information, write to:

Arlene Hope, Library Service Program Officer, J. F. Kennedy Federal Building, Rm. 1309, Government Center, Boston, Mass. 02203

Guide to OE-Administered Programs, issued annually. From: Editor, American Education, U.S. Office of Education, Washington, D.C., 20202 (single copies are free). The 1978 Guide should be ready for the Jan.-Feb. 1978 issue.

National Audiovisual Association, "The A-V Connection: The Guide to Federal Funds for Audiovisual Programs." 152 pages from NAVA, 3150 Spring St., Fairfax, Va. 22030

FOOTNOTES

1. Krueger, Robert, "These Schools Rent Films for $.75 per Title," Audiovisual Instruction, January 1977, p. 19.

2. Dannenbaum, Joan. "From Media User to Media Advocate," Media & Methods, September 1976, pp. 24-28.

REFERENCES

ALA Washington Newsletter, June 30, 1977, October 11, 1977. From: ALA Washington Newsletter, 110 Maryland Ave., N.E., Washington, D.C. 20002.

Egan, Catherine. "Putting the Bard on the Small Screen," Sightlines, Fall 1977, pp. 8-11.

Kuhns, William and John Carr. Movies in America: Teaching in the Dark. Dayton, Ohio: Pflaum/Standard, 1973, pp. 12-13.

Chapter 6: SHOWING THE FILM

CONDITIONS TO CHECK

Always remember that getting the right film is only part of the game, for unless you show it under the right conditions, with the right equipment, and in the right setting, your efforts will be minimized. Film makers spend a lot of time and money making films; you should try to do your best in projecting them. We take a great deal of time to teach and to learn public speaking, and teaching or giving a lecture, yet no one is ever really taught how to show a film. Watching a film must be a total experience. It differs from watching television because of the setting. The room is dark, the picture large, and total absorption with the picture is possible. Here are some of the steps you can take to make your film showings the kind of experience you want them to be.

1. The room you are using should be as dark as possible. All light leaks should be plugged, with as little light penetrating as is feasible. Heavy drapes are better than shades or venetian blinds for ease of operation and maintenance, acoustic effects, decorative value and ventilation. If nothing else is available, use the black plastic sheeting used in gardening. (You'll find it in any Sears catalog and in most hardware stores.) However you "kill the light," devise a system which can be put into operation quickly and effectively. Remember, darkness is necessary for a decent showing, but some young children are frightened at first by the dark. They forget about this after watching a few films, so have the lights on when they enter the screening room and explain what is going to happen.

2. Ventilate the room! Warm, unventilated rooms put people to sleep. If you must choose between air and darkness, choose air. Again, drapes are better for this than any other method of darkening a room.

3. Permit younger children to go to the bathroom before starting a film. If facilities are far away, leave time for this. Even with older groups, try to give time for bathroom visits before the showing begins to avoid interruptions.

4. Comfortable seats are a must. The longer the film the more important this becomes. If the seats in the room you are using are uncomfortable, push them against the wall and let your class sit on the floor. Students should be able to relax wherever they are sitting.

5. Children are not generally disturbed by other children talking aloud during the movies. Especially during scary parts, it may help some of the younger ones to share their thoughts with a neighbor. Often they are better able to cope effectively with vociferous peers than the teacher, and it may be a good idea not to interfere with this natural process.

6. There are a few times of day which are worse for showing films than others. Avoid using films right after lunch, in the late afternoon, or on half days before a holiday. Friday afternoon (when most films are used) is another bad time if you want your class to get the most out of the film showing. Avoid using films as fillers. This may destroy their effectiveness as an educational tool.

7. Films can be screened during class time, but it is important to leave time for discussions. Although continuity is most important, if a film is too long to show during one period, it is better to show only half of it each day, and leave time for discussion.

8. Whenever possible place the projector in a booth or behind a barrier. Unless you are fortunate enough to have a quiet machine, and most school machines are noisy, the noise of the machine will interfere with the sound, which should be clear, as well as easily understood. Young children who have never seen a projector or don't know how one works will enjoy watching you load the machine. Let them see it a few times to satisfy their curiosity.

9. The screen should be as large as possible. It should be proportionately as large as a commercial theatre screen. Usually the only place where you can achieve the best conditions and find the largest screen is in the

auditorium, but if you have a small group it is better to give up the advantages of the auditorium screen for the classroom.

10. Have someone operate the projector for you who knows how. This will leave you free to attend to other details necessary to show the film. Most schools have a crew to run the projector. Students in grades four and up can be trained to have pride in handling the equipment and to get satisfaction from doing a good job. If you restrict the number of children on your crew, it becomes a more select group and easier to teach. Training is necessary, for not all projectors in a school work the same. "I have a projector at home" indicates only that the child can operate his own projector. Make sure your crew knows where the machines are stored, where all the spare parts are, and the procedures necessary for showing a film.

TRAINING A CREW

Once you have such a crew, members can teach each other, and you need only check them periodically.

1. Teach your crew not to rewind the film while someone is talking or a discussion is going on.

2. Beware of leaving cords where people can trip over them in the dark.

3. Know where the light switches are.

4. Have a power cord and extension cord with the projector so that it can be placed for best screening results. Know where the outlets are.

5. Know how to locate spare parts, such as projection and exciter (for soundtrack) bulbs, and spring belts for take-up and rewind (used on many old school projectors).

6. Check the take-up reel to make sure it is the proper size for the film.

7. Try to have the projector at the correct height, so that the audience will not cast a shadow on the film.

8. The best placement for the speaker(s) is above

the screen towards the side and at an angle directed towards the audience. Since few classrooms have speakers on the wall, make sure to place the speakers so that maximum sound reaches a maximum number of students. Only machines with detachable speakers will permit you to place it in front of the audience and off the floor to improve sound quality. If your projector has a speaker jack, you can use a good hi-fi speaker to improve the sound.

9. Focus the lens so that the beginning of the film is not lost. Once the focus is set, you should not have to focus again. If showing color and b/w films, you must focus separately for each one, since there is a difference between what is focused for b/w and for color owing to the different film stock used.

Have all the procedures organized so that the film can start within minutes after your class enters. Have your crew feel they are running a real theater! Like driving a car, once learned, these procedures quickly become habitual and take a minimum of attention.

Remember when purchasing equipment, the easier it is to operate, the more use it will get, and the cost may be less initially. The less chance of making mistakes in loading, etc., the less wear and tear on equipment and materials, the more successful the "show" will be!

Checklist for Projector

Attach a note prominently to the projector:

Make Sure You Know How to Operate the Machine! Make Sure You Have:

1. Extension cord with 2-prong adapter plug (since room may not take 3-prong plug of projector outlet).
2. Pick-up reel.
3. Extra bulbs stored close by.
4. Spring belt.

Before Starting the Film:

1. Check height of screen.
2. Check height of projected picture.
3. Focus.
4. Know where light switches are. Check proper

voltage for room.

5. Check cords (if any) to make sure no one can trip over them. If necessary, wrap them around a table leg to keep them out of the way.
6. Check volume of sound (if dialogue, preset sound level for that).
7. Place speaker properly.

Checklist for Projectionist

Place this list where projectors are stored:

1. Don't use a projector unless it is in good running condition. Have it checked and cleaned at least two times a year.
2. Don't show a sound film on a silent projector.
3. Keep dirt out of the machine. Sprockets and film gate should be cleaned regularly.
4. Focus, set sound volume, check to see that sprocket teeth fit into sprocket holes on film.
5. Check film loops or the picture will not project smoothly.
6. Follow threading diagram and try out the system before projecting an entire film.
7. Three feet of film can be ruined in five seconds. Turn the motor off as soon as trouble develops!
8. Use clean reels. Make sure your take-up reel is of the proper size and securely fastened on the projector.
9. If film breaks, keep all the film. Do not show it again until it is repaired. Do not fasten the break, just overlap the film on the take-up reel. Mark down the break to notify the distributor or whoever owns the film.
10. Store film in a cool, dry place (55° -70° F).

REFERENCES

Eastman Kodak. Audiovisual Projection (S-3), Photo Information Department 841, 343 State St., Rochester, N.Y. 14650.

Eisler, Michael. "Criteria for Choosing Hardware," Previews, December 1973.

Hoelcl, Gisela. "Projection," University Film Center, Newsletter Supplement, vol. 3., no. 4.

Kuhns, William and John Carr. Movies in America: Teaching in the Dark, Dayton, Ohio: Pflaum/Standard, 1973, p. 14.

Parlato, Salvatore and Dolores. Audiovisual Advisor. The Audiovisual Advisor, Box 25, Market Station, Buffalo, N.Y. 14203. 1964.

Tieman, Philip. "Standards for Educational Equipment," Sightlines, March/April 1972, p. 16.

Chapter 7: USING FILMS

INTRODUCTION

A sound philosophy of film use should be formulated by everyone using them. It is not hard to come by, but it takes some knowledge of what's available in the field, some expertise in choosing and using both hardware and software, and an ease of access to the materials. It is important to know the difference between film study and film use in setting goals and objectives for oneself and one's classes. A course in film study uses films as a basis of the curriculum and discusses film as an art form. Students view films, discuss and analyze them, react to them, and perhaps write a critique. They study the films in depth, study techniques used by the director, as well as what he is trying to say. Film use, on the other hand, is the use of films and other non-print media as part of the regular curriculum, in English, social studies, science, language art, art, etc. Teachers and librarians need not be film enthusiasts to use film, rather anyone can do so effectively if they have received proper training.

Not enough has been said about teacher resistance to using film and television in the classroom. Teachers see a threat to their status, as well as interference with classroom control, schedules and content, with the introduction of non-print media. When films and television programs outdo a teacher's performance, their fears of competition become real.[1*] By creating a network of communication between film and television producers and those using media, much of the existing mistrust could be alleviated. When teachers learn to use films effectively, when they learn to use only those providing materials and expertise they could not present as well, and when films are truly incorporated

*Footnotes to Chapter 7 begin on page 147.

into the curriculum, media use will be accepted by all teachers, as well as librarians.

This chapter will concentrate on film use, rather than film study (although mention will be made of both) because teachers often find more difficulty in this area. Films are an occasion for an educational encounter. Whatever is done with them by the teacher and his or her students, is what does or does not work. Teachers must therefore try different approaches when using films as well as when using any other method of teaching in order to try to reach all students.

Our sad observation of the school scene is that films are "in" at most schools, but for the wrong reason. Teachers seem to be saying: "Since everyone is using films, and everyone is watching television (a startling amount daily), let's make our teaching a little easier and watch films too." Some statistics:

1. By the age of 14, children will have watched 22,000 hours of television or more but by the time they graduate from high school, they will only have spent 12,000 hours in the classroom.[2]

2. They are likely to have read more than 200 books, but will have seen more than 700 films at the movies or on television.

3. More American homes are equipped with television than with indoor plumbing.

4. The television set in the average American home is on for an average of 6.5 hours a day, 365 days per year.[3]

Even in those special schools where films are being used as part of the curriculum, too often one still gets the feeling that one or two enthusiasts are pushing films and film "units." Where there are no workshops for the school faculty, no PTA gatherings to discuss films, and no teachers' guidelines for film use (other than those sometimes included with the films), film use will be limited and less successful when used at all. Often there is no change from year to year in "how" the films are used (although the menu of films does change). Teachers must become aware of the many excellent films available and how these would enhance their programs before they can do a good job in this area. Saddest of all, even in the choice of films some schools have done poorly. Some have used overpowering works, which have not helped the cause. Still others choose films which do not necessarily appeal to the students, and teachers find themselves doing entirely too much of the talking. (With no involvement or participation on the part of students, and no interaction between teacher and student, films may become crutches for poor teaching methods.) Some films are too long and some use lecture methods that often bore students. There are scheduling difficulties, and some teachers feel if they have two films they must show them both, thus postponing discussion, or perhaps eliminating it entirely. Full-length features are shown over a period of two or three days, making follow-up activities extremely difficult. In showing feature films, teachers may find that some children have already seen the film, which may complicate the situation. Generally, short films are recommended to give time for discussion after showing the film. It is unfortunate that many teachers have such a compulsion about using any and all films their school rents, borrows or owns, and others feel guilty about using films as though time spent showing media is cheating taxpayers, thus ignoring the variety of educational experiences available to students.

In communities where there are valuable resource people in the field of film making, such as producers and directors, writers, reviewers and animators, they are often not called upon for the expertise they could supply. Keeping parents and the community involved is not only a good idea, but a valuable source of information and perhaps media, for film makers are generous in loaning both their films and skills to local schools.

It is extremely important not to set rigid guidelines about when, why, where and how the films are to be used and taught. At the same time, when films are actually used some structure is necessary for lessons to be successful. One must guard against using some of the more popular films over and over again, for they may become as entrenched as some of the books we have been using. Since movies are only 75 years old and until fairly recently were produced mostly for entertainment, we must take care in identifying film "classics." In this regard we must also avoid pushing our film taste on our students. Again, not every film is going to produce magic results with every class, but, whereas many of us are prepared for this with books, we are not prepared to have students show lack of interest in a film we have chosen for them.

Not every student will want to watch a film or take a film course. Even here, for some, the demand will have to be created. Watching a sensitive film is not going to get a sensitively stated response from every student in the class. Many of them simply don't have that kind of vocabulary, and just watching the film won't give it to them. It is unfair to expose students to a film and expect reactions they are unprepared and untrained to give. Sophisticated levels of appreciation and taste take time to develop. Although films are a way of reaching some students we have been unable to reach in other ways, it is good to remember that the student who comes to school motivated and who wants to learn will also do better in the area of film. Using films means using them regularly. There is little benefit when a class gets to see a film only as a "special treat."

FILM DISCUSSIONS

Many students who do not usually make contributions to class discussions have found it easier to talk after seeing a film. They have been stimulated by what they have seen and have made serious and useful contributions to discussions because they find nothing in films to frighten them, and they have a chance to speak without being wrong. Students who usually stumble over words often are eager to express their views after watching what, in their opinion, was a good film. The "right" film has been used to reach students when other media have not been able to.

Discussions usually don't just "happen." Leading discussions skillfully must be learned. A good discussion should illuminate, not kill by over-analyzing. To fully appreciate a film, it is helpful to try to understand what film makers are doing and how they are doing it. A film is often better able to demonstrate a certain skill or fact than a teacher can, for in preparing the film more material and personnel were available than a teacher has access to. A film may often not have been produced for the specific purpose you are using it, which makes preparation necessary for both teacher and student. There may be a difference in the way the students look at a film if they know that they will be asked to discuss it.

How to lead a discussion is treated in many books. Workshops by skillful discussion leaders are valuable whether these be other teachers or parents. Many local League of Women Voters chapters have experts in this area who are willing to lead such workshops. Discussion is not analysis, for that may be meaningless to students and may even irritate them. Teachers should not be tempted to use events in the film to bolster their own moral code whether traditional or avant-garde, for this may well close communication between teacher and student. If you the teacher have a stockpile of questions to spark discussions when all else fails, check them carefully to see if they are applicable to any topic. If the answer is yes then they can be applied to any film. Lacey feels that it is difficult to avoid teaching because we are used "to rewarding comments that advance discussion toward preordained conclusions or in preordained directions."[4] It is also extremely difficult for teachers to change their methods of teaching, and it may take time as well as a willingness to do so. Learning to accept students' feelings may be one of the most difficult tasks teachers set for themselves. It may sometimes be difficult to avoid letting the discussion become a free-for-all "rap" session with the teacher taking the role of just another student. When this happens open attacks on parents, teachers, the school, etc. may result and it becomes difficult to re-channel the discussion.

Using Discussions

Lacey gives many excellent ideas for film use and discusses the different roles teachers can take.[5] To start a discussion he suggests recalling one sound or one image from a film which in turn will recall other images and sounds, and the class will thus learn how others see. This technique avoids straying from the film while often leading to expanded discussions. It also avoids excessive analysis and permits the film itself to continue working on the audience.

If the point of discussions is to permit emotional and intellectual growth to take place in students, the feelings the movie provoked, and the resulting perception of self on the part of the student is what's important. In learning what each of us sees, the students acquire new tools in communicating with each other.

For young children (grades K-2) it is often necessary to talk a little about the film before showing it. If they cannot read, they will want to know the title of the film. You may want to comment about the subject of the film and explain a particularly puzzling part. If you plan to discuss the film with this age group, try to have help in the room so you can divide the class into small groups (no more than 7 or 8). This help can be parents, aides, or older youngsters. With the very young, discussions often grow out of film-related activities but discussions alone as a follow-up don't always work.

If there are behavior problems, they may be helped by using films, but they may also be exacerbated. If a class is not used to discussions or ready for them, the leader must proceed slowly. Perhaps other approaches will work better at first.

Leading Discussions

Discussions are a way of exploring the feelings a film has aroused or noting specific points the film made, such as in a science class. Pivotal questions will elicit responses. The questions may be simple ones:

"What did you like best?"

"Why?"

"Who was your favorite character?" "Why?"

"Do any of you ever feel like this character?"

"What didn't you like about the film?" "Why?"

"Did you understand the film?"

"What was the film trying to show us?"

Often something the discussion leader wanted to say will come out in the discussion and be more valuable when contributed by a member of the group. You, the leader, must know how to cool down more vocal students and follow up profitable ideas without dominating the discussion. Try not to let one student take over. This might keep the more sensitive students from commenting freely.

If the group or class is new, it may be helpful to have each member write down three or four questions he or she would like to discuss. These can be handed to one student who will act as a discussion leader by reading the questions. This is good pedagogy especially if the students don't know each other.

If the discussion drags, play "devil's advocate." If the group seemed to like the film, mention all the things you disliked. If they seemed to dislike the film praise it. This makes for lively discussion, but make sure you tell your group what you did and why, or they may distrust your opinion in the future. Taping students' discussions and then showing the same film at the beginning and again half way through the semester or unit to compare the reactions of your class, will show them their growth during the year.

Using films without the soundtrack and having students interpret their meaning makes for interesting discussions. If this can be done by the teacher as a "fun" project, when the film is shown a second time, with the soundtrack, interesting things can happen.

If the discussion does not go the way you planned, if it lags, or if you feel it has not been successful, be flexible. Try another approach or perhaps another film on the same topic.

When teaching film as art, it is important to stress the art of the film above the subject matter. This may not be the case when using a film as part of the curriculum. Anyone can watch, enjoy and discuss a film, but if there are social implications and these are understood as well so much the better. When a film is used as part of a unit there may be a conflict. Must the students find the "inner meaning" of the film or can they just enoy it? A class trained to perceive techniques (see Chapter 3) such as color, composition, setting and rhythm will be able to discuss the films with more sensitivity.

Using non-narrative films often forces viewers to use their eyes and minds to draw conclusions. Many children find it easier to concentrate when there is no narration. Here is an opportunity for students and teachers to ask questions together. It may be necessary for the class to prepare together for watching such films. Sometimes there is a lack of factual background, making a trip to the library before seeing the film a necessary part of the lessons. Films should be related to other aspects of learning. If the class is well prepared, non-narrative films will lead to better discussions than other films. If there is disagreement on what was seen, show the film again or the particular section under discussion.

Discussing films is an excellent preparation for film making. Examining and analyzing a film will show students the problems involved in film making as well as what the producer is trying to say. The ability to respond verbally is an added skill discussions can develop, and often reading and writing become outgrowths of it as well. Again non-verbal films can be used with many grades and often in more than one subject area.

Ed Schuman of Dimension Films was quoted in the Fall 1972 issue of California School Libraries: "A good film should provoke an active learning experience that takes place AFTER the film is shown." He wants his films to excite, make curious, provoke, disturb, so they will make the audience "feel compelled to discuss, write, draw, inquire, to do something active and perhaps discover and learn." PIGS (11 min., color), THE COW (11 min., color) and RAINSHOWERS (14 min., color for the lower grades from Churchill Films are just a few examples of Mr. Schuman's excellent work in this area.

Remember that each group is different, and that the interaction of the group and its leader varies at different times of the day, week or year. The many ingredients mentioned previously vary from individual to individual and from group to group.

MORE IDEAS FOR USING FILMS

Run the film a second time, without sound. (Actually most short films should be shown at least twice.) Use a tape recorder to tape the comments the students made while the film was being shown and use that tape as the soundtrack when showing the film again. Have your class write either a narration for the film or dialogue, and then tape and use it. Making your own sound tape for a silent movie whether you use voices, music or sound effects is always a good activity. Using a tape recorder while showing a film, without having your class know about it, and then replaying it can be fun, but make sure no one is offended.

FILM USE IN THE ENGLISH CURRICULUM

Writing

Films can be used to actually teach composition. Compare camera techniques with writing skills. Think of films as a new language. Just as modern English differs from Middle English, if you, the teacher, learn the language of television and films, you can then use this language to help your students acquire new skills. Interpret some of the new vocabulary in a written assignment about a given film. Writing is a skill which should be taught as well to give films structure when students begin making their own films. Without a script chances for success in film making are doubtful at best (see Chapter 8 on Film making).

Have your class write reviews overnight of a film they have seen that day. Discuss the reviews the next day. Do not use any specific questions and see how many good reviews you get and how many criticisms. If the film is a feature film, see if you can find professional reviews. The New York Times and Saturday Review film reviews are kept on microfilm by many public libraries and are good sources for this. Some film catalogs print at least excerpts of reviews. Compare these with the reviews your class has written.

Language Arts

Young children respond very well to nonverbal films by painting, making collages, sculpturing, making puppets and, of course, making their own films, filmstrips and transparencies and drawing on film directly. For language arts, writing stories and plays based on the film are good activities. Dancing, story-telling, puppet shows and plays are yet other film-related activities. Check with the art teacher for available materials. If there is a budget problem, use newspaper, paper bags and found objects. See issues of School Arts for creative ideas. Show a variety of films to younger groups to give them a range of subjects and ideas to paint, draw and make clay models about. Sometimes the creative efforts of young viewers clearly

---

On opposite page: THE VIOLIN, from Learning Corporation of America.

relate to the films; at other times there is no obvious relationship. Try to avoid giving prescriptive directions so they will really express their own thoughts and feelings, almost like showing their own film to you.

Here is a sample list of films which may be used in language arts programs. Whenever you find such a list, try to add some titles you have liked. Perhaps you have already made your own list and are no longer dependent on the opinions of others.

A KITE STORY, from Churchill Films

Non-narrative stories like WINTER OF THE WITCH (22 min., color); THE MERRY-GO-ROUND-HORSE (18 min., color); THE THUNDERSTORM (9 min., color); THE VIOLIN (20 min., color) and CLOWN (15 min., color) from LCA lead to discussions and story writing and story telling. Many of the films considered classics, such as GOLDEN FISH and RED BALLOON also belong here. Other non-narrative films are: ALPHABET (6 min., color, animation, McGraw-Hill); THE DAISY (6 min., color, animation, Macmillan); THE MOLE AND THE HEDGEHOG (10 min., color, animation, McGraw-Hill) and other films about the mole (the mole has long been a favorite with European children); BIGHORN (10 min., color, NFBC), a spectacular documentary of the Rocky Mountain Bighorn sheep; SUNDAY LARK (12 min., b/w, McGraw-Hill); A VISIT FROM SPACE (10 min., color, animation, McGraw-Hill); and two films from Churchill, THE KITE STORY (25 min., color) and RAIN SHOWERS (14 min., color) are excellent for initiating discussions, writing and other activities for the lower grades.

RAIN SHOWERS, from Churchill Films

Other suggested films: THE LITTLE GIRL AND THE GUNNY WOLF (6 min., color, animated by the children who narrate the film, ACI); PADDLE TO THE SEA (28 min., color, producer NFBC, distributor McGraw-Hill); THE STORY OF PETER AND THE POTTER (19 min., color, NFBC); LEAVES (13 min., color, Paramount); DUET (9 min., color) and THE FENCE (7 min., color) from BFA;

ANATOLE (8 min., color, animation, Macmillan); MADELINE (7 min., color, animation, LCA); THE SHOEMAKER AND THE ELVES (13 min., color, animation, Coronet); THE CATERPILLAR AND THE WILD ANIMALS (7 min., color, animation, Perennial Ed.); NO TALKING (6 min., color, part of a series, Screenscope); THE MAGIC BALL SERIES (7 films, 14 min., animation, Eccentric Circle);

MOLE AT THE ZOO, from Phoenix Films

PEPPERMINT STICK SELECTION (Films Inc.) starring such Hollywood favorites as Rex Harrison, Agnes Moorhead and Debbie Reynolds, based on books like Charlotte's Web, Charlie and the Chocolate Factory and Dr. Dolittle, and on and on, including a list "Films to Liven a Language Arts Program" by Carol Emmens, in the February 1975 issue of Previews magazine, Films Kids Like, edited by Susan Rice, and Maureen Gaffneys' More Films Kids Like, as well as the monthly insert in Sightlines, "Young Viewers: Children's Films."

WHITE MANE, from Macmillan Films

Many so-called "children's films" which have been mentioned earlier could be added to this list. Make your own additions, and don't forget to get suggestions from fellow teachers, librarians and your students.

Story Telling

There are a variety of ways in which films can be used in story telling. The simplest way is to have the children retell the story. This can be varied by giving more than one child an opportunity to speak by breaking up the story into sections. Telling a story, keeping the events in sequence, is a good learning exercise. Another activity is to have the entire class participate by drawing a picture of whichever image they remember best.

Give the class a topic sentence and then ask them to tell or write a story, using part of the film, their imaginations or an event or image called to mind by the film. Have children tell or write a story about something in their homes or in their lives which related to the film. This can yield interesting results.

Related Art Activities

Combining language arts and art is fun and the related activities can be varied. The youngsters can write their own script and then do the illustrations with their own art work. Making puppets for their own plays, costumes or masks for a skit, papier-mâché figures or simply bringing in puppets and other props from home work well. Relating a film to more than one subject area is easily done in the lower grades.

One obvious way of doing this is to: 1) Show films about animals; 2) Go to a farm and/or zoo; then 3) Try some of the related suggestions mentioned before (e.g., write a story, draw a picture, act out a story).

FILM GUIDES

Film guides often come with the film you have rented or bought. They are written by persons in the field, and in general contain much worthwhile information. We have written field guides (see samples on pages 112-115) but feel very strongly that the best guide is the film itself and a teacher who comes to the film experience with a background of film watching. To quote Susan Rice, "Most of us who teach film suffer a kind of schizophrenia--the lack of rigidity in this still-new field offers us real opportunities to touch the root feelings of the kids we work with. The absence of an established curriculum allows us to exercise imagination and eccentricity in our teaching. At the same time there is an insecurity about expertise; a longing for explicit criteria and pre-packaged materials that will sustain the traditional distance between teacher and student."[8] Probably because this feeling exists in most of us, guides lean towards a more structured curriculum and classroom, without some of the openness so necessary for a successful film program, one in which students learn to analyze what they have seen as well as how they feel about their film experience. If you feel you must use film guides, try to see them only as check-references.

FILM PACKAGES FROM DISTRIBUTORS

In the same category as film guides but intended for Film Study courses are those film packages set up by companies to encourage teachers to buy or rent a group of films. The group rate is lower than the rental for individual films, and since they are already chosen for you, the selection saves your searching for the right combination. But remember the selections are not yours! Pyramid has five such groups of films, McGraw-Hill has "The Mini Course on Film Study" and other companies will put film groups together for you. Films Inc. has a special film teaching program consisting of "Film Extracts," "Shorts" and "Film Units." Leading names in the field helped to choose the films and write guides. The catalog for this program "The Film Forum" was written by William Jones and tells the how, whys, etc. of holding a forum at your school. Janus Films and Perspective Films have put together a very ambitious program "The Art of Film" using excerpts from feature films. The program comes in 6 film volumes, each approximately 20 minutes, and covers screenwriting, the camera performance, music and sound, editing and directing.

Perhaps it will be necessary sometimes for a school or teachers to rent such packages. They were chosen by experts, are well-documented and are always accompanied by film guides or a course of study. However, teachers, librarians and other group leaders must build up confidence in their own and in their group's ability to pick what is best for them.

Contemporary Films
McGraw-Hill Films
film guide

407812

A VISIT FROM SPACE

Produced by
Zagreb Film

10 minutes
color animation
LC #74-702073

recommended for use in
Women's Studies, Guidance, Language Arts, Art, Science

intended audiences
Pre-School to Grade 3, Libraries

guide written by
Hannah Elsas Miller
M.A. Teachers College, Columbia University. M.S. in Library Science, S.C.S.C., New Haven. Children's film specialist, film consultant and film critic. Former NYC teacher. Westport, Conn.

objectives

1. To show that the appeal of a film is in no way related to the sex of the star.
2. To teach children to relate to people who are different from themselves.
3. To encourage children to use their imaginations in their play.
4. To teach children about our galaxy and outer space.
5. To entertain children.

summary of the film

This timely cartoon tells what happens when an earthling (a little girl) meets a young inhabitant of a distant planet. For those of you interested in women's rights, here is one of the few films in which the star is a girl!

A little girl is trying to get apples off a tree but, try as she will, the tree is too tall and the apples are out of her reach. Finally, she ties a basket to a kite, flies up to the apples in the basket, and picks all of them off the tree. She is interrupted by a strange flying object which cuts the string of her kite. Two little "people" step out of the vehicle after it lands but are frightened by the kite which lands on one of them, causing the other one to take off in their spacecraft.

The little girl finds her kite as well as the creature from space. At first, they are frightened of each other but, on further examination, begin to enjoy each other's company. They try to explain who they are in a charming, non-verbal way and finally shake hands and set off together. The person from outer space eats most of the apples and he and the little girl have a good time together until she is called by her mother. The word "mother" is written on the screen in many languages but her friend from space only points up to the sky and cries for his. He tries to climb up to rejoin her and, finally, using an umbrella to pump air and the kite to fly him in a basket, he rises up to return to his planet and his mother.

At the end of the film, we are shown a trail of apple cores to indicate that our friend returned "home."

after viewing the film

Women's Studies

1. Was the child from outer space a boy or a girl?
2. Have you seen many other films in which a girl was the star?
3. Do most movies give boys and girls equally important roles? If not, why do you think this is so?
4. Do you prefer movies with girl heroes or boy heroes? Does it really make a difference?

Guidance

The two children in the film were VERY different and did not even speak the same language. They looked different from each other, they dressed differently, and came from different planets.

1. How did they manage to communicate with each other?
2. How did they play together?
3. Did their differences bother them? Did it help them to enjoy each other more?

Language Arts

1. Read a report to the class about an unidentified flying object which was seen somewhere in the United States. Discuss this with the class and ask them to write or tell stories about a UFO they have "seen."
2. Have the class tell the story of the film.
3. Write or tell a story about "when my friend from planet X came to visit me . . ."

Art

1. Have children draw or paint pictures they remember from the film.
2. Have children illustrate a story they have made up.

Science

1. Have the children write or tell all they know about the astronauts and their space flights. How long did it take to get to the moon? What did they have to wear on the moon? What did they bring back from their various trips? Show pictures and photographs taken by the astronauts, such as those in National Geographic (Dec. 1969, p. 735-; Sept. 1973, p. 326-).
2. What is a star? Look up the word in a simple encyclopedia. Study some of the simple constellations. Man uses stars to tell time, directions, for surveying, and man learned about atomic energy from studying stars. What do the children use stars for?

for art classes

"School Arts," a monthly magazine published by School Arts, 50 Portland Street, Worcester, Mass. 01608, always has excellent suggestions for creative and imaginative art work which can be done by children of all ages.

related Contemporary/McGraw-Hill films

AMELIA AND THE ANGEL
DOROTHY AND THE KITE
DOROTHY AND THE OSTRICH
MOLE AND THE GREEN STAR
MOLE AND THE HEDGEHOG
MOLE AND THE LOLLIPOP
MOLE AND THE UMBRELLA
A SMALL TRAVELLER

Printed in U.S.A.

Contemporary Films
McGraw-Hill Films
film guide

408571-9

PAINTINGS

produced by
Short Film Studio, Prague

10 minutes/color animation/LC #78-712718

recommended for use in
Language Arts, Guidance, Art, Filmmaking, Schools and Libraries

grade level
Pre-School through Grade 4

guide written by
Hannah Elsas Miller, M.A. Teachers College, Columbia University; M.S. in Library Science, S.C.S.C., New Haven Children's Film Specialist, Film Consultant and Critic, Westport, Conn.

objectives

1. To appreciate the use of imagination in making up simple stories.
2. To make children aware of the comfortable feelings being at home with their parents can give them.
3. To learn about making animated films.
4. To entertain children.

summary of the film

Two paint brushes are brought to life through the use of animation, and the boy begins to court the girl. They proceed to paint a baby and, with the same magic spot which brought them to life in the film, they bring the baby to life.

"Father" paints a little rocking horse and the boy and the horse go off on a trip. Their magic spot sees a monster and, in trying to get rid of him, gets caught by a pail thrown at him by this same monster. The boy tries to free the spot but is frightened off. Running back to his parents for help, his father paints him a cannon which the boy fires at the monster but the monster survives the attack.

The monster next throws an inkspot at the boy and his father has to paint a raincloud to get raindrops to clean the boy. He sets out once more, this time in a boat provided by his father but the monster creates such big waves the parent brushes have to send a helicopter to rescue the boy. The monster still does not give up and continues to chase the boy until the father paints a chain and ball which finally drag the monster down into a hole made by the father.

The boy frees the spot and floats down to earth using an umbrella for a parachute. He comes home to a new hammock and finally realizes that home is the best place for him.

after viewing the film

Language Arts

1. Tell the story of the film in sequence.

2. Make up a story of a tool or other instrument which came alive. Illustrate the story.

3. Write or tell a story starting with "Once I met a monster ________." Have children illustrate the story.

4. Write or tell a story starting with "Yesterday I saw two pens (shovels, brooms, hammers, etc.) dancing."

5. Have children tell about their favorite toys. Make up stories about them, such as taking a trip on a boat or plane.

Guidance

1. Why is it important for young children to stay close to home?

2. Why do parents want to know where their children are?

3. Are there really "monsters" like the one in the film?

4. What are some of the things youngsters are afraid of? (Thunder, darkness, lightning, storms.) Talking about their fears may help young children learn to cope with them. Just knowing there are others who have these same fears may help them feel better about themselves.

Art

1. Often filmmaking is incorporated in the regular art program. A class can make a film together with each child, or group of children, drawing or painting portions of the film. One example could be making a film of the alphabet, with each student taking one letter and animating a short story about it.

2. Have children draw or paint some of the things the father brush painted for the little boy (boat, rocking horse, helicopter, etc.).

3. Have children draw pictures of their favorite toys. Have them tell stories about them.

Filmmaking

1. This film shows imaginative use of animation and could serve as a good example to start children making their own films. Some questions to ask the group before they start on their films might be: "What other tools or implements could come alive to make such a story?"

2. Children enjoy painting on film, which takes less patience than making animated films. The books mentioned below give instructions for this.

related readings

For teacher use

Andersen, Yvonne, ***Teaching Film Animation to Children,*** Van Nostrand Reinhold Co.

For student use

Andersen, Yvonne, ***Make Your Own Animated Movies: Yellow Ball Workshop Film Techniques,*** Little Brown and Co.

For art classes

"School Arts," a monthly magazine published by School Arts, 50 Portland St., Worcester, Mass. 01608, always has excellent suggestions for creative and imaginative art work which can be done by children of all ages.

related Contemporary/McGraw-Hill films

BABYSITTER
EAST AND WEST, HOME IS BEST
THE MONGREL DOG
SIX PENGUINS
THIS IS ONLY A MOUSE

For information on other related films address inquiries to:

Contemporary Films

McGraw-Hill Films

1221 Avenue of the Americas, New York, New York 10020

McGraw-Hill

Printed in U.S.A.

Most of the big distributors have made up film packages in the area of Human Relations, Film Study and Children's Films. LCA has "A Child's World" catalog consisting of 14 entertainment films. Information includes a short description, length of film, whether b/w or color. "Learn to be Human, " also from LCA, contains such excellent films as BIG HENRY AND THE POLKA DOT KID, THAT'S MY NAME--DON'T WEAR IT OUT, THE SHOPPING BAG LADY, and ANGEL AND BIG JOE. All of these deal with love, loyalty, humor, identity and self-confidence. A Social Awareness series from Films Inc., called "About, " contains 13 films on these topics.

THE SHOPPING BAG LADY, from Learning Corporation of America

"Looking Forward: A Mini-Course in Future Studies" is a series of eight films from McGraw-Hill Films. It includes the film FUTURE SHOCK. "Coping with Tomorrow, " a five-film series from ACI contains such interesting titles as ENERGY; TOWARD THE AGE OF ABUNDANCE and FOOD: SURVIVING THE CHEMICAL FEAST.

Pyramid Films has two 90-minute collections of shorts and two abridged 50-minute versions of each: CINEMA 90 & 50, "A rich and diversified group of shorts especially geared for showing to discussion groups, schools and churches" and PYRAMID 90 & 50, "An entertaining educational and representative example of the short film." Pyramid also distributes the films featured in David Sohn's book, Film: The Creative Eye.

There are other topics dealt with in package deals. LCA has a "Great Themes of Literature" program consisting of six $\frac{1}{2}$-hour films, especially edited from full-length features and introduced by Orson Welles. The film guides offer selections from works of literature that treat the same themes as the films used. There are references to films on the same themes. LCA also distributes SHAKESPEARE: A MIRROR TO MAN (22 min., color) showing scenes from TAMING OF THE SHREW, MACBETH and OTHELLO. International Film Bureau's "The Shakespeare Series" are excerpts, varying in length from $5\frac{1}{2}$-$13\frac{1}{2}$ minutes, staged and costumed as the plays were originally done, by the members of the Royal Shakespeare Company at Stratford-on-Avon. EBEC's "Short Story Showcase" contains five short stories by famous American writers. "Putting the Bard on the Small Screen" by Catherine Egan gives an excellent list of films on Shakespeare (Sightlines, Fall 1977, p. 11).

Also from LCA are eight "made for TV Films" of excellent quality that they distribute as 16mm films. These films can be judged on political, social and moral relevancy, their performers are all of the highest caliber, and all are good discussion starters. The quality of the picture has improved on 16mm, and the skills of the directors and cameramen have become more apparent. TELL ME WHERE IT HURTS (80 min., color) starring Maureen Stapleton, won the 1974 Emmy directors' Award of the National TV Academy; THE AUTOBIOGRAPHY OF MISS JANE PITTMAN (110 min., color) won Cicely Tyson the 1974 Emmy Award for Best Actress; and LARRY (80 min., color) which stars Frederick Forrest as a young man erroneously diagnosed as mentally retarded, are but a few samples.

Most distributors have some films in the category of "Literature" in their catalogs for those teachers who wish to go from film to book or play. There are excellent records of plays and poetry which have been used to spark interest in literature classes (see Chapter 1, p. 19). Making tapes of student actors and filming plays produced by students are other ways of using media in literature classes. "The History of Drama" (20 filmstrips) and "American

THE AUTOBIOGRAPHY OF MISS JANE PITTMAN, from Learning Corporation of America.

Literature: A Survey" (30 filmstrips) from Films for the Humanities look interesting and worth exploring if you are limited to filmstrips.

FILM FESTIVALS

There are many different kinds of film festivals suitable for schools interested in using films. One is a purely entertaining, extra-curricular program showing films the students want to see and for which they pay admission. The films chosen are often feature films and the choice is based on past box-office success. The entire program is run by teachers and students during the lunch hours and after school, and is self-supporting.

Another kind of festival was introduced by the Center for Understanding Media in the spring of 1973 in New York City. It is an experimental program in the use of feature films as a unit in the high school curriculum. Based on the concept that schools are committed to experiment with new forms of learning, students see a number of feature films for which study guides were developed by teachers in the area of humanities, social science, personal growth and family life, art education (film art), science and nature study. In the program groups of students pay $1.00 for a field trip to a neighborhood theater for the screening of a feature film. The screening is integrated in the various disciplines as an element of the curriculum. Students attend the screening with their teachers and return to class to discuss the films. The arrangements with theaters, distributors, etc., are handled by a media person. Theater owners are interested in using their theaters during the slack hours, and distributors can arrange to rent films which are out of circulation for these non-theatrical screenings.

Yet another Film Festival for the lower grades, run during the lunch hour, is made up of short films more suitable for this age group. The films are shown for fun and entertainment, but may carry over to language arts, social studies, etc. Any of the films from the "The Magnificent Six and a Half" series from the British Film Foundation, which are distributed by Lucerne Films, would do well in this category. The British Film Foundation is the only film producer making films only for children. In England many commercial theaters run children's programs Saturday afternoon featuring these films. They are excellent and many of them have been televised on CBS's "Children's Film Festival."

There are some general rules as to the length of films and film programs different age groups can watch with some semblance of attention. For children four to five years old, a 15-minute film is long enough, and a total of 30-45 minutes is the limit (if showing a program). Switch the lights on between films to give younger children a chance to stretch, talk, go to the bathroom, but don't let

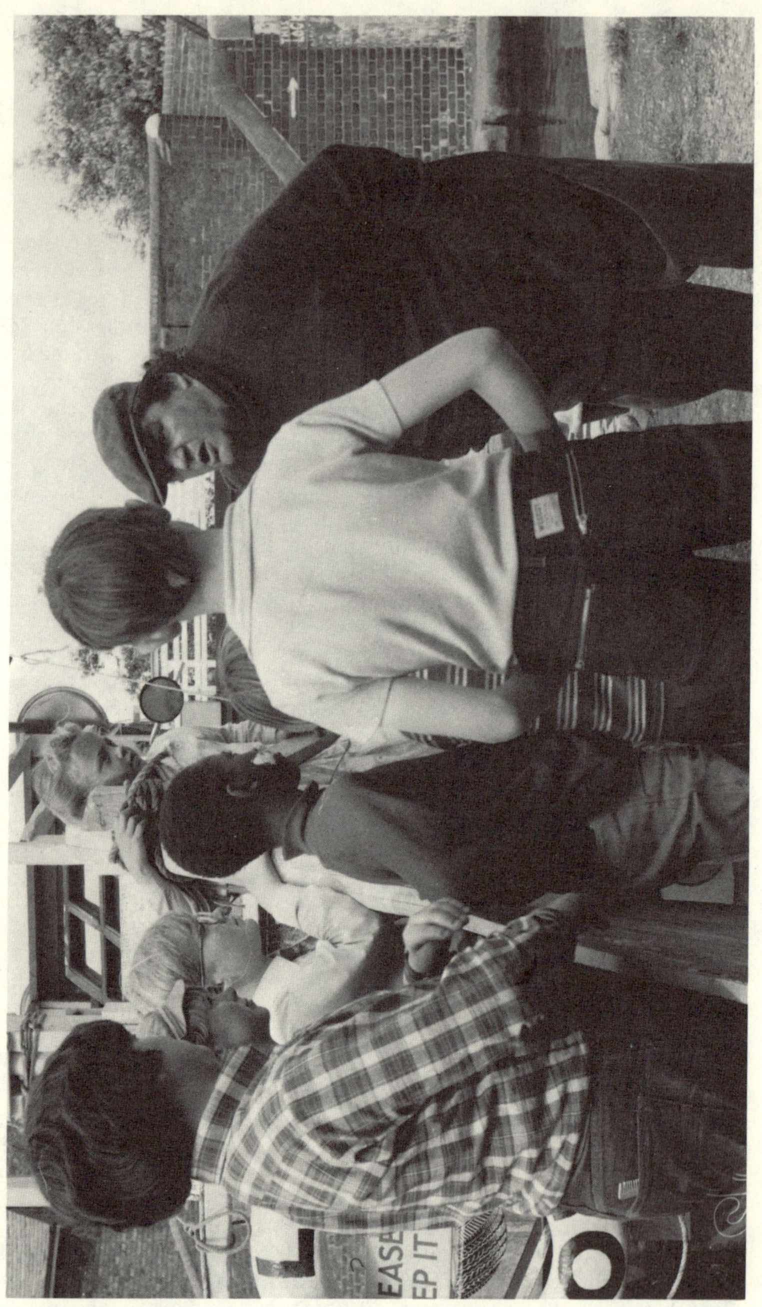

DISCOVERING RUSSIAN FOLK MUSIC, from BFA Educational Media.

them get too active or wound up if more than one film is planned. For groups six to nine years old, 45 to 60 minutes is a good limit to keep in mind. With films which hold the interest of the children, these limits can often be stretched, but the combination of the group, time of day, and place of watching, must be taken into consideration.

Again, there are ready-made lists. In the Jan./Feb. '72 issue of K-eight, in an article "The Children's Film Theatre" by Jean Marzollo and Susan Rice,[10] there is a rather lengthy list of films that the authors have used successfully. Included with the list are tips on how to run a program, including their recommendations on the size of the audience, length of film, program format, how to get films, etc. The list is now in book form, Films Kids Like[11] and is a good book to own. A sequel, More Films Kids Like, edited by Maureen Gaffney can be ordered from the American Library Association (50 E. Huron St., Chicago, Ill. 60611, $8.95). Many of these same films appeared on a shorter list by Frederick Goldman "A

On opposite page: The "KonTiki Kids" episode of the series "The Magnificent Six and a Half," from the Children's Film Foundation; dist. by Lucerne Films.

OVER IN THE MEADOW, from Weston Woods

THE FOOLISH FROG, from Weston Woods

Children's Film Is an Adult Film Is a Children's Film."[12]

Music

Any subject area can be organized into a festival. How about a Music Festival or "Films to Learn Music by." Start the younger children with "sing-along" films: THE FOX WENT OUT ON A CHILLY NIGHT (8 min., color, Weston Woods); OVER IN THE MEADOW (9 min., color,

THE FOX WENT OUT ON A CHILLY NIGHT, from Weston Woods.

Weston Woods); THE FOOLISH FROG (9 min., color, Weston Woods) with a song by Peter Seeger; LONDON BRIDGE IS FALLING DOWN (9 min., color, Connecticut Films) or AMERICAN SONGFEST (42 min., color, Weston Woods). For older students, try THE SYMPHONY OF SOUND (30 min., color, LCA) with Henry Lewis, the conductor of the New Jersey Symphony Orchestra, conducting the Royal Philharmonic Orchestra of London, as he explains the structure of a symphony and the history and development of instruments of a symphony orchestra; W. A. MOZART, CLAUDE DEBUSSY, BEETHOVEN, SCHUBERT, BIRTHPLACE OF BEAUTY, JOHANN SEBASTIAN BACH, all from the

International Film Bureau; THE GUITAR: FROM STONE AGE TO SOLID ROCK (14 min., color, Xerox) a humorous history of the guitar; OPERA WITH HENRY BUTLER (26 min., color, LCA) which demonstrates that opera is a multimedia art form, combining drama, music, painting, ballet, architecture, stage and costume design, and lighting with excerpts from several operas; VIVALDI'S VENICE (27 min., color, Time-Life) shows Venice in photographs and art work to the music of Vivaldi, and PERCUSSION: FROM PLEISTOCENE TO PARADIDDLE, OR, THE BEAT GOES ON (14 min., color, Xerox). Finally, there is BOLERO (25 min., color, Pyramid), a most exciting film. To the pulsating rhythm of Ravel's music, Zubin Mehta and the Los Angeles Symphony Orchestra rehearse and then play the piece. The photography and direction of this film are truly artistic and exceptional. It won an Academy Award in 1974.

CLAUDE DEBUSSY, from the International Film Bureau

To add another dimension to the organ music of Bach try YOUNG MAN AND DEATH (16 min., color, Macmillan) in which Nureyev and Zizi Jeannaire dance and show off their fantastic technique. Students can hear the music of Tchaikovsky, Chopin, Khatchaturian, Rimsky-Korsakov and Strauss, as well as learn more about ballet in SATIN SLIPPERS (32 min., color, Films Inc.). Other films on the dance, with music serving as a background are GRADUATION BALL (27 min., color); MERCE CUNNINGHAM (13 min., color); THE MOOR'S PAVANE (16 min., color), all from Films Inc.; THREE BY MARTHA GRAHAM SERIES (85 min., color, Pyramid, 3 films); and from Phoenix Films ALVIN AILEY: MEMORIES AND VISIONS (54 min., color, 1974) produced by WNET/13; APPALACHIAN SPRING (31 min., color) to the music of Aaron Copland and DANCER'S WORLD (30 min., color) also about Martha Graham.

BEETHOVEN, from the International Film Bureau

Social Studies

An International Film Festival for Social Studies can present films about foreign countries.[13] There is a wealth of films about children of foreign lands available which have much educational material to recommend them. A series on Comparative Cultures from LCA explores the differences in the cultures of the world. TWO FACTORIES: JAPANESE/AMERICAN (23 min., color) presents a study of the two factories and shows how very different the attitude and relationship of management and labor is in these two countries. TWO FAMILIES: AFRICAN/AMERICAN does the same with two families, their structure and the place of each family member. Films Inc. has a "Man and His World Series" containing films about all the continents. The series is ongoing and new films are added continuously.

From CBS's "Children's Film Festival" comes SKINNY AND FATTY (45 min., b/w, McGraw-Hill), a Japanese film; BLIND BIRD (45 min., b/w, McGraw-Hill) from Russia, which tells of a young Russian boy, Vassia, and his blind pet pelican, Pelka; JOANJO: A PORTUGUESE TALE (12 min., color, Paramount), for the very young; and the "Many Americans" series (8 films) from LCA. NIKO: BOY OF GREECE (21 min., color, ACI) was made with love and affection for that country and its people. SAMOAN VILLAGE (15 min., color, AIMS), for middle elementary students, gives a more realistic view of the South Pacific islands than one usually gets from a film. PEOPLE OF VENICE (16 min., color, Churchill) is one of the more informative films in this group, particularly valuable because it touches upon some of the problems which could be overlooked because of the beauty of the city of canals. FLOATING MARKET (11 min., color, ACI) about canals, shifts the scene half-way around the world to Bangkok, Thailand. COUNTRY OF ISLAM (16 min., color, Churchill) features Mustafa, a Moroccan boy who leaves his village in search of formal education. His journey to the city gives us a glimpse of Morocco, its economy and the Islam religion. CHILDREN OF ISRAEL (14 min., color, IFF) presents young Israelis of different backgrounds in school, in a synagogue, in an arts and crafts class on a kibbutz, and on a very crowded beach. YUGOSLAV FARM FAMILY (14 min., color, IFF) points out the fiercely independent spirit of the

---

On opposite page: YOUNG MAN AND DEATH, from Macmillan Films.

farmers who have opposed collective farming in spite of governmental pressure. The family in this film lives on the Dalmatian coast in a 600-year-old house. LABOLA (26 min., b/w, McGraw-Hill), for upper elementary children, documents the many changes South African natives are facing. "Child Life in Other Lands" from Films Inc. is a series of eight films worth exploring and "Families," a series of five films from Churchill, compares different cultures.

For older students there is an unusual film FROM THE FIRST PEOPLE (45 min., color, 1976) which tells about an Eskimo Community who decided what was to be filmed. The harsh realities of life in the Arctic in the village of Shungnak are shown. The film was made by Sarah Elder and Leonard Kamerling who also made ON THE SPRING ICE (45 min., color, DER) and AT THE TIME OF WHALING (38 min., color, DER).

Documentary Educational Resources (DER) also distributes films by Rouch and Bunnel about developing countries; a series called "The San Film Series" is about the people of West Africa, and there are films about the culture of the Yanamamo Indians of Venezuela and Brazil. The International Film Foundation (IFF) distributes an "African Village Life Series," and an excellent film about the Scandinavian countries of Norway, Sweden, Finland, Denmark and Iceland called SCANDINAVIA: UNIQUE NORTHERN SOCIETIES (24 min., color, 1976).

There are several films about Indians for the lower grades: A SONG FOR DEAD WARRIORS (25 min., color, 1973, Tricontinental); OUR TOTEM IS THE RAVEN (25 min., color, BFA); ARROW TO THE SUN (10 min., color, animation, Texture); BALLAD OF CROWFOOT (10 min., b/w, McGraw-Hill); and CHARLEY SQUASH GOES TO TOWN (4 min., color, animation, LCA).

An amusing animated series called "Basic Concepts in Social Studies" from LCA teaches many concepts simply in a story form to the lower grades. WHY WE HAVE LAWS: SHIVER, GOBBLE AND SNORE (7 min., color); WHY WE USE MONEY: THE FISHERMAN WHO NEEDED A KNIFE (8 min., color); WHY PEOPLE HAVE SPECIAL JOBS: THE MAN WHO MADE SPINNING TOPS (7 min., color); WHY WE HAVE TAXES: THE TOWN THAT HAD NO POLICEMEN (7 min., color); and WHY WE NEED READING:

THE PIEMAKER OF IGNORAMIA, are some of the films that make up this amusing series.

WHY WE NEED READING: THE PIEMAKER OF IGNORAMIA, from Learning Corporation of America.

Films about minority groups for younger students in story form such as LET THE RAIN SETTLE IT (11 min., color, Franciscan Communication Center), a subtly understated film on race relations in the South; THE BLUE DASHIKI: JEFFREY AND HIS CITY NEIGHBORS (14 min., color, EBEC) about a young black boy in a big city; WHO DO YOU THINK SHOULD BELONG TO THE CLUB (17 min., color, animation, Stephen Bosuston); and FIRE IN THE STREETS (19 min., color, Arthur Mokin Prod.) about a fire in a city ghetto and the people who were there together, all avoid racism and are recommended for classroom showing.

An interesting UNICEF study is presently underway, headed by Anne Pellowski, Director-Librarian of the Information Center on Children's Culture. The study is using non-print media (mostly films) and games to test whether children's attitudes towards foreign cultures can be influenced by exposure to films and activities native to the country being studied. There is a test group of 100 children

THE BLUE DASHIKI, from Encyclopaedia Britannica Educational Corporation.

in public and parochial schools in New York City and a control group of 100. The study, with a complete filmography, will be published in 1978 or 1979.[14]

Among those films which trace the history of a country from its beginning to modern times, the ones created by Julien Bryan (IFF) are perhaps the best known. For example, his CHILDREN OF ISRAEL uses animation to take us back 4000 years to Biblical times. Documentary footage tells of the years between 1900 and 1948 when the state was founded. Films about immigrants to this country, such as A STORM OF STRANGERS (27 min., b/w, Macmillan and Paramount), narrated by Herschel Bernardi contrasts the early Jewish immigrants on New York's Lower East Side with more recent immigrants to the same neighborhood; and LAND OF IMMIGRANTS (16 min., color, Churchill Films) which concentrates on the major waves of immigrants and their reasons for coming here.

Current and Controversial Topics

For classroom use there are the many films on environmental studies, such as VENICE POLLUTED (16 min., color, Texture) or a no-nonsense look at the problems of obsolete transportation systems CITIES IN CRISIS (8 min., color, Universal Education & Visual Arts), THE END OF GAME (28 min., color, Phoenix) or WHERE DID THE COLORADO GO from the Nova series (69 min., color, Time-Life).

There are some excellent films on energy, including two distributed by McGraw-Hill: ENERGY and WE WILL FREEZE IN THE DARK.

For older groups, have your class pick a topic of current interest, (e.g., race relations, alcohol, drugs, male/female roles). You, the teacher, must be objective and listen to all points of view. If the topic chosen by your class is one you are not well-versed in, get help. Ask another teacher who has more expertise to combine his or her class with yours. Call on a parent or member of the PTA to come in. Use your community resources, special volunteer groups, or special interest groups to send representatives. Have your class prepare the outline of a scenario they would write. Pick a short film to show on this topic, and discuss the different approach used by the

CHILDREN OF ISRAEL, from International Film Foundation

film maker and by the class. You might vary this by picking up two short films, one good and one bad, and sit back and listen to the reactions of your students. Don't always finish the film. Stop halfway and have your students finish with their own written versions.

Wherever possible bring in local color to match the subject of the film. If the film is on drugs, have students bring in articles about your local drug rehabilitation centers and programs, etc. Try to relate the film to what you have already covered in class or what you plan to do next.

The recent concern about the male and female roles in our society today represents but one of the new areas which have been introduced into our lives, and thus into the curriculum. MASCULINE OR FEMININE: YOUR ROLE IN SOCIETY (18 min., color, Coronet) is an in-depth study of today's changing society. Many conflicting viewpoints, on many levels, and on various aspects of male and female identification are presented. The viewer is left to reach his or her own conclusions. EVERYTHING NICE (20 min., color, BFA) shows the process of consciousness-raising, during which women develop new expectations for themselves and a sense of self-worth, along with a new consciousness of what it means to be female. Other and newer films on this topic are: A PLACE FOR AUNT LOIS (17 min., color, Wombat); A WOMAN'S PLACE IS IN THE HOUSE (30 min., color, Texture, 1976) about a Lesbian State Senator; MEN'S LIVES (43 min., color, New Day Films, 1974) exploring sex roles of men and women from a man's point of view; and A MAN (21 min., b/w, Polymorph) which shows a men's consciousness-raising group dealing with the death of the father of a member of this group.

In especially sensitive areas, or those where there may be some conflicting opinions, it may be useful to set up a preview group representing different points of view of the community, faculty, and parents of a particular school. You need to know the point of view of the film, and/or film maker, and if the film shows a bias, you must be aware of it, and include this information in your introduction. Honesty, accuracy, and authenticity, as well as objectivity, should be a must in this type of film. It is always a good idea to permit parents to screen the film before their children see it in the classroom. Set up procedures whereby a child can be excused if parents do not wish him or her to see a film, hard as this is to swallow sometimes,

A WOMAN'S PLACE IS IN THE HOUSE, from Texture Films.

especially if you know that a particular youngster would benefit from seeing a film.

ABOUT SEX, from Texture Films

ABOUT SEX (23 min., color, Texture) is a light-hearted but outspoken treatment of a serious topic, done in a way that teen-agers can accept. It will help them to acquire healthy attitudes about their sexuality, but since it may be controversial, it needs to be previewed as suggested above. TEEN SEXUALITY: WHAT'S RIGHT FOR YOU (29 min., color, Perennial Education, Inc., also available on video-cassette) is about a trip to a birth control clinic by a class visiting New York City, and how 2 of the young people are personally involved with the topic of the film. WE BELIEVE IN MARRIAGE (30 min., color, Family Films, 1975) is about a young couple living together without being married and the reaction of the young woman's parents. FOUR YOUNG WOMEN (color, 20 min., See Saw Films) discusses abortion and birth control on a personal and ethical level.

Other films about the sex roles in our society, such as HE AND SHE--THE FABLE OF ELI NOYES (10 min., color, animated, LCA) a clay animation spoof of the typical roles our society assigns to men and women, shows with a lighter-touch what could happen if they were permanently separated; A TOKEN GESTURE (8 min., color, animation, produced by NFBC, distributed by McGraw-Hill) is a satirical look at the more subtle forms of discrimination with a surprise ending; MRS. COP (16 min., color, Eccentric Circle), about a woman police officer and the pros and cons of her job; SYLVIA, FRAN AND JOY (25 min., color, Churchill), which explores the life style of the traditionalist, the liberated woman, and one who is in transition; and ANTONIA: A PORTRAIT OF A WOMAN (58 min., color, Phoenix Films), which tells the story of a 73-year-old conductor who is still seeking the opportunity to lead a major symphony orchestra.

SUGAR AND SPICE (32 min., color, Odeon) is recommended for parents and teachers and talks about encouraging nonsexist socialization among children.

Here is a sampling of films on other contemporary topics to be explored:

Parenting: ARE YOU READY FOR THE POST PARTUM EXPERIENCE (17 min., color, Parenting Pictures, 1975); and CHILDREN AND BABIES (20 min., color, Polymorph) asks four women "Do you want to have children?"

Childbirth: BIRTHDAY THROUGH THE EYES OF MOTHER (20 min., color, Lawren Productions).

Divorce: CHILDREN OF DIVORCE (37 min., color, Films Inc., 1976) an NBC film with narration by Barbara Walters, MOTHERS AFTER DIVORCE (20 min., color, Polymorph), and ME AND DAD'S NEW WIFE (33 min., color, Time-Life) an ABC after school special.

Rape: NO TEARS FOR RACHEL (27 min., color, Indiana U., 1974), about the failure of the judicial system and about the society which often tries the victim; and NOT A PRETTY PICTURE (83 min., color, Films Inc.).

Battered women: BATTERED WOMEN: VIOLENCE BEHIND CLOSED DOORS (23 min., color, J. Gary Mitchel Film Co.) told by some of these women; and WIFE BEATING (27 min., color, Films Inc.) which examines the psychology of this social problem, and the emotional and physical repercussions on women and their children.

CIPHER IN THE SNOW, from Brigham Young University.

Child abuse: A very special, poignant film about a neglected child, CIPHER IN THE SNOW (24 min., color, Brigham Young U.), tells of a boy no one remembers, and WHAT ABOUT THAD (16 min., color, Brigham Young U.) an open-ended film about a shy, troubled youngster. Child abuse is treated in A CRY OF PAIN (15 min., color, Mass Media Ministries, 1977) and CHILDREN: A CASE OF NEGLECT (Macmillan).

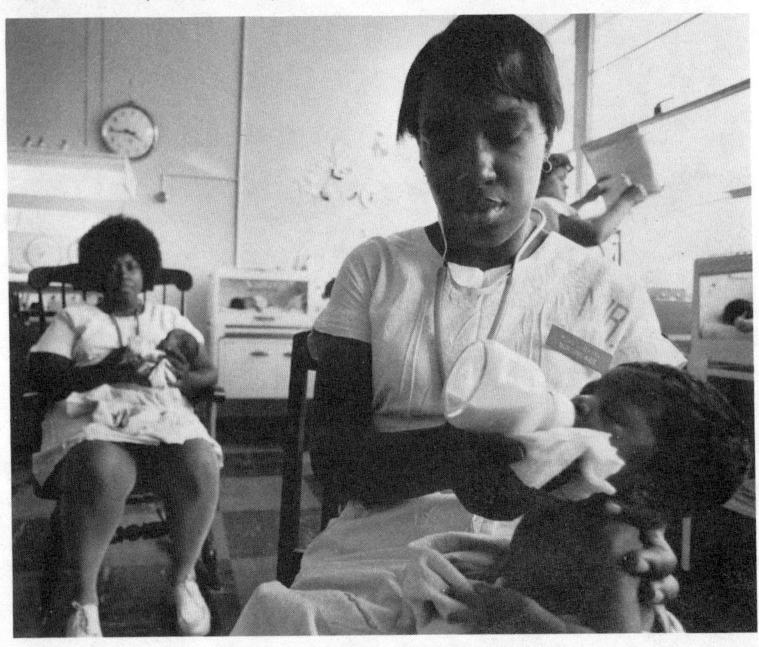

CHILDREN: A CASE OF NEGLECT, from Macmillan Films.

Suicide: SUICIDE AT 17 (19 min., color, Lawren Prod., 1977); and DO I REALLY WANT TO DIE (31 min., color, English subtitles, Polymorph) in which a number of people who thought about and attempted suicide talk about this.

Death and dying may be considered a controversial topic when viewed with young people. A very positive approach, and an excellent film about a young athlete who died from cancer, but not before making a lasting contribution to the children of a town, is JOHN BAKER'S LAST RACE (34 min., color, Brigham Young U.); WHERE IS DEAD (19

JOHN BAKER'S LAST RACE, from Brigham Young University

min., color, EBEC, 1975) is good for teacher education classes; THE RIGHT TO DIE (56 min., color, Macmillan 1975) interviews dying patients and HOW COULD I NOT BE AMONG YOU (29 min., color, Benchmark) is about a young leukemia victim who discovers a new freedom when told he has six months to live.

Old age: PEGEE (28 min., color, Phoenix) a story of love reaching an old, senile grandmother in a nursing home; NOBODY EVER DIED OF OLD AGE (66 min., color, Henry Street Settlement); and SENIOR POWER--AND HOW TO USE IT (19 min., color, Wm. Brose Production, 1975), a positive look at old people and how they can handle potentially dangerous situations.

Drug and alcohol abuse is yet another topic to approach with care. CROSS COUNTRY HIGH (14 min., color, Barr) about the use of alcohol and peer pressure for younger children; THE D.W.I. DECISION (Driving While Intoxicated) (25 min., color, Lawren Production, 1977); US (28 min., color, Churchill) in which adult pill takers and young users talk about each others' behavior; IT'S ONLY BOOZE (28 min., color, Films Inc., 1976) about April, age 13, and her drinking problem; MARY JANE GROWS UP: MARIJUANA IN THE 70s (52 min., color, Films Inc., 1976) an NBC film; and DAVID: OFF AND ON (42 min., color, Films Inc., 1973) in which Martha Collidge looks at her brother David, who at 21 has been an alcoholic and a drug addict.

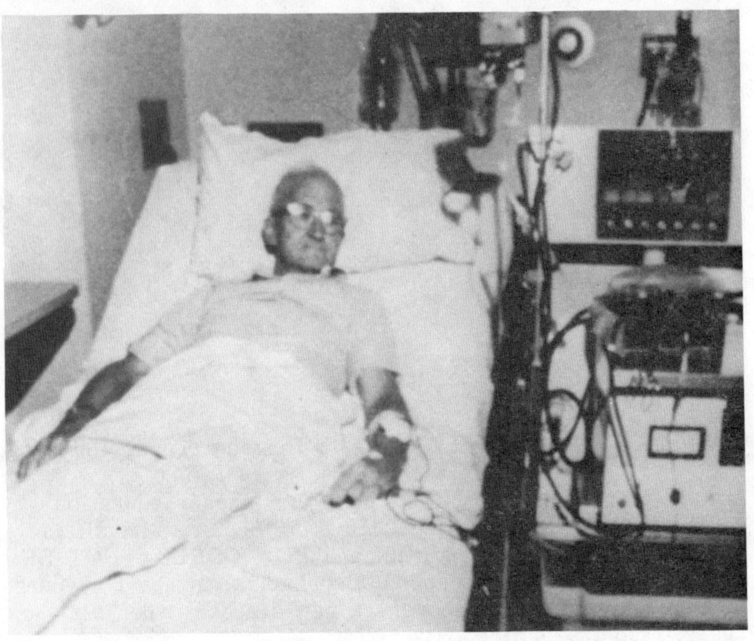

THE RIGHT TO DIE, from Macmillan Films

Crime: In stark black/white animation PRISON (10 min., prod. NFBC, distributor McGraw-Hill) paints a very grim picture of what it's like behind barred doors. The shutting of these doors makes for a soundtrack that calls on all of the senses in this film about the futility of life in prison. Excellent for junior high school and up, for crime prevention, sociology, and prison reform.

Runaways: WALKIN'S TOO SLOW (26 min., color, Bandanna Media, 1976) and ROBIN ... A RUNAWAY (32 min., color, Filmfare).

It should be emphasized that these topics must be explored with students if they are to be properly prepared for life, and if we want them to know we really care. Some of the guidelines for these films must be different than for others, but remember, using them is more challenging, and more satisfying.

Many communities have local film makers, writers, directors, reviewers or film "buffs." Invite them to discuss some special aspect of film. Make sure to meet with your guests before they speak to your class so that the meeting doesn't turn into a lecture. Offer them a list of topics to speak on so you can prepare your class, or ask them to give you a brief résumé. If the talk is to include specific films, make sure everything is ready to show these. Don't permit broken or missing equipment to cause embarrassing situations.

Sometimes a film you have chosen "bombs." Remember young people tend to be honest and avoid polite cliches used by some adults. In the past, teachers evaluated films in terms of the amount of information they contained. Educational films were expected to teach, but often the students became so bored with these films that none of the information was transferred. If the film is no good or if it just doesn't work with your group, admit it. Admit your disappointment but don't compound the negative effect of the film by being negative yourself. Create a positive atmosphere by helping the students state why the film failed. Perhaps they'll want to rewrite the script, so help them with that! Learning why the film didn't work can become a learning situation for teacher and class.

USING NEWSPAPERS, RADIO AND TELEVISION

To teach your class to become critical media consumers, set up an entire course of study with raw materials from the press, radio or television. Use your opaque projector to project news stories, magazine advertisements, political pamphlets and other printed material. Use a tape recorder to tape commercials from radio and television, and if your school owns a video-tape recorder, tape commercials from television. Often local television stations have commercials on 16mm film, which they will lend you free of charge. If no other source is available, try your students. You will be amazed how many of them are able to repeat commercials verbatim. The May 1973 issue of Media & Methods contained a list of learning activities, as well as sources and journalism reviews for a unit on "The Language of Deceit" or "Telling It Like It Isn't."

Video and How to Use It Positively

Pre-teens are analytical about themselves and their own families. Since favorite TV programs often involve families, use these as starting points for discussions. Here are some possible questions from "Commercial TV as a Classroom Tool" by Robert Geller:[15]

> How do characters arrive at choices?
> Who makes decisions?
> Who provides leadership, understanding, love?
> What role, if any, does laughter, jealousy, anger play in the family?
> If there is no mom, or dad, how does the single parent compensate?
> How do the kids function in that family?
> Is there one family, one parent you'd like to adopt for a month, one you'd hate most to live with?

Responses can be fed back to the classroom in discussions about ethics, culture, history, literature, psychiatry, communication and self-awareness.

How about making up questions about some of the programs about doctors to help "exorcise some fears, notions and myths about the healers?"

Younger children have a great need to talk out the things that frighten and confuse them, such as pain, suffering and death. Using TV shows as a starting point may transform a possible negative experience into a positive one. There tends to be more variety on TV than in films. Make use of this.

Ann Christine Heintz in her article "Using What Kids Watch on TV"[16] tells of a special program conducted at St. Mary's Center for Learning in Chicago in which they try to "capture the network of myth and meaning in television literature and to exploit the strength rather than damn its violence or mediocrity...." Those who conducted the program at St. Mary's found that students who participated in

TV-oriented discussions or assignments concerning prime time shows were rarely shy or under-achieving, even though the classes are a mix of teen-agers and adults. Finding abstract concepts--oppressions, integrity, maturity, justice, hypocrisy, revenge, ambition, courage[17]--can readily be done without worrying about the specific content of programs watched.

OTHER AREAS IN EDUCATION WHERE FILMS ARE VALUABLE

Special Education

Special Education is expanding rapidly in most school systems. There are excellent films in this area available from special sources and commercial distributors. The Journal of Learning Disabilities[18] carries regular reviews of some of these films. Spectator, a publication of The National Association of Elementary Principals, carried an article "Films About Learning Disabilities," in the Fall 1974 issue.[19] (Check the catalogs of Aims and Brigham Young University, as well as Lawren Productions for films in this category; see Appendix E.) A film about mentally retarded children, INTERNATIONAL SPECIAL OLYMPICS (28 min., color, from Special Olympics Inc., 1701 K St., N.W., Washington, D.C. 20006), is worth mentioning here, as is THE MUSIC CHILD (2 parts--30 and 15 mins., color, Benchmark), an unusually frank, but at the same time sensitive, film about using music therapy with nonverbal children to achieve some kind of communication.

Teachers' Workshops and In-Service Courses

Films and other media should be used in workshops and in-service courses. "Selected Films for Teacher Training, In-Service Programs and Workshops" appeared in National Elementary Principal magazine in April 1971.[20] The list includes films on learning disabilities, film making, guidance, etc.

A book by Mariann Pezella Winick, Films for Early Childhood: A Selected Annotated Bibliography,[21] lists many films which have been used by the author in courses in Early Childhood Education. The author found most students

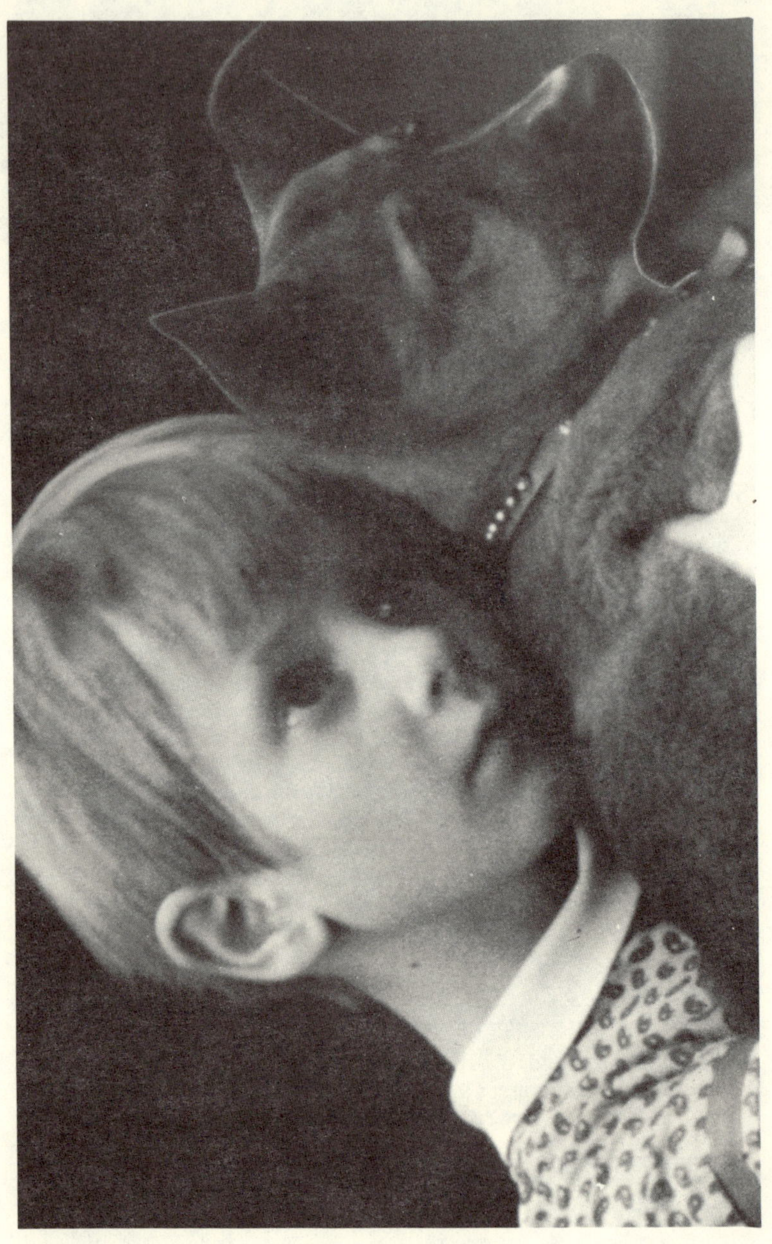

preferred "film observations" to on-the-spot observation, indicating that their attention was focused by the camera, and that they could learn more about a specific situation in this way rather than dissipate their attention over an open field. The author's comment on film use is interesting to note: "In the area of training students to observe, film offers an incomparable medium. The camera's eye is the eye of the observer. It is present for certain visual registrations. The eye of the beholder must follow the eye of the camera. Yet what extraordinarily different responses we get from a group viewing a film. The value of this is that the teacher is now in the position of observing the thoughts and attitudes of students by coming to grips with their modes of attending to a specific document, the film. Written and reading assignments can help give such insight, but systematized observation experiences help to see growth over the course of a semester in a way that no other medium makes possible."[22]

The Child Day Care Association of St. Louis publishes Annotated Film Bibliography which devotes over two thirds of its list to "Films on Child Development." This list, and "Films on Curriculum" are arranged by subject area.[23]

The areas of guidance and human relations are important ones when thinking of using films. Whether used as discussion starters or to make a definite point, films are invaluable.

THE ROLE OF THE ADMINISTRATOR

It is a wise administrator who checks each order before it goes out to find out when and how the equipment and material are to be used. When visiting classrooms, the administrator should check utilization of equipment and offer suggestions and demonstrations on how it can be used or arrange for exchanges between teachers. Obviously, workshops and in-service courses should be arranged by administration for the benefit of all the teachers, and while teaching such courses the use of a/v aids will demonstrate very effectively what the administrator means. Team teaching is a big help in the area of effective media use, as is pairing users with non-users.

On opposite page: THE LOST PUPPY, from Churchill Films.

CONCLUSION

Try to find fresh materials and ideas, as well as films that haven't been taught to death. Try short films rather than features so there will be time for discussion and perhaps time for more than one film on some topics.

There are still teachers who stand next to a screen with a pointer or flashlight to call the attention of the class to a particular act or scene. Others leave the lights on so students can take notes. Yet others show films just because they happen to be in the building, and they try to justify non-existing relationships between film and curriculum. We don't think children will stop watching movies because of any of these, but we can damage the effectiveness of film use in the classroom. A real "no-no" is to discuss a film the class hasn't seen. The teacher who justifies note-taking by, "It's the only way I can get the class to pay attention," has either not paid enough attention to the physical conditions under which the films are shown or has chosen the "wrong" film for this particular group.

Although the supplementary value of films is almost universally accepted, most librarians and teachers do not have their use as instructional media as one of their goals. In the past few good films and filmstrips for classroom use were produced in the U.S. This is changing with more and more excellent films for classroom and entertainment being produced both here and abroad. American made, so-called "children's films" are still a comparative rarity, but when found they are often gems. The producers of "classroom films" are just beginning to listen to teachers and students, and have been slower in changing their format although changes can be seen there too as more creative film makers enter this field.[24]

Films should never be used as just a "filler" for all good films are educational, even if chosen for fun and entertainment.

Since much of the language of the young is made up of visual and aural components, sometimes called "the language of the streets," teachers might do well to begin to integrate some of that form and technique into the curriculum. Chaucer and Dante dropped Latin for English, perhaps we will similarly have to adjust our language, if not quite as dramatically, and hopefully without lowering our expectations and standards. We would never advocate substituting films for teachers as some media people have suggested, but observing some classrooms one does become tempted. Films should be used where other techniques are not as effective. Some things can be said best with films, and there is where their biggest impact lies, and where films can contribute the most.

Films must remain an open medium, one that is used by those who want to, and those who can be creative in its use. Often when using films teachers and students become colleagues, exploring and discovering together. Those who are open to new ways and new ideas also know the new language of the media, and have been using it right along. We sincerely hope that a new horizon of film use is approaching.

FOOTNOTES

1. Schramm, Wilbur. "The Researcher and the Producer in ETV," _Public Telecommunication Review_, July/August 1977, p. 14.

2. Burmester, David. "The Language of Deceit," _Media & Methods_, May 1973, p. 23. ("Updated John Culkins' statistics as gathered from research papers, books and speeches by one author.")

3. Jones, Tom. "Getting It All Together," _The Film Forum_, Films Inc., 1972, p. 1.

4. Lacey, Richard. _Seeing with Feeling_. Philadelphia: W. B. Saunders Co., 1972, p. 45.

5. Lacey, _op_. _cit._, pp. 43-48.

6. Lacey, _op_. _cit._, pp. 26-54.

7. _School Arts_. George Horn, editor. (Printers Bldg., 50 Portland St., Worcester, Mass. 01608).

8. Rice, Susan. _Media & Methods_, Oct. 1973, p. 11.

9. Brennan, William, Jr. "Theatre School Film Program," _Media & Methods_, Oct. 1973, p. 14.

10. Rice, Susan and Jean Marzollo. "The Children's Theatre," K-eight, Sept./Oct. 1971, pp. 36-40.

11. Rice, Susan, compiler and editor. Films Kids Like. Chicago: American Library Association, 1973. (Being updated.)

12. Goldman, Frederick. "A Children's Film Is an Adult Film Is a Children's Film," K-eight, Nov./Dec. 1971, p. 43.

13. Miller, Hannah. "International Film Festival," K-eight, Sept./Oct. 1971, pp. 49-52.

14. Anne Pellowski in a conversation with the author Nov. 1977.

15. Geller, Robert. "Commercial TV As a Classroom Tool," K-eight, Jan./Feb. 1973, p. 91.

16. Heintz, Ann Christine. "Using What Kids Watch on Television," Media & Methods, March 1976, pp. 42-43. (Write to St. Mary's Center for Learning, 2044 W. Grenshaw, Chicago, Ill. 60612, for further information.)

17. Heintz, op. cit., p. 43.

18. Journal of Learning Disabilities. (101 E. Ontario St., Chicago, Ill. 60611).

19. Miller, Hannah. "Films About Learning Disabilities," Spectator, Fall 1974, pp. 14-15. (National Association of Elementary School Principals, 1801 North Moore St., Arlington, Va. 22209).

20. Miller, Hannah. "Selected Films for Teacher Training, In-Service Programs and Workshops," National Elementary Principal, Apr. 1971, pp. 68-72.

21. Winick, Mariann Pezella. Films for Early Childhood: A Selected Bibliography. Early Childhood Education Council of New York City, 196 Bleeker St., New York, N.Y., 1973.

22. Winick, op. cit., p. 2.

23. Child Day Care Association of St. Louis. Annotated Film Bibliography: Child Development and Early Childhood Education. 915 Olive St., St. Louis, Mo. 63101. (Due to lack of funds there are only a few copies left, and the lists were never updated.)

24. McDavitt, Joan, Bill Speed and Linda Strauss. "California Librarians Rap with Filmmakers," Film News, vol. 33, no. 2, March/April 1976.

INFORMATION ON THE EFFECTS OF TELEVISION WATCHING

Barnouw, Erik. Tube of Plenty: The Evolution of American Television. Oxford University Press, 1975. The development of television as a dominant factor in American life, and as a shaper and reflector of American culture and society.

Berger, Arthur. The TV-Guided American. New York: Walker & Co., 1976. The cultural role and significance of selected, popular television programs. What they show about American life and values.

Bogart, Leo. The Age of Television: A Study of Viewing Habits and the Impact of Television on American Life. 3rd ed. Frederick Ungar Publishing Co., Inc., 1972. Analysis of viewing habits of Americans. Shows impact of television on politics, economics and education. Bibliography.

Laybourne, Kit. "A Television Atlas," Sightlines, Winter 1977/78, pp. 8-10. A summary of the effects of television watching. Each statement is supported by bibliographic data.

Liebert, Robert H., Jon M. Neale and Emily S. Davidson. The Early Window: Effects of Television on Children and Youth. New York: Pergamon Press, 1973. Three psychologists examine the contents of programs and commercials, and show the effects on the behavior, social attitudes and psychological development of young people. Bibliography.

Miles, Betty. Channeling Children: Sex Stereotyping in Prime-Time Television. Princeton, N.J.: Women on

Words and Images, 1975. Analysis by women.

Winn, Marie. The Plug-In Drug. New York: Viking Press, 1977. Based on interviews with families, child specialists, and teachers, the book shows the negative effects of addiction, and gives some answers on how to control the "drug."

REFERENCES

Books

Anderson, David R. and Gary Wilburn. Visualize. Instructor's Manual. Dayton, Ohio: Pflaum/Standard, 1971, p. 51, "Appendix F." "Conducting a Discussion After a Film." Gives good advice on how to lead discussions.

Brown, Roland. A Bookless Curriculum. Dayton, Ohio: Pflaum/Standard, 1972. A description of a media oriented curriculum for the "non-learner" in English classes. A year's lesson plans are detailed.

Feyen, Sharon (ed.). Screen Experience: An Approach to Film. Dayton, Ohio: Pflaum Publishers, 1969. Analytical history of different types of films. Suggestions for film series and program.

Friedlander, Madeline S. Leading Film Discussions. League of Women Voters (817 Broadway, New York, N.Y. 10003), 1972, $1.50. A guide to using films for discussions, training leaders, finding the right film, program planning.

Gaffney, Maureen (comp.). MORE FILMS KIDS LIKE. ALA, 50 E. Huron St., Chicago, Ill. 60611. 1977. $8.95.

*Goldman, Frederick and Linda R. Burnett. Need Johnny Read? Practical Methods to Enrich Humanities Courses Using Films and Film Study. Dayton, Ohio: Pflaum Publishers, 1971. A detailed study of why and how to teach with films.

Hoban, Charles F. The State of the Art of Instructional Films. The ERIC Clearinghouse on Media and

Technology, Stanford University, Stanford, Cal., 1971. Definitions, developments, and research in the field.

Jones, William. The Film Forum. Films Inc. catalog, 1972. "Why Teach Films?" Discusses organizing budget, schedule and film selection.

Kuhns, William. Exploring the Film. Dayton, Ohio: Pflaum/Standard, 1971. Intended to be used as a text in a film study course, using the method of concentrating on specific elements of films.

*Kuhns, William and John Carr. Movies in America: Teaching in the Dark. Dayton, Ohio: Pflaum/Standard, 1973. To help film teachers organize and teach a course in the history of American movies. A resource book with the most complete bibliography. Pp. 11-12 deal specifically with discussions. Recommended!

*Lacey, Richard. Seeing with Feeling. Films in the Classroom. Philadelphia: W. B. Saunders Co., 1972. Developed from articles in the Independent School Bulletin and Media & Methods. Provides approaches for all teachers to teach film study. Tells how to use films, what to expect from students and gives various exercises to help get started on a program. Recommended!

Laybourne, Kit (ed.). Doing the Media, A Portfolio of Activities and Resources. (Contact Peter Haratonik, Media Studies. Program New School For Social Research, 66 5th Ave., N.Y., N.Y. 10009 for information.) Project to develop flexible curriculum to serve as models in elementary and secondary schools to train teachers and develop teaching materials.

Limbacher, James (ed.). Using Films: A Handbook for the Program Planner. New York: Educational Library Association, Inc., EFLA 17 W. 60 St., New York, N.Y. 10023, 1967. (Out of print, being revised.) What makes a good film? Presenting a film program. Teaching film appreciation. Includes a list of organizations offering free films by Frank J. Leahey.

*Linton, Dolores and David. Practical Guide to Classroom Media. Dayton, Ohio: Pflaum/Standard, 1971. Suggestions for improving media study. Plans for integrating media into the curriculum. Discusses tapes, radio, records, still photography, film and television.

Mallery, David. Film in the Life of the School. National Association of Independent Schools, 4 Liberty Sq., Boston, Mass. 02109, 1968. Discussion of practices and possibilities. Annotated list of old and new films of special interest to schools.

Rice, Susan and Rose Mukerji (eds.). Children Are Centers for Understanding Media. Washington, D.C.: Early Childhood Educational International, 1973. (Available from Association for Childhood Educational International, 3615 Wisconsin Ave., N.W., Washington, D.C. 20016.) $3.95. Discusses media projects which teach children how to use the necessary equipment for media production. Media activities in the schools and television are used as a source of literacy.

*Rice, Susan (ed.). Films Kids Like. Published for the Center for Understanding Media by the American Library Association, Chicago, Ill., 1973. A list of films--just what the title states. Also tells how to run a children's film theater. (Look for updated version to be published in 1978.)

*Shillaci, Anthony and John Culkins (eds.). Films Deliver: Teaching Creatively with Films. New York: Citation Press, 1970. This book consists of 15 papers describing what films can do for teachers and students. New concepts and approaches to film study. How it's all being done today. Programs incorporating films and television into English and social studies. The nitty-gritty of films in education. Appendices. Recommended!

Sohn, David. Film Study & The English Teacher. A professional paper prepared for the University of Indiana Audio-Visual Center, 1968. A good "how-to" paper.

Sohn, David (ed.). Good Looking: Film Studies, Short Films and Film Making. Philadelphia, Pa.: North American Publishing Co., 1975. A Media & Methods book. A collection of essays on the state of film study. Part II contains views and reviews of short films. Part III: film making.

Valdes, Joan and Jeanne Crow. The Media Works. Dayton, Ohio: Pflaum/Standard, 1973, $4.95. Ways of examining seven of the mass media for the secondary school student.

Periodicals

Brown, Roland. "Moral Dilemma, A Teaching Unit for Slow Learners," English Journal, Nov. 1971, pp. 924-6.

Doty, David. "I Liked the Part Where...Kids Responding to Films," K-eight, May/June 1972, pp. 34-35.

Foley, Helen. "To Sing the Streets: Using a Community Film Program to Teach Composition," English Journal, Nov. 1971, pp. 1101-8.

Gilmore, Hugh. "What Film Teaching Is NOT," Media & Methods, Sept. 1970, p. 41.

Holloway, Ronald (Rev.). "A Guide to Films for Discussion and Film Study," Contemporary Films/McGraw-Hill Catalog, 1221 Avenue of the Americas, New York, N.Y. 10020.

Isaacson, David. "Film Study in the High School English Curriculum," English Journal, Apr. 1973, pp. 651-8.

Jones, Emily. "The Art of Using Films," International Film Foundation, Inc. Catalog Supplement, 475 Fifth Ave., New York, N.Y. 10017, 1973-74.

Miller, Hannah. "A Little Bit of Sugar Helps the Medicine Go Down," K-eight, May/June 1972, pp. 40-41.

Miller, Hannah. "Films About Learning Disabilities," Spectator, National Association of Elementary School Principals, Spring 1974, p. 13.

Miller, Hannah. "Films to Learn Music By," K-eight, Jan./Feb. 1973, pp. 102-5.

Miller, Hannah. "International Film Festival," K-eight, Sept./Oct. 1971, pp. 49-52.

Miller, Hannah. "Selected Films for Teacher Training, In-Service Programs and Workshops," National Elementary Principal, Apr. 1971, pp. 68-72.

Oksner, Robert M. "Television and the Elementary School: Some Good News, Some Bad News," Sightlines, Winter 1977/78, pp. 1142.

Rice, Susan and Jean Marzollo. "The Children's Theater," K-eight, Jan./Feb. 1972, pp. 36-40.

Schisgall, Jane. "The Creative Use of Multimedia," Teaching Exceptional Children, Summer 1973, pp. 163-5.

Winick, Mariann Pezella. Films for Early Childhood: A Selected Bibliography. Early Childhood Education Council, 196 Bleeker St., New York, N.Y., 1973.

Chapter 8: MAKING FILMS

INTRODUCTION

Marshall McLuhan has observed that for the first time in the history of man the information levels outside the classroom are higher than those inside. Teachers not only compete with television, radio, movies, records, books, photographs, telephones, tapes, magazines and computers, but with commercials which cost $50,000 a minute to produce, and "Sesame Street" and "The Electric Company" which have invaded the lives of our children in and out of school. Since schools must acknowledge the existence and influence of this new media, it would follow that children should be viewing and discussing a variety of films and television programs, that they are creating films, videotapes, photographs, and writing about them in the classroom.

It must be obvious to any observer of the education scene that in many schools this is just not so. Whether from ignorance or fear of the unknown, for whatever reason, teachers do not arrive on the job equipped to handle the new media as they are equipped to handle books. The U.S. is behind many European countries and Canada where film education has been accepted for years. Most teachers do not know much about film making (just as many film makers do not know enough about schools and how they operate). In this chapter we hope to provide the framework for film and other non-print media production. Since there are many books and films on the topic we will try to be brief but there is a lengthy bibliography and filmography at the end of the chapter for those looking for information.

It may not be enough sometimes just to look at movies. For many students it also becomes important to take part in the process of creating. John Culkin's advice on avoiding boredom in watching films is to go out and make them. He said, "Passivity before a TV screen gets solved by activity behind a camera or film editing."[1*] Making films gives students confidence for writing and expressing themselves, while offering outlets for creativity, imagination and excess energy accumulated in sitting passively. But it is expensive. Before embarking on film making or a VTR program with a class, know what it is you want to accomplish, see if there are other ways of doing it, and be sure to check your budget.

The AECT (Association for Educational Communications and Technology; see Appendix A) Convention of 1974 had as its theme "involvement." Many of the leaders of this convention feel that until educators and students become more involved in the making of materials, their use will not become universal as it should, given the "mediatmosphere" we live in and the advanced state of the technology we use. In the elementary schools, with their self-contained classrooms, we find that film can be and is integrated into the regular curriculum. There film viewing can be naturally related to writing and language arts, film making and art. Elementary school children seem eager to try their hand at film making. In the high schools where there is film making, it is often limited to a few students as an individual study project, or as part of an English report. Very few schools have active media centers where students can sign up to do "film reports," make slides and records, and work with media as part of their regular curriculum. Yet, as one teacher said: "Film making as a language arts project comes closer to engaging every student in a real learning situation than anything I've tried in eight years of teaching."[2]

Books, magazines, and organizations stand ready to assist teachers willing to branch out into film making. Students should be encouraged to use this creative medium to express themselves, for visual literacy is part of the educational establishment, whether recognized or not.

Only when all teacher training and library schools make media training part of the required curriculum, will future teachers and librarians come to the teaching situation with realistic expectations about films and film use.

---

*Footnotes to Chapter 8 begin on page 190.

FILM MAKING AS A LEARNING PROCESS

Teachers who have tried film making with elementary and junior high school age students give the following reasons why it is a real learning experience[3] (most of what follows can be applied equally to VTR):

1. It is a completely new method of communications for most students, and since none have experienced failure in using films, they approach it with a more positive attitude.

2. Everyone and every talent is needed. Actors, artists, cameramen, electricians, mathematicians, writers, recorders, organizers, clean-up people, directors and spectators, all are a necessary part of the process.

3. Movies are a permanent record, and can be played over and over, not like a play which is finished once the performance is over.

One teacher noticed these evidences of learning: Ego involvement of every student; improvement in grammar and communication skills; improvement in organizational skills; attempts at predicting results of visual stimuli; pride in a product produced through group effort; and discovery of film as a new way of seeing.

PROBLEMS HELPED BY INVOLVEMENT IN FILM MAKING[4]

Many problems resolve themselves when even a difficult class makes a film, but it is a wise teacher who will not expect problems to disappear.

1. Disagreement and arguments over who should handle equipment and who is to blame for mistakes are solved by children who want to see the project succeed. Because they are truly interested, they at first help solve each other's disagreements, and eventually everyone becomes so involved the arguments may stop altogether.

2. Children with disabilities find there is something they can do, even if it is only to keep track of everyone else.

3. Students who have always experienced failure before find they may be good at some aspect of film making.

4. Show-offs are sometimes good actors and comedians.

5. Rivalries over who can be cameraman, director, producer, etc., tend to resolve themselves when participants find out how hard the job is, and how much patience is needed. They may even offer to share the job and to take turns.

6. Creativity suddenly becomes important, and students with ideas are welcomed instead of being made fun of.

7. Those who have not achieved academically may find areas to achieve in, thus getting support for other school work.

8. Absenteeism is markedly decreased since everyone wants to be part of the project.

Teachers involved in film making have learned that sensitive and imaginative students make sensitive and imaginative films, but the converse is also true. Dull students can make insensitive and dull films.[5] The magic that does occur behind the camera is that students begin to see, acquire a sense of power, become aware of their capabilities and gain confidence. An excellent film made by the Bank Street College of Education (610 West 112 Street, New York, N.Y. 10025), CHILD'S EYE VIEW (21 min., color), describes how a group of children ages 5-9 became aware of their neighborhood while attending an after-school program, where they used cameras. They lost some of their fears and mistrust of their neighborhood and the people in it, and finally became more "open" to future learning through the use of film and cameras.[6]

INTRODUCTORY PROJECTS TO FILM MAKING

Be sure before embarking on any film making project that you have at least read some of the literature written by those who have tried it (i.e. Media & Methods articles). Speak to teachers who have made films with classes, and observe classes making films. Make your own film. Catch as many mistakes as you can before they happen.

Photography

Photography can be used as an independent activity or as an introduction to film making. People have been taking photographs for nearly 150 years. In 1888 the first "push-button" Kodak camera was introduced by George Eastman. Today teachers and students are able to use cameras in the classroom that may sell for as little as $.65.[7]

Cameras help children to see the world around them and to tell about it in the pictures they take. They enjoy using machines and this is a truly independent, individualized activity. Black and white film is inexpensive when bought in bulk, and developing film is quite simple. There are many creative activities one can do with cameras. Pictures of one's family, school or neighborhood taken to illustrate a written story, make the assignment a more challenging one. Close-up shots are always fascinating, whether of something in nature, someone's eye, a person, etc.

Through the use of photographs teachers have found an easier interdisciplinary approach to teaching. A science class that goes out into the fields to photograph details of flowers and trees can be accompanied by their English teacher who can assist in the picture taking and help the class write about their pictures. Poetry lessons can be geared to pictures of nature as well as moods suggested by photographs. Photography is a means of self-expression, of focusing on what is being studied, and of sharing one's experiences with others.

One source of information on photography is School Arts.[8] Since student use of cameras is increasing and a minimum of technical competence is required, students can help in producing instructional materials, such as slides, tape sets, and filmstrips. By preparing a script, and with a short period of instruction in basic photography, students using their own cameras can do such a project.[9] Wherever possible the school should supply film, flash bulbs, and pay for and make arrangements for processing. When tapes are to be used for a soundtrack, these should be provided as well.

The results of teacher evaluation of one such project were the following:[10] 1) The enthusiasm of involved students was high; 2) The involvement of teachers and students was excellent; 3) The photographic quality was generally good; 4) Outdoor shots were generally better than indoor ones; 5) Teacher assistance at the script-planning stage was the major factor determining the success of visualization and continuity; 6) Teachers felt the media preparation helped students become better informed in the particular subject area they were working in; 7) The media produced was a strong motivation at the time it was made; 8) The media produced could be used in future teaching.

It is useful in the elementary grades to teach children that photographs and films say things, just as words do. Have your class pick out the subject of a picture, a slide, or one frame of a filmstrip. This is sometimes harder than it sounds. Ask what ideas or moods are being communicated. (This will also show how one can communicate without words.) Since pictures and films communicate many different feelings, visual images, moods, etc., each individual's response may differ. There is no one correct response, but everyone should be able to feel good about what they saw. This activity can be followed with one where the children make up their own pictures or filmstrips, using illustrations from magazines, or pictures they have drawn, thus communicating with each other with their own work.

Another simple activity to embark on with your class, before they begin to get into film making, is to use leaders from a 16mm film. You can buy blank leaders in most camera stores. Run the blank leader through a projector, so the children can see there is nothing on it. Lay it down flat on top of paper and scotchtape it in place. Using felt tipped pens and crayons, or scratching with pins, have your students make designs or write their names on the blank leader. Run it through the projector again so that the children can see their homemade movies. Older children may want to add sound by using a record or tape. This is one way of explaining that it takes 24 frames of film to make one second's worth of a movie on the screen and that skill and patience are needed. (You might even get in a math lesson on the use of a ruler.) An added benefit from using photography is that slides used in making a presentation can be stored in the library or media room for future use. They are valuable resource materials.

HOW TO INVOLVE STUDENTS

For some students just learning that films don't just "happen" is a revelation. They can learn this by talking to someone who has made a film and by watching amateur films or by making their own. One way of starting a project when working with a class is to ask those students who want to make films to form groups of from five to eight students. (This will ensure that every member of the group will have a real responsibility.) The groups then begin to decide what type of film they wish to make, documentary, animation or live-action. One teacher reported that each year there seems to be a favorite subject (anti-drug, ecology, monsters, etc.). It is a good idea for the teacher to remain in the background at this stage of the project.

Having chosen the type of film and the subject, the group is ready for a script, and for assigning the roles and responsibilities of each member of the group. All films need a producer who is responsible for the entire production. This includes making decisions as well as arranging for "location" shooting. In a larger group there may also be a co-producer. For animation films the art director is responsible for the over-all production.

Decisions need to be made about black and white film vs. color, as well as the length of the film. (One standard 50-foot roll of super 8 film runs 200 seconds.) Another assignment is that of the cameraman. All of the cameramen must be shown how to use the available equipment and given a chance to operate the camera to be used. With younger children it is sage advice to let all the participants see and handle the camera and other equipment before the actual project begins, to eliminate the "gimme" stage. By emphasizing what the equipment can do, as well as how easily it can break, much careless handling can be avoided. If all groups are using the same camera no student will want to be responsible for holding up the shooting schedule of the entire class.

In the process of translating written scripts into visual images individual ideas will appear. No two students are going to interpret the script in exactly the same way. This may result in much rewriting, an excellent language arts lesson. Once the script is finished and accepted by the group, props are collected, scenes rehearsed, and the group is ready to begin shooting. Here is a good opportunity to go out into the community, and by working with different sectors, students may even attempt to narrow the "generation gap." You must be prepared for groups going out of the classroom and the building, unless they are making an animated movie. You must be prepared, as well, for filming which takes more than one 45-minute period. However you handle these problems, check first to make sure your administration and other teachers will go along with your ideas and will be cooperative in helping the children with their projects.

The film is not finished until it has been edited, spliced, and run and re-run to be criticized and/or praised by the entire group, the teacher, and the entire class. Editing out any segment of film they have made is difficult for children. Watching the film many times with different groups will help them see the film as others do, and cutting thus becomes much easier. Truffant suggests, "There is no limit to what can be done. There are no rules." His advice on preparing to make films is to go to the movies and sit through the same picture, if it's a good one, as many times as possible.

The scriptwriter is responsible for transforming ideas into visual images. Francis Ford Coppola (THE GODFATHER), who is both a writer and a director, once said, "When people go to see a movie, 80 percent of the effect it has on them was preconceived and precalculated by the writer."[12]

In much of the film making going on in our schools, there is a lack of emphasis on the written part of film. There must be a structure for a message to be communicated, and this discipline should become part of film work. The unplanned, improvised and spontaneous action some young people are filming can work only once, if at all, and then only because it seems different. Even technique, if well used, soon begins to bore general audiences if it is used for its own sake. This is a point that cannot be overemphasized! Every project we have described here has been founded on some structured activity. In schools where students are permitted to make films without planning or guidance, too often the activity begins and ends as a "fad." Since there are many activities which foster concomitant learning of skills that can and should be included in film making (i.e. writing, mathematics, etc.) teachers who want such projects to succeed must work, and work hard to help students. The tool should never become the master!

MAKING YOUR OWN VIDEOTAPES

Television programs which are based on the interests and personal lives and school work of students, when exposed to the community, can be helpful in establishing stronger bonds between school and community. They can be used to give the community insights into the viewpoint of students, and to show the wide span of student opinion, life style, ambitions, which in general mirror much of the adult community. Many schools make their programs available to PTA groups, as well as community and church groups.

Exploring newspaper articles, radio and television programs, a construction site, a hospital, a supermarket, or a library, can make for a lively program if properly planned and prepared. Exploring the hows and whys of any such topic can offer excellent learning experiences. Interviewing people by writing out possible questions is an exercise in writing and verbal skills. John LeBaron, in his article, "Television: Production for K-12" tells of a community related project done under his direction by a group of 9-11 year olds.[13] He discusses the work of two groups, one operating outside the school, the other working inside by bringing community resources into the school. The types of learning by the children included:

1. Exercising their writing and verbal skills.
2. Planning, organizing and problem solving.
3. Interaction with important members of the community outside the school.
4. Sharpening of questioning skills, and improving the art of visual communication.
5. Use of mathematics.
6. Use of graphic arts.
7. Information retrieval, transmission and communication.
8. Self-analysis and self-criticism.
9. Collaboration with peers.
10. Involvement in selection/rejection process as part of a group, in making judgments, compromises and collective decisions.
11. Distinguishing the important from the unimportant.
12. Learning to improvise creatively and extemporaneously.
13. Defining the need for social interaction by hosting guests in their school.

Welby Smith recommends "a utilitarian approach to video" in his article "VTR: A Tool Not a Tent Show."[14] He describes in some detail one elementary school's approach to stimulating children with reading difficulties, that in turn had an impact on the entire school. One third grade class was given the assignment to write a book on the basic operation of a VTR. Using their manuals as guides, the students proceeded to tape other classes. Those who wrote the manuals then taught others how to use the VTR. Eventually some of the student teams became experienced enough to receive requests for taping sessions. They then asked those using their "taping services" to set up objectives, diagrams, choose shooting locations and prepare a checklist of needed VTR components for the production. A post-production conference with the person making the original request was added, giving an opportunity for evaluation.

Physical education teachers and coaches have taken advantage of video to tape games, both classroom and competitive, to show where a team or class needs improvement in skills. Dance presentations, as well as dramatic ones, when taped make criticism easier and help to preserve the work done by students. The opportunity to analyze and evaluate skills from videotapes is one of the most valuable contributions of this media.

Before purchasing a videotape recording system know what your objectives in using it are, and don't buy more than you need. You may find it relatively easy to get funds to buy a system, but remember you also need a staff to run it. Underutilizing the equipment is a waste of money, so start small. The systems are expandable, and you can always add cameras, switching equipment, lights, and editing capability. Once you understand how to use the basic components, camera, monitor, microphone and videotape recorder, you should be able to utilize them effectively. Above all, know what you want to do!

STARTING A MEDIA CENTER

If you are in charge of starting a production facility in your school here are some points to remember:

1. Decide what to do, when and how to do it, and who will do it. Don't start before the project is defined. Plan ahead! This includes equipment, space, staff and money you will need.

2. Survey the faculty to see what kind of services they need and want, and more important what they are willing to help with. Involve as many as are willing to help in the planning.

3. Use public relations techniques to inform students and faculty of new materials and equipment. Give talks, display your materials, hold fairs and festivals.

4. Train student aides in use of equipment to work with other students and faculty.

5. Set goals and objectives so you can explain to the faculty, administrators and even the Board of Education if necessary what you plan to do.

6. When buying equipment, check to see what your school already has and what can be built in-house. You may need help when purchasing new equipment (see Chapter 2). Look at other schools who have working media centers. Check workshops, professional film makers, your local camera store and anyone who is knowledgeable in what is really needed. Look around your school for teachers who have some experience in film making. You will need a media specialist, and the more competent the person you find the more help you will get. Experts in your community are usually most willing to help with time and advice, and sometimes equipment. Above all, keep in touch with the faculty of your school.

7. Don't start operating on a grand scale. Start slowly with one project at a time. Don't let anyone rush you into making costly mistakes which may jeopardize the entire program.

For further information on media centers, see the following article by Eileen R. Dunyon: "A Curriculum Based Media Program--Describing Media Techniques Developed at Oakdale School in Gordan School District." (ED121287) From ERIC Document Reproduction Services, P. O. Box 190, Arlington, Va. 22210. ($3.50 in photocopy, $.83 in microfiche). When ordering include ED no.

BIBLIOGRAPHY ON FILM MAKING

Most young film makers would rather use the trial and error approach to learning than bother to read books or even watch a film on the subject. Since it is often the most expensive method of learning, and since young film makers rarely if ever have unlimited funds available, sooner or later they must turn to other means, such as books or films. There are some excellent ones on the subject, and students and teachers can choose from among a variety. For some, reading books may be the best way of gathering information, others learn better by using more than one sense and may prefer a film.

The following list of books on film making was compiled over a period of several years with the help and advice of teachers and students. Since the list was made no doubt other books have been published, and some of those mentioned have gone out of print. Whether the books are kept in the library, the English department, by the principal or in the classrooms, students should be encouraged to use them rather than rely entirely on teachers for instruction.

Although no attempt was made to be complete, I apologize in advance for any omissions, which may make this list less useful.

Andersen, Yvonne. Make Your Own Animated Movies: Yellow Ball Workshop Film Techniques. Boston: Little Brown and Co., 1970.

This is by far the most popular book for student use in the elementary and junior high school grades. Based on animation techniques as developed by the author in her workshops with children, the book gives instructions and techniques for animating figures, clay, cut-outs, for painting on film, setting up and using cameras, splicing films, synchronizing sound and pictures, and the use of special effects.

Andersen, Yvonne. Teaching Film Animation to Children. New York: Van Nostrand Reinhold Company, 1970.

Intended for the adult wishing to teach film animation, the book includes all phases of camera work, synchronized sound, price guidelines and evaluation of cameras, projection and editing, films and tape recorders are listed. Directions are included for adapting single frame releases for doing animation work, and animation methods using movable and hinged cut-outs, clay, toys, painted film, constructed forms, live actors and others are given.

Anderson, David and Gary Wilburn. Visualize: Instructors Manual. Dayton, Ohio: Pflaum/Standard, 1971, Student Manual and Instructor's Kit.

A step-by-step approach to visual language, the book contains seven appendixes for use in demonstrating each of the seminars outlined, for film sources, a bibliography, glossary of terms, and procedures for discussing films and for conducting brainstorming sessions. This is part of a kit which contains a student manual and a textbook as well as a student-made film and a set of photographs.

Bell and Howell. Guide to Successful Super 8 Movie Making. From Bell and Howell, 7100 McCormick Rd., Chicago, Ill. 60645.

A "how-to" pamphlet.

Bendick, Jeanne and Robert. Filming Works Like This. New York: McGraw-Hill Book Co., 1970.

A very popular book with elementary and junior high school students, it includes every aspect of film making: budget, cameras and how to choose them, lenses, films, light, sound animation, etc.

Bobker, Lee. Elements of Film. New York: Harcourt, Brace, World Inc., 2nd ed., 1974.

Story and script, image and sound, editing, the job of the director, acting, the contemporary film maker and film criticism are discussed. A brief but good analysis of film making techniques.

Brown, James and others. AV Instructional Technology: Manual for Independent Study. New York: McGraw-Hill Book Co., 4th ed., 1973. Text and Instructor's Manual.

Part of the book is devoted to the theoretical and practical consideration in selecting, producing, using and evaluating media, including film and television.

Communication Arts Books. A series of pamphlets on aspects of film making and video production. Published by Hastings House Publishers, N. Y.

This includes Basic TV Staging, The Use of Microphones, Your Film and the Laboratory.

Cowil, Peter (ed.). A Concise History of the Cinema. New York: A. S. Barnes, 1970, 2 vols.

This is a discussion of films in the U. S. and other countries as seen through the contribution of major movies and their directors. It contains chapters on documentaries, animation and the newer technology.

Garon, Jay and Morgan Wilson. The Family Movie-Making Book. New York: Bobbs-Merrill, 1977.
Hints for home or classroom movies--film making by non-professionals.

Gaskill, Arthur L. and David A. Englander. How to Shoot a Movie Story. New York: Morgan and Morgan Publishers, 1967.
Useful as a teacher reference, the book discusses continuity, simple sequence, different kinds of shots and story editing. More concerned with narrative and dramatic elements than equipment.

Goldstein, Laurence and Jay Kaufman. Introduction to Film. New York: E. P. Dutton Inc., 1976.
Using analytical techniques, the authors have tried to reproduce the original experiences of writers, directors, cameramen, sound men and editors who create a film. An in-depth analysis of every phase of motion picture production. Many illustrations are used. Choosing and Testing a Camera, pp. 569-583; Glossary of Film Terms, pp. 591-604.

Helfman, Harry. Making Pictures Move. New York: Morrow, William & Co., 1969.
For the young beginner, this book gives specific instructions for doing animation. Another book by the same author, Making Your Own Movies (1970) gives a brief history of the background of movies, as well as instructions for shooting titles and other techniques.

Herman, Deldie and Sharon A. Ratliffe (eds.). Radio, Television and Film in the Secondary School. 1973. Available from National Textbook Co., 8259 Niles Center Rd., Skokie, Ill. 60076
This guide provides basic information in specific areas, including planned units, equipment, and bibliographies in media analysis; history of radio, television and film; equipment; physical plant; materials, radio production; television production; and film production.

Huss, Roy and Norman Silverstein. The Film Experience: Elements of Motion Picture Art. New York: Harper & Row, 1968.

Another excellent guide for teachers, as well as older students attempting to make films on their own, the book contains definitive discussions of research films, story boards, continuity, imagery, and all those components necessary to making a film.

Kardish, Laurence. Reel Plastic Magic: A History of Films and Filmmaking in America. Boston: Little Brown and Co., 1972.

For students and teachers, this history of films and film making in America serves as an excellent introduction for a course in cinematography and film history.

Kemp, Jerrold E. Planning and Producing Audiovisual Materials. San Francisco: Chandler Publishing Co., 2nd ed., 1968.

Basic techniques of planning audiovisual material using photography, graphics and tape recording are demonstrated in step-by-step method. The preparation of slide series, filmstrips, films and television programs is discussed. Includes filmography and bibliography.

Kodak. Send for Index to Kodak Information for complete listing of what's available. Eastman Kodak, Rochester, N.Y. 14650.

Kuhns, William and Robert Stanley. Exploring the Film. Dayton, Ohio: Pflaum Publishers, 1971.

This easy-to-read book tries to give the film audience an added awareness of all they are seeing. A short history of the development of the motion picture and an analysis of some of the ingredients, such as sound and color, are followed by examples from actual movies. The final chapter deals with the film making process.

*Kuhns, William and Thomas F. Giardino. Behind the Camera. Dayton, Ohio: Pflaum Publishers, 1970.

Written to provide a foundation in the technique of film making, since competent film making requires knowledge of cameras, lenses, film stock, lighting, and how to work with people. Film making is a tool for expression and communication and the book tries to help with all of these.

Larson, Roger with Ellen Meade. Young Filmmakers. New York: E. P. Dutton & Co., Pb. Avon, 1971.

Describes some teen-age made films and what is needed to make 8mm or 16mm films.

Larson, Roger, Lynn Hofer and Jaime Barrios. Young Filmmakers Foundation: Young Animators and Their Discoveries. New York: Praeger Publishing, 1973.
Introduces techniques and special effects of film making through interview with twelve young, amateur film makers.

Laybourne, Kit (ed.). Doing the Media. Center for Understanding Media, now Media Studies Program, New School for Social Research, 66 Fifth Ave., New York, N.Y. 10011
Described as a "Kind of Whole Earth Catalogue of Media Activities for Children." This is a how-to book which describes projects including all media to develop a series of flexible curriculum for elementary and high schools, to train teachers and develop teaching materials. Suggestions for selling ideas of improving media use, financing programs and getting optimum use out of available equipment.

Lidstone, John and Don McIntosh. Children as Film Makers. New York: Van Nostrand Reinhold Co., 1970.
For older students and teachers, the book covers use of the camera, projectors, organization and supervision of film making, editing, sound animation, and titling. There is a bibliography and a description of a project done by students.

Lindgren, Ernest. The Art of the Film. New York: Macmillan, rev. ed., 1963; pap., Colliers.
The older student may be able to manage this book. It is a short history of movies, the tools used in film making, descriptions of the many different people necessary to produce a film, as well as the necessary techniques and film criticisms.

Linton, Dolores and David. Practical Guide to Classroom Media. Dayton, Ohio: Pflaum/Standard, 1971.
This is a book for those starting out. It will help to keep them from becoming discouraged. There are simple explanations of how film works with some good ideas on demonstrating to students, tips on choosing a project, the nature of film, film criticism, film language, selection of film making equipment, student film making and the rewards of film making.

*Madsen, Roy Paul. Animated Films: Concepts, Methods, Uses. Interland Publishing Co., 1969; distributed by Pitman.
This is considered the most comprehensive text available

on the techniques of animation. The book covers its history, both past and present, with a complete discussion of the many and diverse uses of the animation technique in movies and television, both here and abroad. Subsequent chapters put the language defined in the first chapter to use, with comprehensive discussions of the animation stand, pan and zoom, a filmography, scripts, storyboards, and film styles. Planning and drawing cartoon animations is treated in great detail, and the bibliography is an international one.

Madsen, Roy. The Impact of Films: How Ideas Are Communicated Through Cinema and Television. New York: Macmillan, 1973.

Analysis of all aspects of cinema, television, videotape. Includes impact on audiences. Bibliography.

Malkiewicz, Kris J. Cinematography: A Guide for Film Makers and Film Teachers. New York: Van Nostrand Reinhold Co., 1973 (pap.).

Tells of the work of the cameraman and discusses techniques of sound recording, cutting and production logistics. Discusses technical aspects of equipment. Includes bibliography, glossary.

Manchel, Frank. When Pictures Began to Move. New York: Prentice-Hall, 1965.

This short, easy-to-read history of the motion picture industry explains camera techniques and how they evolved and changed to meet the new needs of our times. The growth of necessary staff and their functions, the story of film pioneers and stars, and a panoramic view of the entire era of motion pictures is made available to the young reader.

Matzkin, Myron A. Better Super 8 Moviemaking. New York: American Photo-Graphic Book Publishing Co., 1967, (pap.).

Contains excellent suggestions for working with Super 8 plus basic needs for film making.

Pfragner, Julius. The Eye of History: The Motion Picture from Magic Lantern to Sound Film. New York: Rand-McNally and Co., 1964.

In story form the struggles and frustrations of the early pioneers in the movie industry are described.

**Pincus, Edward. Guide to Filmmaking. New York: New American Library, Signet Books, 1969 (pap.); Henry

Regenery Co., Publisher, hardcover.

Used by teachers and students as a textbook in classes of cinematography, this is often recommended as the one book to buy if there are budget limitations. It is a production manual and contains explanations about choosing the best camera, and such topics as screening the final product. There are diagrams and tables, and the emphasis is on 16mm, but the differences in using 8mm are discussed.

Quick, John. Handbook of Film Production. New York: Macmillan, 1972.

Begins with a brief history of motion pictures. Explains every aspect of film making with diagrams. Use of equipment and techniques included. High school and up.

Rilla, Wolf. A-Z of Moviemaking: A Handbook. New York: Viking Press, 1970.

A well-written handbook on the basic process of film. Film grammar, lighting, sound, acting, editing, everything but writing, are included.

Roberts, Kenneth and Win Sharples, Jr. A Primer for Filmmaking. Pegasus, 1973.

To help film makers get to know and use the tools necessary in all aspects of technical film production. A step-by-step guide for the older student.

Rynew, Arden. Filmmaking for Children. Dayton, Ohio: Pflaum/Standard, 1971 (text and student handbook).

A practical guide on how a teacher can conduct film making classes on the elementary school level. The Motion Picture Production Handbook for each student gives work rules, examples, samples and illustrations.

Smallman, Kirk. Creative Film-Making. New York: Collier Books, 1969, (pap.).

Film, cameras, lighting and exposure, lenses, editing, recording and mixing sound, special effects and using non-actors, are some of the topics included here. Complete sample scripts, indicating how various techniques can produce desired effects, feelings and ideas, all within a $198 budget, are given.

Sohn, David, ed. Good Looking. Philadelphia: North American Publishing Co., 1976 (A Media & Methods Book).

This book contains sections on film study, short films

and film making. How to use films, what films to use and how to make films is told by the following experts:

Carrico, Paul. "Student Filmmaking: Why and How," pp. 189-204.

Sheratsky, Rodney E. "Easy as 1, 2, 3, (4, 5, 6, 7, 8, 9...)," pp. 205-208. Step-by-step instructions on learning to use a camera and making a film.

Sheratsky, Rodney E. "Freaking Around with Films," pp. 209-216.

Repath, Austin. "Making a Movie," pp. 217-221.

Braverman, Charles. "The World of Kinestasis--How to Make Your Own Complete Sound Movie Inexpensively," pp. 222-225.

Andersen, Yvonne. "The Yellow Ball Workshop," pp. 225-229. "Animation is one of the simplest of film techniques to teach. If six year olds can work in this medium successfully...."

Putsch, Henry. "Student Filmmaking: Type and Technique," pp. 23-232.

Brasso, Russell, "Making Student Filmmaking Work," pp. 233-235.

Many of the articles were written several years ago but are still valid today.

Stephenson, Ralph and Jean R. Debrix. The Cinema as Art. Penguin Books, 1965; pap., Pelican.

This analysis of the various techniques of the cinema is a good tool for teachers, and for students ambitious enough to start film making on their own. The author discusses how images created by the camera differ from reality, and why cinema is really an art form. In depth discussions of space in cinema include shooting angles, depth, cutting, framing, time, double exposure, decor, costumes, make-up, and sound.

Trojanski, John and Louis Rockwood. Making It Move. Dayton, Ohio: Pflaum/Standard, 1973 (separate teacher's manual).

This simple how-to book includes a student handbook and teacher's manual and resource guide. 16mm films to illustrate each type of animation are dealt with in the teacher's manual. There is a chapter on the history of animation, handmade films, puppet and doll animation, object, cut-out, cel animation, kinestasis, pixillation, and motion distortion. "A program for the study and projection of animation pictures by young people." Each chapter of the teacher's manual has a list of print and film resources.

Youngblood, Gene. Expanded Cinema. New York: E. P. Dutton Co., 1970 (pap.).

After an introduction by Buckminster Fuller, the book is divided into four parts. Part I talks about the audience and the myth of entertainment. Part II gives the history of film language. Part III is about the results of new developments. Part IV talks about television as a creative medium and includes interviews with people in the field. The book is for the older student and serious film makers.

Yulsman, Jerry. The Complete Book of 8mm (Super 8, Single 8, Standard 8) Movie Making. New York: Coward-McCann, 1972.

Gives advice on which cameras and accessories are best and how to use them. High school and up.

BOOKS ON VIDEO

Anderson, Chuck. The Electric Journalist: An Introduction to Video. New York: Praeger, 1972.

Bensinger, Charles and the Editors of Photography Magazine. Petersen's Guide to Video Tape Recordings. 1973 (from Petersen Publishing Co., 8490 Sunset Blvd., Los Angeles, Cal. 90069).

Most complete and useful guide to using video. Answers many questions, explains equipment, editing, video productions, etc. Step-by-step instruction on how to play back tape, parts necessary to using VTR and care of tapes and recordings.

Efrein, Lawrence. Video Tape Production and Communication Techniques. 1971. Tab Books.

Ewing, Sam and R. W. Abolin. Don't Look at the Camera. Shortcuts to Television Photography and Filming. Blue Ridge Summit, Pa. 17214. Tab Books, 1973.

Gilliom, Bonnie Cherp and Ann Zimmer. ITV: Promise into Practice. Educational Media Center, Ohio Dept. of Education, 518 South Wall St., Columbus, Ohio 43215 (Attention G. R. Bowers), 1972 (Xerox hard cover).

The bulk of this book discusses the pragmatic use of ITV. Programming and studio production techniques, as well as hardware requirements are discussed. Includes an evaluation of teaching with television.

Hurrell, Ron. Manual of TV Graphics. New York: Van Nostrand Reinhold, 1973.

Kuhns, William. Exploring Television. Chicago: Loyola University Press, 1971.

*Mattingly, Grayson and Welby Smith. Introducing the Single Camera VTR System: A Layman's Guide to Videotape Recording. New York: Charles Scribner's Sons, 1971, 1973.

This simple, but comprehensive book is an excellent guide to using VTR system. From discussions of why one would use such a system, to detailed analysis of the camera, video-cassette recorders, technical standards, production standards, the Port-a-Pac, and a glossary, this is one of the few books on the topics for student use.

McAdam, Robert J. and Charles Vento. Portable Video Tape Recorder. A Guide for Teachers. National Education Association, 1201 16th St., N.W., Washington, D.C. 20036, 1969.

Utilizing PVTR, operation of the equipment, and differences in available equipment are the basis of this book.

Millerson, Gerald. The Techniques of Lighting for TV and Motion Pictures, 1972; Basic TV Staging, 1974; The Technique of TV Production, 9th ed. 1972; TV Camera Operation, 1973. Communication Arts Books, New York: Hastings House.

Moore, Frank J. A Guide to the Use of Closed Circuit Television (CCTV). Center for Effecting Educational Change, Fairfax County Schools, Bailey Crossroads, Va., 1970 (Xerox hard cover).

Tells what a CCTV system consists of, what it can be used for, and projects. Includes a short bibliography.

Murray, Michael. The Videotape Book: A Basic Guide to Portable Television Producting. Taplinger Productions, 1975.

Robinson, Richard. The Video Primer. Quick Fox Inc., 33 W. 60th St., New York, N.Y. 10023, 1974.

Weiner, Peter. Making the Media Revolution. A Handbook for Video-Tape Production. New York: Macmillan Publishing Co., 1973.

Videofreex. The Spaghetti City Video Manual. A Guide to Use, Repair and Maintenance. New York: Praeger Publishers, 1973.

A manual for people who want to be more self-sufficient with video hardware. It is divided into four sections: Theory, Systems, Maintenance, and Not So Basic Maintenance. It contains a bibliography on understanding basic video equipment and learning to work with it.

FILMOGRAPHY ON FILM MAKING

The following films on film making were chosen because we believe they are helpful to the young film maker. They can be used together with books or alone, but the watching of films about film making plus actual experience can cause amazing things to happen.

Since no one film ever satisfies everyone's needs, a variety of approaches are suggested.

FILMMAKING FUNDAMENTALS (15 min., Films Inc., 1972) describes a junior high school class project which was part of a communications workshop. The project shown is that of a 13-year-old boy making his own film. He explains the fundamentals of a storyboard, use of the tripod, distance and zoom lenses, focusing, speed, single frame, trick photography, lighting, titling, and editing, including cutting and splicing. He does all of this while making a movie about a cowboy on a ranch. The appeal is to younger students.

Two films on the subject come from the International Film Bureau. A FILM ABOUT FILMMAKING (17 min., 1971) is a step-by-step analysis of making a live film. Shooting scripts, clothes, settings, types of shots needed, as well as equipment such as cameras, film, and light meters are demonstrated. On-location planning of actual shooting, editing and functions of various crew members are also included. The finished product is clearly analyzed. The film is a humorous one. MAKING A SOUND FILM (10 min., 1973) is for the older student. It discusses the different types of sound possible, such as synchronized sound, and voice-over-voice. Tape recorders, cameras, editing techniques, and equipment and the use of music are presented in a way which makes learning about them most interesting.

BASIC FILM TERMS, from Pyramid Films

UNDERGROUND FILM (23 min., ACI Films, 1971) features Chick Strand and her work. More than 2000 underground films are produced here each year, and there is a strong bond between those who produce these films and those who view them. There are distributors working with only young film makers, and special theaters which show their films. The film is addressed to the 5600 students now majoring in film making at colleges all over the U.S. (as of 1974), and shows these often outspoken young people what is happening in this field.

Pyramid Films distributes some excellent films. BASIC FILM TERMS: A VISUAL DICTIONARY (15 min., 1970) is one of the best films about the basic language of film making as used in writing, shooting and editing. Script terminology, kinds of shots, lenses and their effects, camera angles and movement, sound, and optical effects are defined and demonstrated as used in an actual movie in the making. Camera movements, types of lenses used and explained. The one minute script at the end of the film, which is the finished product, is very funny, as are the "out-takes," those scenes which are usually never used, but which are shown here. FRAME BY FRAME (13 min., 1973) is about the art of animation. Examples of frame-by-frame photography, using colored paper between actual pictures to create a flicker film, and drawing on tracing paper and directly on the film are but two of the techniques, which are exaggerated to really make an impression on the viewer. STUNTMAN (11 min., 1972) shows a man being hung, shot, going through a window, and jumping off a roof. The "hows" of the stunts are explained, as well as the training necessary to stay in shape to do the stunts.

MOVIE STUNTMEN (28 min., color, LCA) views five Australian movie stuntmen. They reveal their emotions as well as techniques used to achieve their feats.

SIX FILMMAKERS IN SEARCH OF A WEDDING (15 min., Pyramid Films, 1970) tells of six different approaches used to film the same wedding. One film maker concentrates on the family life of the groom, another segment is done in the style of a home movie, including some of the errors often found in such films. Yvonne Andersen and her Yellow Ball Workshop contributed an animated version of the wedding. Yet another photographer concentrated on the rehearsal, and the last segment shows the wedding album of stills done by the local photographer. Young film makers can get a host of ideas about different ways of treating any one subject.

THE SCREEN PLAY (15 min., Pyramid Films, 1972) gives the details of writing a screen play, how to type it, what to include and what to leave out. By showing an actual scene and analyzing it simultaneously while showing pages of the script, the film is most helpful for those wanting to learn this aspect of movie making. BASIC LIGHTING (5 min., Pyramid Films, 1971) covers intensity, direction and specularity of lighting. CONTINUITY I (5 min., Pyramid Films, 1972) covers camera positions, action axis, and compressions of time and space, using the changing of an automobile tire as an example. CONTINUITY II (5 min., Pyramid Films, 1972) discusses both controlled and uncontrolled actions (i.e., the arrival of an airplane) and how the film director can adjust to these. WORTH HOW MANY WORDS (5 min., Pyramid Films, 1972) really demonstrates how spectacular the movie camera can be. The film goes back and forth in history, with shots of Abraham Lincoln alternating with the blasting off to the moon, nature shots, shots taken through a microscope, and shots of people of

BASIC FILM EDITING, from Pyramid Films

foreign lands. Together they show the student the immense wealth of material available, and the power of the camera in capturing it. All of the films have guides which contain the complete script, and all are available in 16mm as well as super 8.

In HOW TO MAKE MOVIES YOUR FRIENDS WILL WANT TO SEE TWICE (10 min., color, Benchmark) Murray Suid has made a film primer using an actual movie to demonstrate the language of film.

Two films that can be borrowed free of charge from

BASIC FILM PHOTOGRAPHY, from Pyramid Films

Kodak are BASIC MOVIE MAKING (14 min., color, 1973) and HOW WINNING TEEN-AGE MOVIES ARE MADE (28 min., color, 1974). Both explain basic techniques and the second shows segments of the completed works.

THE FIRST MOVING PICTURE SHOW (7 min., color, Phoenix Films) is a good film to use in film making workshops. Clay and graphic animation, as well as other techniques are used.

THE MAKING OF A DOCUMENTARY (22 min., color, producer CBS News, distributor Carousel Films, Inc.) takes the viewer through all the pre-planning and research stages, into the actual shooting and final editing, to the end result. Techniques covered are lighting, cross-cutting, jump cuts, reverse shots and sound. THE TELEVISION NEWSMAN (28 min., color, Pyramid) a film by Charles Braverman, shows a day in the life of an ABC news reporter. The need for directing and editing skills under deadline pressure are examined.

THE ELECTRIC FLAG (15 min., Pyramid Films, 1973) asks whether in an election for public office the campaign controls the medium, or the medium controls the campaign. With footage from THE CANDIDATE we see how the film came very close to a real campaign by using simulated sets, and professional campaign advisors. The role of the media specialist and pro-man are shown in the work they do in political election campaigns.

SPECIAL EFFECTS (13 min., color, Pyramid) is a behind-the-scenes demonstration of the most common mechanical effects used in film making. It covers snow, frosted windowpanes, rain, lightning, fire, bullet holes and flaming arrows.

ANIMATION: A LIVING ART FORM (10 min., color, Aims, 1971) talks about the 400,000 still pictures and millions of photographs it took a professional Hollywood studio to produce the cartoon "Shinbone Alley" starring Carol Channing and Eddie Bracken. The script through storyboard-animation, adding sound and editing, and the composite print are examined here.

SANDMAN (4 min., color, Eccentric Circle) was produced by Eliot Noyes, who also created CLAY and THE ALPHABET, to explain the technique of sand animation.

FRANK FILM (9 min., color, Pyramid), a winner of over 200 awards, shows in collage animation the myriad of possibilities of that type of film making. The double soundtrack, one of Frank telling us about his life, the other a stream of words in free association is also unique. A film to be seen many times to be fully appreciated.

GENE DEITCH: THE PICTURE BOOK ANIMATED (25 min., color, Weston Woods) explains how books are transferred into animated films. The narration is, unfortunately, slowed down for youngsters, but the film is a good one to show how the many components of such a film are put together.

A really unusual film, IN QUEST OF COCKABOODY (43 min., color, live action and animation from Cranbrook Ltd., One Broad St., Guilford, Conn. 06439), is a documentary about the making of the short COCKABOODY by John and Faith Hubley with Yale Art students and faculty members of the Yale Child Study Center. An analysis of

GENE DEITCH: THE PICTURE BOOK ANIMATED, from Weston Woods

animation and its capability to exaggerate reality is shown. Editing of the soundtrack by the Hubleys as well as the editing of hundreds of original drawings by Tissa David to make the final film are used to demonstrate the creative process in making an animated film.

Films by Young Filmmakers

There are a number of films about young film makers making films while working in a group. These try to show some of the fundamentals necessary to working in this medium. THE YOUNG ART: CHILDREN MAKE THEIR OWN FILM (Van Nostrand Reinhold, 1965) was photographed by students of the Collegiate School in New York City. It tells how to set up and run a film program, and what the results look like. The same company distributed LET'S MAKE A FILM, taken at Yvonne Andersen's Yellow Ball Workshop in Lexington, Mass. Children are shown working with movable and hinged cut-outs, clay, toys, and paint on film, constructed forms and live actors. Made by this pioneer in the field of animation and children-made films in 1965, it still ranks as one of the best on this topic.

EDEN, from "Plum Pudding," a product of Yellow Ball Workshop.

FILM CLUB (28 min., Youth Film Distribution Center) is a film teacher's diary of a summer program conducted on New York City's Lower East Side. Teenagers making their own movies and showing their work on a Moviebus are seen through the eyes and camera of their instructor, Mr. Barrios.

In MOVE (15 min., Benchmark Films, 1970) nine and ten year olds make short, animated films. It was photographed in a classroom in the Amidon School in the District of Columbia. The hows and whys of animation are drawn and narrated by the children. They use drums to illustrate how pictures can be made to move, tell about making sound effects, and finally show some of their films. The film is accompanied by an excellent and detailed guide.

CHILD'S EYE VIEW (21 min., color, Bank Street College of Education, 1969) describes how a group of children, aged 5 to 9, in an after-school program, became aware of their own neighborhood by using film and camera. The film does much more than that, however, for it describes how the camera helped a teacher to "open" this group of children to further learning.

MINI MOVIE MAKERS (10 min., color, Para., 1971) stars 7- to 12-year-old film makers at the Henry Street Settlement in New York City and shows them making animated films using the simplest techniques and drawings, as well as drawing directly on film.

The "Young Filmmakers Series" (LCA, 1973) is a group of three films expressly produced for the lower grades. THE HANDY DANDY DO-IT-YOURSELF ANIMATION FILM (11 min., color) won the Blue Ribbon Award at the 1974 American Film Festival, and teaches simple animation through demonstrations by three children using a super 8 camera. THE HANDY DANDY DO-IT-YOURSELF EDITING FILM shows how the children organize and edit footage shot in the second film and shows the final product. There is a manual, consisting of a 24-page student workbook and a 6-page teacher's guide.

IN THE MIDDLE, from "Newton Mini-Films," a product of Yellow Ball Workshop.

FRAME BY FRAME: THE ART OF ANIMATION (13 min., color, Pyramid) explores different kinds of animation as made by grade school film makers. Frame by frame techniques, still picture filming, flicker filming, cut-out animation, cell or drawn animation, direct images on film and time sequence filming are shown.

THE AMERICAN SUPER 8 REVOLUTION (31 min., color, IFF, 1972) is recommended for teacher training for it shows a super 8 film production by a fifth grade class. It is not only a film about film making, but the story of the film is about the American Revolution, thus showing how history and film making can be combined in teaching 10 and 11 year olds.

Films About the History of Films

The history of movies is told in many films. ANIMATED CARTOONS (17 min., Film Image, 1947) is the history of animated movies. The earliest picture-showing equipment, like Plateau's Plenakisticope (1832) and Reynaud's Praxinoscope (1877) are used to show the development of the art of animation. Also from Film Image, BIOGRAPHY OF A MOTION PICTURE CAMERA (21 min., 1947) continues where ANIMATED CARTOONS stops, with Edison's Kinetoscope and Lumiere's Projector. In these films we see that it used to take pounds of equipment, and at least half an hour to take one picture, and how large audiences would gather to watch 40 seconds of a moving picture.

THE FIRST TWENTY YEARS (5 parts, 17-22 min., Pyramid) represents 100 motion pictures selected from more than 3000 films that were restored from the Library of Congress paper print collection. The project took Kemp Niver (the author of The 1st Twenty Years, Pyramid, $7.50), over 10 years.

FILM: THE ART OF THE IMPOSSIBLE (27 min., LCA, 1971) explains the creative aspects of the art of film making. Analyses of sequences from well-known films are used to show how the impossible became real by using simple editing techniques. Michael Ritchie, director of DOWNHILL RACER, shows scenes from his own film, as well as scenes from POTEMKIN, LAWRENCE OF ARABIA, KING KONG and BIRTH OF A NATION, analyzing the camera work and the necessary psychology to be used on the audiences to make the impossible seem real.

THE EYE HEARS--THE EAR SEES (25 min., producer BBC, distributor LCA, in 2 parts) is the story of

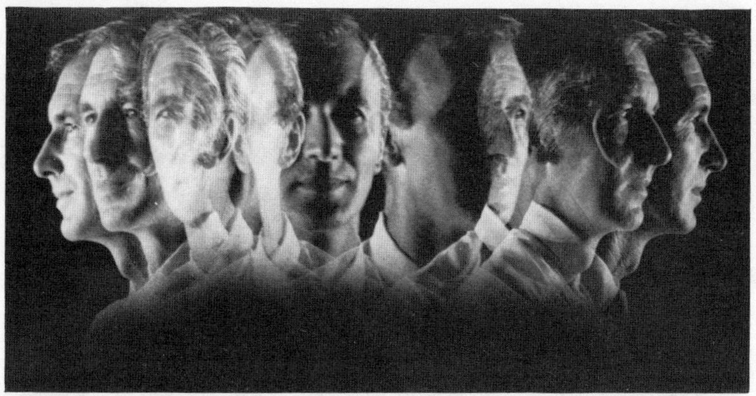

THE EYE HEARS--THE EAR SEES, from Learning Corporation of America.

Norman McLaren of the National Film Board of Canada (who invented his own tools and techniques and had a tremendous influence on other animators). The first animated film using his technique of drawing directly on film, by-passing the camera, was HEN-HOP which McLaren did in 1942. He shows how he makes his films, some of which may take as long as a year to finish. Examples from FIDDLE-DE-DEE and LA POULETTE GRISE demonstrate much of what he tells the viewer. Experiments with animation with people, such as NEIGHBORS and PAS DE DEUX which he made in 1967 (where even the soundtrack is drawn on the film directly) provide more examples for the viewer to understand McLaren's belief that "the most important thing in film is movement." THE LIGHT FANTASTICK (57 min., color, NFBC) is a detailed retrospective of the development of animation films as done by the National Film Board of Canada. Norman McLaren's hand-drawn-on-film and pixillation techniques; Evelyn Lambart's cut-outs; Lotte Reiniger's shadow puppets; and Ryan Larkin's visual improvisation are featured.

PUPPETS OF JIRA TRNKA (26 min., color, Phoenix) details how the puppets are drawn, the script (both written and drawn) prepared, how the puppets are made, sets designed and constructed, costumes sewn, and the film directed. We see how each movement of the puppets must be

---

On opposite page: THE PUPPETS OF JIRI TRNKA, from Phoenix.

BASIC TV TERMS, from Pyramid Films

carefully timed. Excerpts from Trnka's films demonstrate some of the above.

Films About Television

Pyramid distributes "The Television Workshop" featuring six films on the history, technology and current development in television: TELEVISIONLAND (12 min., color) a Charles Braverman film; ELECTRONIC RAINBOW (23 min., color) an introduction to television; BASIC TV TERMS (17 min., color) a "Video Dictionary"; MAKING OF A LIVE TV SHOW (25 min., color) also by Braverman; TELEVISION NEWSMAN (28 min., color); and SIXTY SECOND SPOT (25 min., color). These come with a film guide by David Sohn and a bibliography.

For a more complete list see Linda Artel's article, "Films About Television," (Sightlines, Winter 1977/78, pp. 17-22).

MAKING A LIVE TELEVISION SHOW, from Pyramid Films

FOOTNOTES

1. Miller, Hannah. "A Working Media Center: An All Media Approach to Learning," Audiovisual Instruction, February 1974, pp. 59-60.

2. Magarrell, Elaine. "A Process Not a Product," K-eight, September 1973, p. 18.

3. Magarrell, op. cit., p. 20.

4. Bogojavlensky, Ann and Donna Grossman. "How to Involve Students in Filmmaking," K-eight, April 1973, pp. 29-42.

5. Gilmore, Hugh. "What Film Teaching Is Not," from the book Good Looking, David Sohn, ed., p. 3.

6. Harris, Robbie. "Child's Eye View," K-eight, February 1972, pp. 13-15.

7. Greenberg, David. "Shoestring Cameras," K-eight, September/October 1971, pp. 28-30.

8. Cole, Robert. "Photography: Basic Equipment & Layout II," School Arts, January 1974, p. 11.
   "Photography: Basic Darkroom Layout, Equipment, Part I," Dec. 1973, p. 39.
   "Developing and Printing b/w Film," Feb. 1974, pp. 6-7 (information sources from manufacturers of film equipment, books, pamphlets).
   "Making Photographs," Mar. 1974, pp. 6-7.

9. Eastman Kodak. Index to Kodak Information. From Kodak, Rochester, N.Y. 14650. Contains list of pamphlets and films on every aspect of photography. Includes sources of materials.

10. Oh, Choong-Youl. "An Idea Whose Time Has Come: Student Preparation of Instructional Materials," Learning Resources, a supplement of Audiovisual Instruction, January 1974, pp. 2-3.

11. Witsch, Michael. "A Primer on Cameraless Filmmaking," Media & Methods, January 1976, pp. 38-39.

12. Alpert, Hollis. "Mirror to the World," S/R World, September 7, 1974, p. 37.

13. LeBaron, John. "Television: Production for K-12," Learning Resources, a supplement to Audiovisual Instruction, January 1974, p. 4.

14. Smith, Welby. "VTR: A Tool Not a Tent Show," Media & Methods, May/June 1977, p. 28.

SOURCES OF INFORMATION

Organizations (see Appendix A for descriptive details)

American Film Institute, John F. Kennedy Center for the Performing Arts, Washington, D.C. 20566.

Association for Educational Communication and Technology (AECT), 1201 16th St., N.W., Washington, D.C. 20036.

Educational Film Library Association (EFLA), 17 West 60th St., New York, N.Y., 10011.

Periodicals

American Cinematographer, published by American Society of Cinematographers, 1782 N. Orange, Dr., Hollywood, Cal. 90028.

American Film, published by AFI, John F. Kennedy Center for the Performing Arts, Washington, D.C. 20566.

The Animator, published by Northwest Film Study Center, Northwest Art Museum, Southwest Park & Madison, Portland, Ore. 97205.

Audiovisual Instruction, published by AECT, 1201 16th St., N.W., Washington, D.C. 20036.

Factfile, published by American Film Institute, John F. Kennedy Center for the Performing Arts, Washington, D.C. 20566 (pamphlets).

Film News, 250 East 57th St., New York, N.Y. 10019.

Media & Methods, published by North American Publishing Co., 134 N. 13th St., Philadelphia, Pa. 19107.

School Arts, 50 Portland St., Worcester, Mass. 01608 (for photography only).

Sightlines, published by EFLA, 17 West 60th St., New York, N.Y. 10023.

Today's Filmmaker, 250 Fulton Ave., Hempstead, N.Y. 11550.

REFERENCES

Photography

Beatrice, Laura. "The Overhead Projector: A New Approach," K-eight, January/February 1972, pp. 33-34.

Bohr, Joei. "Say It with Pictures--A Creative Photography Workshop," Media & Methods, January 1977, p. 55.

Cole, Robert. "Photography: Basic Darkroom Layout I," School Arts, December 1973, p. 39 (includes sources of information).

Cole, Robert. "Photography: Basic Equipment and Layout II," School Arts, January 1974, p. 11.

Cole, Robert. "Developing and Printing B/W Films," School Arts, February 1974, pp. 6-7. (Sources of detailed information on chemicals, as supplied by manufacturers of films, equipment, and in books and pamphlets.)

Cole, Robert. "Making Photographs," School Arts, March 1974, pp. 6-7.

Eckhardt, Ned. "The Learning Potential of Picture Taking," Media & Methods, January 1977, pp. 48-53.

Greenberg, David. "Shoestring Cameras," K-eight, September/October 1971, pp. 28-30.

King, Warren. "Winning Student Photographs," Media & Methods, January 1977, pp. 56-61.

Linton, Dolores and David. Practical Guide to Classroom

Media. Dayton, Ohio: Pflaum/Standard, 1971. Chapter 9 "Still Photography."

Oh, Choong-Youl. "An Idea Whose Time Has Come: Student Preparation of Instructional Materials," Learning Resources, a supplement to Audiovisual Instruction, January 1974, pp. 2-3.

Osler, Bobbie. "How to Make Pinhole Cameras," K-eight, January/February 1972, pp. 30-32.

Speight, Jerry. "Shooting with a Creative Eye," School Arts, December 1973, pp. 36-37.

Witsch, Michael. "A Primer on Cameraless Filmmaking," Media & Methods, January 1976, pp. 38-39.

Wiseman, Robert. "A No-Camera Slide Program," Media & Methods, January 1977, pp. 63-64. (Tells how to make slides by a process called "lifting.")

Video

Brown, Mary. "Video and Cable--A Bibliography and Source List," EFLA Supplement, 1973. (Lists books, pamphlets, articles, periodicals, film organizations and agencies, and sources of videotapes for sale and/or exchange.)

Darby, Jim L. and Libby Mulder. "The Tri-County Regional Library's Program in Video and Cable TV," Previews, November 1975, pp. 6-8.

Drukker, Leendert, "Video Playback, Battle for the TV Screen: Progress Report on Disc, Video-tape and Super 8 Film Players," Popular Photography, October 1973, pp. 43-44.

Eisler, Michael H. "A Primer of Projectuals," Previews, October 1974, pp. 7-9.

Kaplan, Don. "Understanding Visual Continuity," Media & Methods, October 1976, pp. 48-50.

Laffel, Jeff. "Made for TV Movies--A Whole New Ball Game," Film News, September 1974, pp. 16-20.

LeBaron, John. "Television: Production for K-12," Learning Resources, a supplement to Audiovisual Instruction, January 1974, pp. 4-5.

Reynolds, James. "Wanted a TV Crew," Audiovisual Instruction, December 1976, pp. 40-42.

Russel, Gail. "The Electric Rainbow Co.," K-eight, January/February 1972, pp. 22-24.

Smith, Conrad. "The Early History of Animation: Saturday Morning TV Discovers 1915," Journal of the UFA, XXIX, 3 (summer 1977), pp. 23-35.

Watson, Elizabeth and Brenda D. Maloney. "AV Licensing Brings Kids and Media Together," Previews, October 1975, pp. 7-9.

Wright, Dan C. "An Inexpensive Way to Improve Your Videotapes," Media & Methods, January 1976, p. 45.

Film Making

Alpert, Hollis. "Mirror to the World," S/R World, September 7, 1974, pp. 37-38.

Belica, Michael. "Filmmaking III, Starting a Local Production Facility from Scratch," K-eight, September/October 1972, pp. 33-34.

Becker, George. "Make a Movie Without a Camera," School Arts, December 1973, pp. 141-5.

Bogojavlensky, Ann and Donna Grossman. "How to Involve Students in Filmmaking," K-eight, March/April 1973, pp. 29-42.

Covert, Nadine and Fern McBride. "The Minnewaska Report: Symposium on Child-Made Films," Sightlines, Fall 1977, pp. 2-3.

Duggan, Robert and Frank Ross. "Good Film Conferences Make Good Neighbors," Media & Methods, December 1970, pp. 42-43.

Flinchbough, Todd. "Move It," K-eight, January/February 1972, pp. 25-28.

Forman, Rose. "Czech Film Festival," Film Library Quarterly, Fall 1969, p. 23.

Gardner, Paul. "Alumni of Film School Now Star as Directors," New York Times, January 30, 1974, p. 24.

Halleck, Dee Dee. "There's Gold in Them Thar Hills: Prospecting for Child-Made Films," Sightlines, Fall 1977, pp. 7-8.

Harris, Robbie. "Child's Eye View," K-eight, January/February 1972, pp. 13-15.

Hofer, Lynne. "Young Filmmakers," Film Library Quarterly, Spring, 1969.

Lasser, Michael. "More Than Photography, Less Than Panacea," Audiovisual Instruction, May 1972, p. 8.

K-eight editorial, "Technical Tips," March/April 1973, p. 35.

Lee, Rohama. "The Common Denominator Is Service," Film News, April/May 1974, pp. 6-7.

Magarrell, Elaine. "A Process Not a Product," K-eight, September 1973, pp. 18-22.

Mallery, David. "Films in the Life of the School," National Assn. of Independent Schools, October 1968.

Maynard, Richard. "Educational Film Teachers," Scholastic Teacher, April 2, 1973.

Miller, Hannah. "$65 Buys a Film Library," K-eight, September 1973, pp. 47-48.

Miller, Hannah. "A Working Media Center: An All Media Approach to Learning," Audiovisual Instruction, February 1974, pp. 59-60.

"Reactions to the Symposium on Child-Made Films," Sightlines, Fall 1977, pp. 11-12.

Roman, Donald. "Communi-Capers, The Thing Is Coming," K-eight, March/April 1972, pp. 46-48.

Rose, Joyce. "Filmmaking. Making a Movie Without a Camera," K-eight, September/October 1972, pp. 26-27.

Scheff, Thomas W. "Getting Started in Animation," Media & Methods, September 1976, pp. 42-44.

Sutton, Ron. "Secondary School Film Study: Moving from Prescription to Description," Sightlines, March/April 1973, pp. 6-8.

Filmographies

Limbacher, James. "Movies About Movies," Service Supplement, Sightlines, March/April 1971.

Limbacher, James. "More About Movies," Service Supplement, Sightlines, March/April 1973.

Parker, David L. "A Filmography of Films About Movies and Movie-Making," (rev. ed.), Eastman Kodak, 1971.

APPENDIX A

Organizations Actively Engaged in Helping Teachers, Students and Librarians in the Areas of Film Use, Film Making and Film Study.

The following list of organizations should be helpful to those who want more training and information in the area of film. Those who are looking for others with whom they may share ideas will also find this kind of information.

THE AMERICAN CENTER OF FILMS FOR CHILDREN, c/o Division of Cinema, University of Southern California, University Park, Los Angeles, Cal. 90007. (213) 741-6071, Richard Harmetz, Executive Director.

The Center was founded in Oakland in 1964, but did not become really active until 1969, when it joined the Los Angeles County Museum of Art in the First International Children's Film Festival to be held in the U.S. Now an annual event, it has helped the Center to grow in importance in the area of quality film programming for children. The Academy of Motion Pictures is helping the Center through its Scholarship and Grants Committee, to expand its Information Service. With a proper staff, this service is now able to answer specific questions and give data on films. There is a circulating film program, "Highlights of the International Children's Film Festival," and children-made films are sponsored in the International Muse Contest. In 1974, for the first time in the history of the UNESCO sponsored International Muse Contest, the grand prize winner was an American, as were three other prize winners.

The purpose of the Center is to hold film festivals for children, exhibitors, critics, distributors, film makers and educators, to make them aware of what is being done in their own country and abroad. The Center also promotes film education for young people, children's film making projects, research and the lobbying for easier distribution of children's films. Its aim is to get quality children's films shown in theaters and on television in the United States.

(There are 17 independent Centers in countries all over the world, all dedicated to working in the areas of quality films for children. In addition there is the Children's Film Foundation in England. Founded in 1951, and originally supported by the entire film industry, it is now an independent film making company, whose films lead the world in the production of films for children. These films are exported to 30 countries, the U.S. being one of their smallest markets.)

There are children's film festivals held in Teheran, Iran; Gijon, Spain; Gottwaldov, Czechoslovakia, just to mention a few in which children help to judge films. Czechoslovakia has three film studios devoted to making films for children. Other Eastern European countries are also very active in this field. The United States is far behind European countries in making films for children.

AMERICAN FILM INSTITUTE (AFI), The John F. Kennedy Center for the Performing Arts, Washington, D.C. 20566. (202) 833-9300. Membership $15 a year, $10 for educators.

The AFI was founded in 1967 as an independent, nonprofit organization by the National Endowment for the Arts, a federal agency. Its purpose is "to preserve the heritage and advance the art of film and television in America." Initial funding came from the National Endowment for the Arts, and was matched by the Ford Foundation, the Motion Picture Association of America, and individual and private corporations.

According to its brochure, AFI does the following: Preserve and catalog motion pictures; conduct conservatories to train film makers; fund independent film makers through the Independent Filmmaker Program (IFP); provide guidance to film teachers and educators through its National Education Services program; operate a repertory movie theater in the John F. Kennedy Center in Washington, D.C.; and help institutions present classic film programs.

<u>Publications:</u> 1) <u>American Film: Journal of the Film and Television Arts</u>, a monthly magazine, contains articles on the stories behind films, scope of the film, the art of film, previews, articles about directors, finances of movie making, and discussions of television; 2) <u>AFI Catalog of Feature Films</u>, two volumes, 1921-30, 1961-70; 3) AFI Guide to College Courses in Film and Television; 4) <u>Fact-</u>

files... currently available for $2 to members, $3 to others. Available titles: "Film and Television Periodicals in English," "Student Film Festivals and Awards," "Careers in Film and Television," "Guide to Classroom Use of Film," "Women and Film/Television," "Children and Film and Television." Six others are forthcoming as of this writing.

Seminars and Workshops: These are conducted periodically on the teaching and use of film and television in schools and colleges.

AFI Center for Advanced Film Studies provides intensive workshops for teachers, librarians and researchers. These include courses in screenwriting, film production, directing, production management, cinematography and editing. There is a program in the art of film making for those with some proficiency, and an Education Liaison with colleges and universities on various aspects of developing curricula in film and television.

AFI Life Achievement Award: A major fund-raising effort through the sale of tickets, this award has been given annually since 1973.

ASSOCIATION FOR EDUCATIONAL COMMUNICATION AND TECHNOLOGY (AECT), 1201 16th Street, Washington, D.C. 20016. Membership $30 a year.

AECT began in 1923 as the Department of Visual Instruction of the NEA. Now an autonomous, professional association for those actively involved in using technology in instruction, its members are media librarians, specialists in schools and colleges, principals and school administrators, those working with media in the armed forces, museums, businesses, libraries and hospitals. "Members carry out a wide range of responsibilities in the study, planning and application, and production of communications media for instruction." These include films and filmstrips, computer assisted instruction, and books and pamphlets on facilities and equipment. Extensive bibliographies on visual literacy, films and books are available from AECT. Films can be rented through the NEA AV Studio, 1201 16th Street, Washington, D.C. 20036. Conventions are held annually in cities across the country, where films are shown at workshops and lectures. There is always an exhibit of educational technology and equipment at these conventions.

Publications: 1) *Audiovisual Instruction*, the official AECT magazine, is published monthly, and included in membership dues. Special articles appear regularly, addressed to teachers, librarians, AV directors and coordinators, on innovative instructional programs (see Appendix C for details); 2) AV Communication Review, published four times a year, is a more scholarly journal, addressing itself to research workers, theoreticians, graduate students and AV personnel; 3) etc., a monthly, membership newspaper, carries the latest information on workshops, conferences, job opportunities, new publications, and up-to-date information on happenings in the media field.

4) Instructional Resources, included in Audiovisual Instruction as a special section, contains "practical, step-by-step information focusing on the 'how-to' aspects of media"; 5) Who's Who in the Media Field, is an annual membership directory and date book of the AECT.

Special publications on media and library programs, developing the profession, media personnel, instructional materials, and visual literacy, research and theory, are published regularly and sold to members at discounts.

Films and Filmstrips are also available to members at discounts.

ASSOCIATION OF AUDIO-VISUAL TECHNICIANS (AAVT), P. O. Box 9716, Denver, Colo. 80209. (303) 534-5671, Elsa Kaiser, Executive Manager.

AAVT serves AV technicians in areas like "exchanging information on repair, modification, lubrication, disassembly and reassembly of AV equipment, descriptions of special tools and techniques..., and in finding resources of parts, tools, and services and production information."

Publications: 1) Fast Forward, a monthly newsletter; 2) Annotated Directory of Parts and Services for Audiovisual Equipment, up-dated every two years, covers parts sources for the equipment of 855 manufacturers.

Activities: The first national meeting with the National Audio-Visual Assn. will take place in Houston in January 1978. A joint meeting with AECT will take place in Kansas City in April 1978.

CENTER FOR UNDERSTANDING MEDIA, now the MEDIA STUDIES PROGRAM, New School for Social Research, 66 5th Avenue, New York, N.Y. 10011. (212) 741-8903, Peter Haratonik, Director.

For the past two years, the center's main activity has been the development of a Masters of Arts in Media Studies at the New School. Many of the former members of the Centers are teaching in the program.

EDUCATIONAL FILM LIBRARY ASSOCIATION, 43 West 61 Street, New York, N.Y. 10023. Membership dues vary according to the size of the institution, and whether it is educational or commercial. Single membership, $15, Nadine Covert, Editor.

EFLA was incorporated in 1943 as a nonprofit membership organization, to serve "as a national clearinghouse for information about 16mm films and other nonprint media, including their production, distribution and use in education, the arts, science, industry and religion." They are a source of information on nontheatrical films through their programs of publications, evaluations, workshops, reference service and sponsorship of the American Film Festival. The Board of Directors is elected by the membership, three from each major group; college and Universities; schools; and general and adult groups, including public libraries and nonprofit organizations.

Publications: 1) Sightlines, the official publication since 1967, appears five times a year, and includes the following features: News and articles on films and film production, utilization and current development in the field; "Who's Who in Film Making" featuring one outstanding film maker in each issue; "Filmlist" giving new releases available from distributors; "Service Supplement," selected subject lists of films in areas of current interest; "Feature Films" listing new featurelength 16mm and 8mm films; The EFLA Bulletin, four times a year (new); and "Children's Film Supplement," prepared by the Media Center for Children.

2) Filmographies, sometimes first issued as a service supplement, on such topics as "99+ Films on Drugs," "Aging"--an annotated list of over 150 films, and "Alternatives"--150 films on education, life-styles and religion; 3) Manual of Film Evaluation, by Emily Jones; 4) University and College Film Collections, listing over 400 libraries including personnel, budget, and size of collection; 5) Educational Media Organizations, a descriptive directory of U.S. and Canadian film and television organizations; 6) Museums with Film Programs, listing over 500 museums; 7) Films for Young Adults, and 16mm Distributors Handbook geared to independent film makers.

Evaluation Program: Published on 3x5 cards, in sets of 36, the evaluations are mailed to members ten times a year. The "Film Evaluation Guide," a cumulation of all evaluations published from 1946-64, 1964-67, and 1967-71, is also available.

American Film Festival: The first festival was held in 1959 with 400 entries to be judged. Since then the number of entries has more than doubled, and over 500 volunteer specialists are involved in the judging each year. Only non-theatrical films, distributed by American companies are entered, and final competition is divided into some 35 categories. Prizes, including the "Emily Award" for the film with the most number of points, are given to the most highly rated films. Blue ribbons are awarded to the winners in each category, and these are then circulated to public libraries and colleges across the country on the "Blue Ribbon Circuit." The program guides of the festival lists all entries with a short synopsis, running time, distributor, etc. This is the one festival held in the U.S. that enables teachers, librarians, media people and film buffs an opportunity to view this many films at one time, and people from all over the country, including film makers and distributors attend.

Workshops: These have been added to the EFLA program since 1963. They are held in large cities on such topics as film evaluation, film production, film library administration and film making.

Information Service: Reference files provide members with information by telephone, in person and by mail. The library is open to the public three days a week.

ERIC CLEARINGHOUSE ON INFORMATION RESOURCES, School of Education, Syracuse University, Syracuse, N.Y. 13210. (315) 423-3640.

"ERIC is a national system which makes available unpublished, hard-to-find documents on all phases, levels, and subject areas of education. Sixteen Clearinghouses (each focuses on different facets of professional education) locate, acquire, and organize these materials for use by educators, researchers, and others interested in the field. The system is supported by the National Institute of Education of the U.S. Department of Health, Education and Welfare.

"The focus is on personnel, personnel development, strategies, systems, procedures, materials, and equipment used in these areas. Included are the following specific topics: Libraries; Learning Resource Centers; Information Science; Instructional Design, Development and Evaluation; Systems Analysis; Community Information Systems; Instructional Media; Information Transfer; Mastery Learning; Simulation and Gaming; Programmed Instruction; Information Brokering.

"The Clearinghouse is also concerned with the delivery of information and instruction through media: Television, computers, radio, films, microforms, holography, other audiovisual devices."

Publications: 1) Resources in Education, a monthly index; 2) Current Index to Journals in Education, articles relevant to its scope are selected, indexed and annotated. Available by subscription from Macmillan Information, 866 3rd. Ave., New York, N.Y. 10022; 3) A Comparison of Guides to Nonprint Media, by David Rawnsley, (Ir-); 4) Instructional Television: The Best of ERIC 1974-75, by Warren Siebert (Ir-12); 5) Budgeting for School Media Centers: An Annotated Bibliography, by David Loertscher, (IR-14).

On-Going Programs: Each of the 16 Clearinghouses on University campuses all over the country does the following within its scope (write to ERIC for complete list): 1) Acquisition, indexing/abstracting of documents and journals in scope areas; 2) Publication program (see samples above); 3) User services program--Inquiries by mail, telephone or in person are answered or referred to the proper source.

MEDIA CENTER FOR CHILDREN, 43 West 61 Street, New York, N.Y. 10023. (212) 757-1850, Maureen Gaffney, Director. (Formerly part of Center for Understanding Media).

Publications: 1) Young Viewer, a quarterly supplement to Sightlines since Fall 1977 (see EFLA) containing "articles, interviews, reports on books and workshops relevant to children's media, and brief reviews of films/videotapes/performances/exhibits designed for kids." 2) More Films Kids Like, ed. Maureen Gaffney, published by the American Library Association, (50 E. Huron Street, Chicago, Ill. 60611), sequel to Films Kids Like by Susan Rice (due in 1978); 3) What to Do When the Lights Go On: Recipes from the Children's Film Theater, to be published in 1978.

Activities: 1) Children's Film Theater (CFT); 2) Mid-Winter Conference on Children's Films, including film viewing and workshops on children's film making.

PRIME TIME SCHOOL TELEVISION, 120 LaSalle Street, Chicago, Ill. 60603. (312) 368-1088, Irving B. Harris Chairman. Membership $19 a year.

"PTST is a national, nonprofit organization which works to encourage teachers and parents to take full advantage of the learning opportunities offered by evening television programs. PTST produces and distributes study materials on television specials and series programs on both commercial and public television."

Publications: Prime Time School Television, an insert in Media & Methods, (see Appendix B) lists programs, their contents and guides on how to use them. It contains: Monthly study guides on select television specials that include program synopsis, teaching activities and resources; Program calendars listing all special programs; Special offerings, such as a guide to the NOVA series in 1977, and a guide to the best movies seen on TV in 1977; Handbook/ Feedback pages to exchange teacher's television activities that have been used successfully in the classroom; and during the 1977-78 school year there will be special units on economics, values education and advertising.

TELEVISION INFORMATION OFFICE, 745 5th Ave., New York, N.Y. 10022. James Poteat, Librarian.

Supported by major television networks, individual commercial stations, educational stations and the National Association of Broadcasters, TIO sponsors research projects, develops annotated bibliographies of primary sources of information on television, studies on meaningful children's programming, etc. It provides separate services for its sponsor stations.

Publications: Teacher's Guides to Television, published twice a year, contains study guides to programs of educational value. From Teacher's Guides to Television, Bx. 564, Lenox Hill Station, New York, N.Y. 10021. For a complete list of publications write TIO, 745 5th Ave., New York, N.Y. 10022 (the list was being up-dated at the time of this writing).

UNIVERSITY FILM ASSOCIATION, Temple University, Philadelphia, Pa. 19122. Timothy J. Lyons, Editor.

UFA is engaged in "furthering and developing the potentials of the motion picture medium for purposes of instruction and communication throughout the world; encouraging the production of motion pictures in the various educational institutions; engaging in the teaching of the art and science of motion picture production and techniques, film history, criticism, and/or related subjects; serving as a central source of information on film instruction and film production by educational institutions; and providing means for the sharing of ideas on the various activities involved in teaching film courses, in producing and distributing motion pictures and allied materials."

Publications: 1) Journal of the University Film Association, a quarterly magazine; 2) Digest, the Vice-President's newsletter, published several times a year; and the

UFA membership directory, a bi-annual biographical roster.

Activities: 1) Annual Conference, since 1946, usually held during the third week of August. Includes previews of University produced films, both professional and student made, workshops, seminars and demonstrations; 2) Clearinghouse for exchange of information for film teachers.

APPENDIX B

Primary Sources of Film and Television Reviews

THE BOOKLIST, American Library Association, 50 East Huron Street, Chicago, Ill. 60611. $24/year, semi-monthly, Sept.-July, since 1905. Paul Brawley, Editor.

Regular Features: Review of Films and Filmstrips, and Multimedia Kits (reviewed in-house); 8mm Loops; Audio-cassettes reviewed by outside reviewers; Occasional review of videocassettes; Consultant groups (librarians, media specialists, and curriculum specialists) cooperate with the staff in evaluating the media ranging from pre-school to adult, in all subject areas; Only recommended items are listed, and information includes distributor, year of release, running time, price and rental price, age (usage); Compilation on special topics, as well as cross-media reviews on outstanding non-print material.

"The Booklist is a buying guide to current materials (released within the last three months) recommended for purchase by schools, public libraries and other library institutions. Booklist will review materials in all subject areas and for all age levels (preschool to adult), which are available for purchase or long term lease from U.S. producers and distributors. All reviews are written by the Booklist's non-print editor and staff reviewers and selected librarians and media specialists experienced in the evaluation and utilization of media" [Irene Wood, Nonprint Reviews Editor].

FILM NEWS. The International Review of AV Material and Equipment. 250 West 57th Street, New York, N.Y. 10019. $6/year, 5 times a year, since 1939. Rohama Lee, Editor, Publisher. As of January 1978 incorporating Learning Resources, published in Canada by Richard Guerrier.

Articles on the history and use of films in schools and community. Signed critical reviews of new and older films, previewed by people in the field of education. News of major film festivals, and award winning 16mm films.

Regular Features: "Film Reviews"; "Classroom and Community Films"; "Performing Arts"; "Religious and Interfaith," including filmstrips; "Filmstrips," sound and silent; "Records"; "Films and TV Press," newsworthy items; Announcements of film festivals and film events; "What's New in Equipment"; "A-V Calendar."

"Nowhere else will you find so many and such a variety of objective, professional reviews and other information about available A/V materials. Established in 1939, professional, audience-tested reviews. Describes new equipment. Accent on U.S. scene, approached from world viewpoint. Articles by authorities. Covers classroom, public library, government agencies and community use of A/V. Also carries news of 8mm sound. Film News can be purchased with Government Grant Funds" [Rohama Lee, Editor, Publisher].

LANDERS FILM REVIEWS, P. O. Box 69760, Los Angeles, Cal. 90069. Bi-monthly, (Sept.-June), $45, Cumulated Title and Subject Index $5, since 1956, Bertha Landers, Editor.

"Approximately 700 to 1,000 16mm educational films are covered annually, making this a principal source of reviews. Reviews are written by in-house professional staff."

"Landers Film Reviews purpose is to provide a current guide to 16mm films worthy of consideration for purchase by public libraries, school media centers, community colleges and universities, and other users of non-theatrical films. Full mediagraphic data is consistently provided, along with intended audience recommendations, content of film, technical quality and comment on how well the producers have accomplished their stated purpose of the film. In addition LFR lists film festival winners, and new multimedia instructional materials under producer or distributor name. Each issue is indexed by subject and by title with Source Directory of Producer/Distributor addresses" [Bertha Landers, Editor].

*MEDIA & METHODS, published by North American Publishing Co., 134 N. 13th Street, Philadelphia, Pa. 19107. $9/year, 9 times a year. Sept.-May/June, since 1965. Anthony Prete, Editor.

---

*If there is money in the budget for only one magazine on media, this is the one used most by those in the field.

Regular Features: Editorials--"In Focus"; "Recommended," Films, filmstrips, slides; "Prime Time School Television," insert listing program synopses, guides on how to use them; "Mediabag," may include films, filmstrips, television programs, recordings, tapes, prints or hardware reviews and recommendations; "Thrifttips," (occasional) information on inexpensive and free films and their sources.

Media & Method has been called the "most imaginative magazine in the secondary school AV field." Films are reviewed by practicing teachers and librarians. Articles written by experienced teachers give helpful hints on using media. Only favorable reviews are printed. Media & Methods publishes books on media, such as Good Looking, edited by David Sohn, and conducts workshops such as the one on video production at "Video Expo-New York '77."

"I think film is an immensely powerful medium--its place in the classroom is no less important than books. M&M has been a major force in spearheading the films in high school movement. We were the first education magazine to introduce McLuhan and Culkins to secondary teachers. Our commitment to media usage recognizes no primacy of any single medium, but encourages the use of games, films, tapes, etc., as they best fit a particular context or issue. We have a wide network of teachers who alert us to new materials, plus an active marketing director who is in touch with film distributors. We are always open to anyone who approaches us to screen or discuss their films" [Frank McLaughlin, Editorial Director].

PREVIEWS, News and Reviews of Non-Print Media, R. R. Bowker Co., 1180 Ave. of the Americas, New York, N.Y. 10036. $7.50/year, 9 times a year, Sept.-May. Phyllis Levy, Editor.

Regular Features: "16mm films," reviewed by subject areas; "Filmstrips" (sound and silent) reviewed by subject areas; "Slides"; "Spoken Words"; "Prints"; "Kits"; Semi-annual list, "Audiovisual Guide: A multi Media Subject List."

"Previews, which began publication in September 1972, is attempting to provide the most comprehensive coverage available on all non-print materials. We have requested all audio-visual producers/distributors to send us all their items immediately upon release. We publish reviews for all audiences, preschool through adult. All our reviews are signed by an individual, which we believe lends credibility to the review. In addition, both favorable and negative reviews are published in Previews. We believe that the use of non-print materials in the classroom is a necessary supplement in all areas of the curriculum and aid in the learning process" [Phyllis Levy, Editor].

SIGHTLINES, Educational Film Library Association, Inc., 43 West 61 Street, New York, N.Y. 10023. Membership dues vary, $15 for a personal membership includes magazine and festival guide. Nadine Covert, Editor.

Sightlines contains up-to-date information of interest to film users about films, film festivals, reviews and listings of films available for current distribution, all aspects of film, video, articles on the use of films, filmographies, and annotated listings of films on special topics. Cuts across the entire field of non-theatrical films. "No reviews per se." EFLA Evaluations, published separately, edited in-house. Film reviews prepared by committees across the country.

Regular Features: "Freedom to View"; "Film Review Digest," quotes from film reviews from many sources; "Film List," unevaluative description of new films and filmstrips; "Who's Who in Filmmaking," a profile of a non-theatrical film producer; "Calendar of Events," lists film festivals, workshops, study institutes, competitions; "News Notes"; "Feature Films on 16mm and 8mm"; Children's Film Supplement prepared by Media Center for Children; "Young Viewers."

"We try to publish articles or service supplements (filmographies on a particular subject) on topics that are of concern to our members. Recent articles, such as one on "Films on Death and Dying," and filmographies such as those on "Aging" and "Alternatives" have been initiated in response to frequent inquiries by our members. We also try to anticipate the information needs of our readers whenever possible.

"Films for the classroom should go beyond the use of the old-fashioned instructional film which is strictly didactic and usually dull. There are creative films which lend themselves to a variety of classroom uses. We hope that our articles and film lists will lead teachers to such films" [Nadine Covert, Editor].

APPENDIX C

Professional Journals Which Carry Information on Non-Print Media and Equipment

There will be no attempt at critical analysis of the magazines included here, nor have we attempted to list all the journals that may, from time to time, preview films. We do not feel that this can be done. We did try to include as many subject areas as possible. The type of non-print media reviewed depends on the editorial policy of the individual publication, and may mean emphasis on programs and equipment rather than softwear. We apologize for any omissions, as well as the inclusion of magazines no longer being published. This is a changing field.

Additional periodicals may be found listed in the AFI Factfile Film and Television Periodicals in English (from AFI, the John F. Kennedy Center for the Performing Arts, Washington, D.C. 20566).

AMERICAN CINEMATOGRAPHER, published by the American Society of Cinematographers, 1782 North Orange Drive, Hollywood, Cal. 90028. Monthly, $9/year.

Technical articles on motion picture photography and production; useful for VTR and film making.

AMERICAN FILM, published by the American Film Institute, John F. Kennedy Center for the Performing Arts, Washington, D.C. 20566. 10 issues, $15/year. Editor, Hollis Alpert.

General articles on all aspects of film and television. Useful for video teachers. Regular columns and features include: "Dialogue on Film," with directors, actors, producers and writers; "Explorations," which investigates new trends and technology; "Focus on Education," evaluating the opportunities and progress in that field; "Festival Reports,"

"Books," and "Comments," presenting editorial views.

THE ANIMATOR, published by the Northwest Film Study Center, Northland Art Museum, Southwest Park & Madison, Portland, Ore. 97205. Quarterly, $2/year.

Newsletter with articles on practical aspects of film making and film study.

ATHLETIC JOURNAL, published by Athletic Journal Publishing Co., 1719 Howard Street, Evanston, Ill. 60202. Monthly, $5/year, since 1921. Editor, Lori Fradin.

Prints favorable and other reviews by staff. Reviews films, 16mm and 8mm, filmloops and filmstrips.

AUDIO, published by North American Publishing Co., 401 Broad Street, Philadelphia, Pa. 19108. Monthly, $7/year, since 1947. Editor, Gene Pitts.

Reviews classical, popular and jazz music, and non-musical records. Contains articles concerning installation, construction, and maintenance of audio equipment and new products.

AUDIOVISUAL COMMUNICATIONS, published by United Business Publications, Inc., 750 3rd Ave., New York, N.Y. 10017. Monthly, $11/year, since 1961. Editor, Mike Yukas.

Descriptive reviews of films dealing with communication, training procedures, mostly commercially produced films that are distributed free, on loan. Slanted to industrial and commercial use. "Training Media" column every few months lists audio and video tapes, slides, filmstrips and films used in training programs. Useful for career guidance.

AUDIOVISUAL INSTRUCTION, Journal of the AECT, 1126 16th Street, N.W., Washington, D.C. 20036. 10 times a year, Sept.-May, combined June/July, to all members, dues $30. Editor, Howard Hitchens.

Regular Features: "Clips," news items of interest to readers; "New Products," both software and hardware, as well as changes made in previous products or editions... lists sources of information; "DEMM," Division of Educational Media Management, a column written by different contributors; "RTD," Research and Theory Division; "International Division," news of International Council of Educational Media; "ERIC," a service of the ERIC Clearinghouse on Information Resources at Syracuse University...a review of their services and activities; and "News Notes." Special section on instructional resources.

BACK STAGE, 165 West 46 Street, New York, N.Y. 10036. Weekly, $18/year.

Business aspects of producing television commercials, and films.

BALANCE SHEET, A Magazine On Business And Economic Education, published by South-Western Publishing Co., 5101 Madison Street, Cincinnati, Ohio 45227. Monthly, free to teachers of business education and administrators. Editor, G. Whitney Voiers.

Reviews filmstrips, slides, transparencies and other non-print media in regular column, "Audiovisual Aides." Keeps business teachers aware of interesting items useful in the classroom.

THE BOOKLIST <u>see</u> Appendix B

BROADCASTING, published by Broadcasting Publishing Inc., 1735 DeSalle Street, N.W., Washington, D.C. 20036. Weekly, $30/year.

Feature articles and news items on television, cable TV and radio.

CABLE INFORMATION <u>see</u> FILM INFORMATION

CAMERA OBSCURA, P. O. Box 4517, Berkeley, Cal. 94701. 3 issues a year, $6/year.

Feminists writing on film and film theory.

CATHOLIC FILM NEWSLETTER, published by the Office of Films and Broadcasting of the U.S. Catholic Conference, Suite 1300, 1011 1st Avenue, New York, N.Y. 10022. Twice a month, $10/year, since 1964. Editor, Patrick J. Sullivan S.J.

Reviews theatrical films, TV, filmstrips and video-cassettes. Reviewed by staff, according to rating system. Regular columns: "Educational Resources," "Community Dimensions," "Television," and "TV Programs of Note."

CANYON CINEMA NEWS, Industrial Center Bldg., R. 220, Sausalito, Cal. 94965. Quarterly, $3/year.

Notes and short articles on and by independent film makers.

CLASSIC FILM COLLECTOR, 340 Poplar Ave., Indiana, Pa. 15701. Quarterly, $7/year, since 1962. Editor and publisher, Samuel K. Rubin.

Reviews films regularly, with ratings. Reviews by staff, some contributed by readers. News and reviews of movie related books, magazines and other publications. News of and from distributors. "Disseminates information on the classic film for the benefit of collectors, educators and film buffs."

THE CLEARINGHOUSE: A Journal for the Modern Jr. and Sr. High School, published by Helen Dwight Reid Educational Foundation, 4000 Albermarle Street, N.W., Washington, D.C. 20016. 9 times a year, $10/year individual, $17 institution. Mg. Editor, Janet M. Norton.

Reviews 16mm films, filmstrips and phonograph records. Offers current information on instructional media.

COMMUNITY COLLEGE SOCIAL SCIENCE JOURNAL, published by Community College Social Science Assc., Grossmont College, 8800 Grossmont College Dr., El Cajon, Cal. 92020. 3 times a year, $15/year individual, $20 institution, since 1970. Editor, Dr. Gerald Baydo.

Reviews films and other non-print media to stimulate more and better use of them as instructional aides. Films reviewed by the editorial board whose members are instructors at two year colleges.

EFLA Evaluations--3 by 5 cards--part of the Educational Library services. SIGHTLINES, EFLA magazine (see Appendixes A and B).

EDUCATIONAL & INDUSTRIAL TELEVISION, published by C. S. Tepfer Co., Inc., P. O. Box 565, Ridgefield, Conn. 06877. Monthly, $12/year, since 1968.

For those who need to know how to produce and use TV for instruction/training/communication. Entire magazine is about non-print media, especially video. "Programs-----Off the Shelf" lists new available programs, including short summary of content, price and availability. Teachers' Guides, written by professionals in industry and colleges.

EDUCATIONAL TECHNOLOGY, published by Educational Technology Publishing Co., 140 Sylvan Ave., Englewood, N.J. 07632. Monthly, $35/year, since 1961. Editor, Lawrence Lipsitz.

Contains news of all media, no reviews. Reports on theory and application of technology, both soft- and hardware, in education, government programs, and industrial training. Features regular department on new equipment and materials.

ELEMENTARY ENGLISH, published by National Council of Teachers of English, 1111 Kenyon Rd., Urbana, Ill. 61801. Monthly, Oct.-May, $10/year.

Occasionally reviews films and filmstrips in "Instructional Strategies." Occasional article on film and television.

ENGLISH JOURNAL, published by National Council of Teachers of English, 1111 Kenyon Rd., Urbana, Ill. 61801. Monthly, Sept.-May, $15/year, since 1912. Editor, Stephen Judy.

Covers multi-media. "The Scene" reports on non-text and non-classroom materials. Articles on film use.

FAST FORWARD, published by the Assn. of A-V Technicians, 236 West 13th Ave., Denver, Colo. 80204.

Contains information on current equipment, modifications, use, up-coming conferences. Articles on problem solving, book reviews.

FILM COMMENT, published by Film Society of Lincoln Center, 1865 B'way, New York, N.Y. 10023. Bi-monthly (6 x a yr.), $10/year, since 1962. Editor, Richard Corliss.

Interviews with directors and screen writers. Articles on wide range of subjects, including films and television. Review of books on film subjects. In-depth articles on Hollywood films, Independents, Industry, Television.

FILM INFORMATION, published by the Broadcasting and Film Committee of the National Council of Churches, Bx. 500, Manhattanville Station, New York, N.Y. 10027. Monthly, combined July/Aug., $7/year, since 1970. Editor, Beatrice Rothenbeucher.

Reviews feature films for use by church groups, parents, teachers, and film buffs. Covers about 300 American and foreign films a year. Reviews written by leading Protestant film critics. Include favorable and unfavorable for theatrical releases, only favorable for 16mm.

CABLE INFORMATION, from same source, a monthly newsletter. $10/year.

Information on happenings on cable TV. "Particular attention to community action, creative local programming and innovative use of videotape."

FILM LIBRARY QUARTERLY, published by the Film Library Information Council, Bx. 348, Radio City Station, New York, N. Y. 10019. Quarterly, $10/year, since 1967. Editor, William Sloan.

Reviews films regularly. Reviewers give opinions on 16mm films for library use. Emphasis on noneducational, cultural and documentary films. Occasional video review. Articles on film makers and film making.

FILMMAKERS NEWSLETTER, P. O. Box 115, Ward Hill, Mass. 01830. Monthly, $9/year. Publisher and Editors Suni Mallow and H. Whitney Bailey.

"For professionals and semi-professionals working in film and videotapes in studios, industrial production houses, University film departments, TV stations and corporations."

FILM NEWS see Appendix B

FILM QUARTERLY, published by the University of California Press, Berkeley, Cal. 94720. Quarterly, $6/year, since 1958. Editor, Ernst Callonbach.

Scholarly articles on every aspect of film and film history. In-depth reviews of feature films. Articles concerning trends, historical or biographical aspects of motion picture productions. Interviews with directors. Reviews of books about films.

HIGH FIDELITY and HIGH FIDELITY/MUSICAL AMERICA, published by The Publishing House, Great Barrington, Mass. 01230. Monthly, $8.95/year without Musical America, since 1951. Editor, Leonard Marcus (combined High Fidelity and Musical America $18).

Regular features: "News and Views"; "Equipment in the News"; "Equipment Reports"; "New Releases," reviews written by prominent music critics; "Backbeat," pop music section. Articles about music and musicians, recording artists and techniques. Reviews of classical, theater, and film releases. Featured recordings of classical, theater and film music.

HORN BOOK MAGAZINE, published by the Horn Book Inc., Park Square Bldg., 31 Street & James Ave., Boston,

Mass. 02116. 6 times a year, $14/year (after April 1978). Editor, Ethel Heins.

Non-print reviews written by regular reviewers: reviews of films, filmstrips, record sets, filmstrip/cassette sets, phonograph records in "Audio-Visual Reviews." Reviews only audio-visuals connected with children's literature.

INDUSTRIAL EDUCATION, Macmillan Professional Mag. Inc., 1 Fawcett Place, Greenwich, Conn. 06830. Monthly, (Sept.-June), $9/year, since 1914. Editor, Paul Cuneo.

Lists films regularly--no reviews. Lists AV materials of all types.

INSTRUCTOR, published by Instructor Publ. Inc., Instructor Park, Dansville, N.Y. 14437. 10 issues/year, $14/year, since 1891. Editor, Leanna Landsmann.

"Reviews," a regular column, covers books, films, filmstrips, records, color prints, overhead transparencies and kits on a variable schedule. Only favorable reviews appear. Films are reviewed by William Cuttill of Indiana U. For 1977-78, films were reviewed in September and May, filmstrips in September, December, January, February and April. "TV News," news of special programs.

INTERNATIONAL DEVELOPMENT REVIEW, published by Society for International Development, 1346 Connecticut Ave., N.W., Washington, D.C. 20036. Quarterly, $25 membership in society, $12 Libraries, $7.20 for instructors and librarians, since 1957. Editor, Andrew Rice.

"Media Department" reviews documentaries about developing countries. Critical reviews are written by staff member, Dr. Jean Ackerman, and invited writers from Third World countries.

JEWISH MEDIA SERVICE, on the campus of Brandeis University, Lown Bldg., 415 South Street, Waltham, Mass. 02154. Editor, Amy Kronish.

Lists films, filmstrips and transparencies--annotated.

JOURNAL OF GEOGRAPHY, published by the National Council for Geographic Education, Dept. of Geography, Western Illinois U., Macomb, Ill. 61455. 9 issues/year, (Sept.-May), $12-16/year. Editor, Harm J. deBlij.

Reviews films, slides, filmstrips, film loops, pictures, transparencies, maps, globes, graphs, charts, diagrams, models, field trips, instructional television and tape recordings. "Media Review" provides members with information on sources of media materials, reviews on-going projects, reviews nature and status of media at various levels of geographic education, commercial media materials, and publishes media-oriented short articles.

JOURNAL OF LEARNING DISABILITIES, published by the Professional Press Inc., 101 E. Ontario Street, Chicago, Ill. 60611. 10/year, $16/year, since 1967. Editor, Gerald M. Senf.

Reviews films on special education, super 8 and kits. Includes articles on programs, materials and techniques.

JOURNAL OF THE UNIVERSITY FILM ASSOCIATION, published by the University Film Association, Dept. of Radio-Television-Film, Temple University, Philadelphia, Pa. 19122. Quarterly, $6/year, since 1943. Editor, Dr. Timothy Lyons, film editor, Don Frederickson, Dept. of Theater, Cornell University, Ithaca, N.Y. 14853.

"For those who teach film." Lists nontheatrical motion pictures produced by University film units in the U.S. Articles on motion picture production, projects of University film units, film education, film history, reviews of literature on films, meetings and conferences.

MAN/SOCIETY/TECHNOLOGY: A JOURNAL OF INDUSTRIAL ARTS EDUCATION, published by American Industrial Arts Association, Inc., 1201 16th Street, N.W., Washington, D.C. 20036. 8 times a year, $15/year, since 1939. Editor, Jeri M. Salassi.

"Media Reviews" carries favorable reviews of films, and other nonprint media. Regular column.

Special issues on visual and graphic communication.

MASS MEDIA NEWSLETTER, published by Mass Media Assn. Inc., 2116 N. Charles Street, Baltimore, Md. 21218. Twice monthly, (second and fourth Mondays) Monthly in June, July, August and December, $12/year, since 1964. Editor, Janice P. York.

Reviews 16mm films, feature films available on 16mm, free films, filmstrips, national television programs, videotapes, cassettes, tapes, recordings, slides, kits and organizations. In-house and free lance reviewers, only recommended items are listed. Regular columns: "The Tube," announcements of upcoming TV programs; "TV Viewpoint," television commentary; "Current Cinema," commercial film reviews; "Mediation," multi-media how-to for churches; "What If," simulation games; "Lagniappe," ideas and resources for religious education.

MEDIA & METHODS see Appendix B

MEDIA MIX NEWSLETTER: Idea and Resources for Media Communication, published by Claretion Publ., 221 W. Madison Street, Chicago, Ill. 60606. 8 times a year, $9/year, since 1969. Editor, Jeffrey Schrank.

Valuable for lesser known short films. Newsletter reviewing books, films, videotapes. Editor does reviews.

MEDIUM, published by Jewish Media Service, on campus of Brandeis University, Lown Bldg., 415 South Street, Waltham, Mass. 02154. Editor, Amy Kronish.

Reviews films and other nonprint media on topics of interest to Jewish Educators. Lists only recommended items. Each issue is devoted to one topic (e.g., Fall '77: Bible & Archeology). "Media Scene," current releases. Also distributes films. Send for free catalog.

MODERN LANGUAGE JOURNAL, published by National Federation of Modern Language Teachers Assn., University of Colorado, Boulder, Colo. 80309. Bi-monthly, $9 Individual, $10 institution, since 1916. Editor, Charles King.

Occasionally reviews films, filmstrips, records and tapes. Lists non-print media which "contribute substantially to the mastery of a foreign language and/or provides meaningful insight into a foreign culture."

PUBLIC TELECOMMUNICATIONS REVIEW, published by National Association of Educational Broadcasters, NAEB, PTR 1346 Connecticut Ave., N.W., Washington, D.C. 20036. $18/year. Editor, Olga Zabludoff.

Articles on Educational Television and Television programming.

RELIGIOUS TEACHERS JOURNAL, Box 180, West Mystic, Conn. 06388. Monthly, Sept.-May, $7.50/year, since 1968. Editor, Marie McIntyre.

Films considered must relate to religious education. Multi-media column regularly reviews films, records and filmstrips. Lists only favorable reviews.

Articles on film use, some with bibliographies, for religious education.

SCHOOL ARTS MAGAZINE: THE ART EDUCATION MAGAZINE FOR TEACHERS, published by Davis Publ., Inc., Printers Bldg., 50 Portland Street, Worcester, Mass. 01608. 10 issues/year (Sept.-June), $11/year. Editor, George Horn.

"Resource Materials" list new films, filmstrips, kits about art, and materials directly concerned with teaching art. "News, People, Places, Events" mentions some festivals (e.g., International Crafts Film Festival). Excellent source of art projects, information on photography, media production (limited). Written by teachers for teachers.

SCHOOL PRODUCT NEWS, published by Independent Publishing Co., 614 Superior Ave. West, Cleveland, Ohio 44113. Monthly, controlled circulation, $18/year, since 1962. Editor, Roger Morton.

Contains sections on instructional hardware, software and supplies, AV equipment and storage, and facilities. Includes reviews of all non-print media, done by staff. Factual information rather than evaluative.

SCIENCE TEACHER, published by National Science Teachers Assn., 1742 Connecticut Ave., N.W., Washington, D.C. 20009. 9 times a year (Sept.-May), $20/year membership, since 1933. Editor, Rosemary Amidici.

Reviews films, filmstrips, television programs on related topics. Coordinated by Dr. Glenn Blough, Science Teaching Center, University of Maryland, College Park, Md.

SIGHTLINES see Appendix B

STEREO REVIEW, published by Siff-Davis Publ. Inc., 1 Park Ave., New York, N.Y. 10016. Monthly, $7.98/year, since 1958. Editor, William Anderson.

Reviews of new, classical, and popular discs and tapes. Laboratory test reports on new audio equipment. Information about music, musicians and composers. Artistic performance and quality of recordings are rated.

SUPER8 FILMMAKER, P. O. Box 10052, Palo Alto, Cal. 94303. Quarterly, 8 times a year, $7/year, since 1972. Editor, Joyce Newman.

"The Collector" carries reviews of feature films on super 8. "Take One: Products Review." Articles on "how-to" make films--some excellent ideas. Regular column on "Animation," "Produce & Probe," "Tools & Tricks."

Annual cumulative index of past articles (Jan./Feb. issue).

TEACHING EXCEPTIONAL CHILDREN, published by Council for Exceptional Children, 1920 Association Drive, Reston, Va. 22091. Quarterly, $12.50/year (free to Ass. members), since 1968. Editor, June B. Jordan.

For teachers of gifted and handicapped children. Media reviews sometimes include films for this special group, and classroom follow-up activities. Catalog of Publications and Nonprint Media (rev. 1977).

TODAY'S EDUCATION: Journal of the NEA, NEA, 1201 16th Street, N.W., Washington, D.C. 20036. 4 times a year (Sept.-Oct., Nov.-Dec., Jan.-Feb., March-April), free to members, $2/copy, since 1913. Editor, Dr. Walter Graves.

Regular column "Audiovisual Materials," reviews 5-7 films per issue. Reviews by William J. Cuttill and Beverly Teach of Indiana U. A/V Center, Bloomington. Only favorable listings.

TODAY'S FILMMAKER, 250 Fulton Ave., Hempstead, N.Y. 11550. Quarterly, $6/year.

Technical articles on film making.

TOP OF THE NEWS, published by the American Library Association, 50 E. Huron Street, Chicago, Ill. 60611. Quarterly, $9/year, since 1942. Editor, Mary Jane Anderson.

Publication of the Children's Service Division and Young Adults Service Division of the ALA. News of international events concerning publishing and production of books, magazines, films, phonorecords and other media for children and young adults. Announcements of awards. Occasional article on media use.

TRAINING FILM PROFILE, published by Olympic Film Service, 71 West 23 Street, New York, N.Y. 10010. Bimonthly, $150/year, since 1968 (carries no advertisement). Editor, Walter Carroll.

A review service for films and other media, including all formats. A full page evaluation of each item is given. Films about the world of work and career orientation, including human relations, communication skills, public issues and materials for self-development. Recommended for high school and older students. Reviews done by users of material. Yearly cumulative title and subject index.

WILSON LIBRARY BULLETIN, published by H. W. Wilson, 950 University Ave., New York, N.Y. 10452. Monthly (Sept.-June), $14/year, since 1914. Editor, William Eshelman.

Carries occasional article about media. Regular Column "Cine Opsis," by Jana Varlejs. Reviews films for small and medium size libraries on a topic of current interest. Topic differs in each issue.

APPENDIX D

Sources of Lists of Films in Special Subject Areas

It would be an almost impossible task to attempt to list all the sources of films on selected topics, particularly since new lists are published all the time. In order to acquaint the reader with some of the more accessible lists, the following organizations, books, magazines, bibliographies, etc., are cited as examples of what is available. Wherever possible, lists are mentioned in their subject areas. Many commercial distributors have separate catalogs on such topics as women's studies, sexuality, ethnic studies, art and/or dance, children's films, and literature. Public libraries and university film libraries are often excellent and inexpensive sources of subject lists.

GENERAL

American Film Institute. Factfile: Guide to Classroom Use of Film/Television, from AFI, John F. Kennedy Center of the Performing Arts, Washington, D.C. 20009. April 1977, $3.

Lists sources of films and video for purchase and rental.

The American Museum of Natural History. Margaret Mead Film Festival, from Museum of Natural History, C.P.W. & 79th Street, New York, N.Y. 10024, 1977.

A special list chosen for the Festival by experts on children's films and others.

EFLA: "Super Shorts--The Best of the Recent Short Films" by the staff of EFLA. Media & Methods, Dec. 1976, pp. 16-20.

A select list of over 75 recent short films, grouped by topics.

Freeman, Jan G. Selected Films for Young Adults, 1976, Chicago: American Library Association, 50 E. Huron Street, Chicago, Ill. 60611.

Annotated bibliographies, discussion programs, filmographies, films, library programs for young adults. 35 entries are listed, including title, description, running time, price, producer and distributor. Films were released in 1974 and 1975.

Film News regularly reviews special subject areas such as dance, ecology, etc. Films on religion are reviewed in every issue.

Gaffney, Maureen (editor). More Films Kids Like. Chicago: ALA, to be released in 1978 (see Rice, Susan).

General Service Administration, Washington, D.C. 20409. A Catalog of U.S. Government Produced Audiovisual Materials-1974, free. (Being revised--ask to be placed on mailing list.)

Contains subject headings as well as alphabetical, annotated lists of films, with running time, government department which produced the film, b/w or color, ordering information and price.

Lee, Rohama (editor). Film News Omnibus, vol. 1, Review of 16mm Films. Published by Film News, 250 West 57 Street, New York, N.Y. 10019, $17.50.

A collection of reviews of documentaries, short subjects and feature films in 16mm published by Film News. Contains information on sources, running time, description of films, release date, prizes won, etc. Film lists on Dance," "Science," "History and the Humanities." Subject index.

Limbacher, James. Feature Films on 8mm & 16mm. A Directory of Feature Films Available for Rental, Sales & Lease in the U.S. New York: R. R. Bowker, 1974 (rev. ed.).

Supplements appear from time to time in Sightlines.

Media Review Digest, Pierian Press, 5000 Washtenaw, Ann Arbor, Mich. 48104. 1977, $79.50. A complete service. Write for information.

National Information Center for Educational Media. Index to 16mm Educational Films. From National Information

Center for Educational Media (NICEM), University of Southern California, University Park, Los Angeles, Cal. 90007, 1973. (1977, 6th edition) $109.50.

List of 70,000 annotated short films.

New York Public Library, 1977 Supplement, from New York Public Library Film Library, Donnell Library Center, 20 West 53 Street, New York, N.Y. 10019. $3.

Annotated--lists synopsis, running time, b/w or color and distributor. Pp. 1-64 adult and young adult films; pp. 65- children's films. One of the best lists around.

Parlato, Salvatore, Jr. "A Wealth of Film for Budget Minded Film Buyers." Previews, Sept. 1974, p. 7.

Parlato, Salvatore, Jr. Superfilms: An International Guide to Award-Winning Films. Metuchen, N.J.: Scarecrow Press, 1976, $13.50.

Lists 1500 non-theatrical films from 258 worldwide competitions. Compiler Parlato points out that awards do not always reflect the quality of the film. One reason for this is, that the quality of the jury and the competition vary.

Previews (see Appendix B for publishing data). "Audiovisual Guide: Multimedia Subject List," since 1972.

Lists series and individual titles under broad subject headings. Non-critical in nature, includes all non-print media. Running time, price, grade level, distributor are listed. Appeared 9/72, 5/73, 9/73, 3/73, 3/74, 9/74, 3/75, 9/75, 4/76, 9/76, 5/77. "Best of the Year Filmstrips and Slides Roundup," by Diana Spirt, annual. Previews regularly lists reviews according to subject areas.

Rehrauer, George. The Short Film: An Evaluative Selection of 500 Recommended Films, Macmillan Information, $12.50.

Rice, Susan (compiler & editor). Films Kids Like, published for Center for Understanding Media by ALA, Chicago, Ill. 1973. From ALA, 5 Huron St., Chicago, Ill. 60611.

Schmidt, William D. "Creative Curriculum Films," Sightlines, vol. 10, no. 1, Fall '76. pp. 6-8.

"Analysing the Design of Outstanding Instructional Films." These include "Red Balloon," "Rainshowers," "Occurrence at Owl Creek Bridge," "The Lottery." Top 20 films chosen by film educators in the U.S.

Sightlines (see Appendix B for publishing data).
Reviews special subject areas in depth in its "Service Supplements." Sold by EFLA once they have appeared.

Sohn, David (ed.). Good Looking, Philadelphia, Pa.; North American Publishing Co., 1976 (A Media & Methods Book).
Part 2: "Views and Reviews: Short Films," pp. 65-179, lists films for film study courses. Chapters with film lists by Fred Marcus, Adele Stern, William Sloan, Frank McLaughlin, Ralph Ameli. Some excellent reviews from Media & Methods round out this excellent collection.

Union Catalog of Motion Pictures and Television Manuscripts and Special Collections, published in 1977 by G. K. Hall, Boston, Mass. $25. From Film and Television Study Center, 6233 Hollywood Blvd., Suite 303, Los Angeles, Cal. 90028.
Holdings of more than 70 libraries, museums and colleges, universities and historical societies in 11 Western states. Ninety percent in California institutions.

Vincent, Richard. "A Bibliography of Film Reference Sources," Journal of the University Film Association, XXIX, 3, summer 1977, pp. 43-47.
Indexes to Films includes compilations on films by and about women, collections from New York Museum of Modern Art, Yearbooks of motion pictures, British film catalogs, filmographies of Third World, etc. Pp. 52-54, Directories and Catalogs; pp. 54-55, Film Reviews--lists indexes of film reviews; pp. 55-56, Annuals.

Weaver, Kathleen, Film Programmer's Guide to 16mm Rentals. Albany, Cal.: Reel Research, 1975 (2nd ed.).

ALCOHOL

Resources from National Center for Alcohol Education, from Clarice Leslie, Manager, Instructional Materials Development, NCAE, 1601 N. Kent Street, Arlington, Va. 22209.

AMERICANA

Center for Southern Folklore, 1216 Peabody Ave., P. O. Box 4081, Memphis, Tenn. 38104. Judy Peiser, Director.

Send for catalog--film on Appalachia, etc.

Epple, Ron. "Short Films Americana," Media & Methods, Nov. 1976, pp. 16-18.

List includes "Minorities," "Simple Celebrations," "Food and Fun," "Americans at Large," "Cities," "Coming of Age," "Foibles and Follies."

Ladevich, Laurel and Thomas Swiss. "Resources for the Study of Native Americana," Media & Methods, May/June 1977, pp. 50-55.

List of books, art and music, photographs and films about American Indians. Includes a list of Teaching Resource Materials available from ERIC Clearinghouse on Reading and Communications Skills, 1111 Kenyon Road, Urbana, Ill. 61801.

Woolls, Blanche. "Mixed Media for the Bicentennial," Previews, Dec. 1975, pp. 3-9.

Includes budget-cutting ideas, reviews by librarians, teachers and students.

ANIMATED FILMS

Epple, Ron. "Animation: Alive and Well," Media & Methods, April 1977, pp. 42-46.

"Animator's Animator," "Also But Not Only for Kids," "Allegories and Myths," "Personal Fantasies," "Abstract," "Conceptual," "About Animators."

Segal, Philip. "Animated Films: A History and Filmography," Previews, April 1977, pp. 42-46.

Gives short history and lists the best of the last few years. Filmography and bibliography.

ANTHROPOLOGY

Audiovisual Services, Pennsylvania State University, University Park, Pa.

Film News. "Films About Anthropology," Jan./Feb. 1978, Margaret Mead Festival, Museum of Natural History, New York, N.Y.

National Anthropological Film Center of the Smithsonian Institution, Washington, D.C. 20560.

New York Visual Anthropology Center, 298 5th Ave., New York, N.Y. 10011.

ASIAN STUDIES

Hawkins, John. Teacher's Resource Handbook for Asian Studies, for Communications on Comparative International Studies, from University of California, Los Angeles, Cal., Graduate School of Education, 1976.

Covers all print and non-print media, arranged according to grade levels. Lists books, prints, maps, films, slides, filmstrips, records and tapes. Annotated with sources. Excellent.

Hymes, Jo Ann (ed.). Asia Through Film, Annotated Guide. Project of PACE, Project on Asian Studies in Education, University of Michigan A/V Center. From Center for Japanese Studies, 108 Lane Hall, University of Michigan, Ann Arbor, Mich. 48109, $3.50.

Introduction on how to use films. Annotated list, with evaluation for each film, grade level, source information.

South Asian Studies Department, University of Wisconsin, Madison, Wisc. 53706.

Send for list of films.

ART

Miller, Hannah. "Art in the Making," Children's House, Spring 1977, p. 4.

BLACK STUDIES

African Studies Association. Africa from Reel to Reel, compiled by Steven Ohrn and Rebecca Rilly, for African Studies Ass., 218 Shiffman Center, Brandeis University, Waltham, Mass. 02154.

Annotated, with sources.

Franklin, Oliver. "Black and Ethnic Films," Sightlines, vol. 9, no. 3, Spring 1976, pp. 10-12.

"Building a Black Film Audience," pp. 71-76, includes recent films as well as early classics.

Film News. "Black Experience and the Media," October 1974, 27, 46.

Includes filmography.

Maynard, Richard. The Black Man on Film: Racial Stereotyping, Hayden, $3.50.

Media & Methods, Dec. 1970, a list of films on Black Studies.

Miller, Hannah. "A Little Bit of Sugar Helps the Medicine Go Down," K-eight, May/June 1972, pp. 40-1 (write to North American Publishing Co., 134 N. 13 Street, Philadelphia, Pa. 19107).

BEHAVIOR MODIFICATION

Sightlines. "Films on Behavior Modification," Service Supplement, 1973/74, from EFLA (see details in Appendix A).

CAREER EDUCATION

Film News. "Films About Careers: Part III," Sept. 1974, pp. 26-7.

Seventy-six films, single or in sets, about the world of work and fitting into it.

A Selected List of Motion Pictures and Filmstrips, for sale and rent by the National Audiovisual Center, Washington, D.C. 10409.

CHICANOS

Menyah Productions: write for catalog to El Centro Campesino Cultural, P. O. Box 1278, San Juan Bautista, Cal. 95045.

Check catalogs of major distributors (see Appendix F).

CHILDREN'S FILMS

Divoky, Diane. "Children's Rights," Sightlines, vol. 9, no. 1, Fall 1975.

Author states that most films on this list are geared to adults, and those aimed at children "tend to be patronizing."

Emmens, Carol A. "Films to Liven a Language Arts Program, The Year's Best for Elementary Grade Children," Previews, Feb. 1975, pp. 5-9.

Gaffney, Maureen and Gerry Laybourne. "Film Activities Kids Like," Sightlines, vol. 10, no. 1, Fall 1976, pp. 9-12.

Description of activities, list of film used in Children's Film Theater.

Gaffney, Maureen. "More Films Kids Like: A Preview," Sightlines, Winter 1977/78, pp. 10-12.

Goldman, Frederick. "Children's Films," K-eight, Nov./Dec. 1971, p. 43.

Green, Ellis and Madalynne Schoenfeld (eds.). A Multimedia Approach to Children's Literature--A Selected List of Films, Filmstrips and Recordings Based on Children's Books. Chicago: ALA, 1972. (Order from ALA, 50 E. Huron Street, Chicago, Ill. 60611. $2.50.

Lists books, followed by media produced from books.

Miller, Hannah. "Feature Films for Children," Wilson Library Bulletin, Feb. 1971, pp. 560-71.

Miller, Hannah. "A Case for the Use of Creative Films in the Classroom," Elementary English, May 1974, p. 671.

Miller, Hannah. "Why Children's Films Are Not Rated X," Wilson Library Bulletin, October 1971, pp. 183-4.

Morton, Miriam. "Children's Films at the 1975 Moscow Festival," Sightlines, vol. 9, no. 1, Fall 1975, pp. 9-10.

New York Public Library. See under GENERAL in this appendix.

Rice, Susan. Films Kids Like. See under GENERAL in this appendix.

Rice, Susan. "An Eye for an I," Sightlines, Fall 1974, pp. 3-4.

An analysis of what works and what doesn't work in children's films, and their effects on those watching them.

Sightlines, Fall 1974.

The entire issue is devoted to "Films for Children." Articles and lists include: "Non-Sexist Films for Children," "The Children's Film Foundation," and "Experimental Films for Children: Some Random Thoughts."

As of 1978, Sightlines now carries a section in each issue called "Young Viewers: Children's Films." Edited by Maureen Gaffney of the Media Center for Children, this is an excellent source of information about children's films, articles on film use with young children, and film lists.

CRAFTS

New York State Craftsmen Inc., 27 West 53 Street, New York, N.Y. 10019.

Send for lists of specific films on crafts.

Check catalogs of major distributor.

DANCE

Brooks, Virginia (compiler). "Dance, Report of 6th Annual Dance Festival," Film News, Sept./Oct. 1977, pp. 19-22.

"Dance," Film News, Jan./Feb. 1977, pp. 18-20.

Report on Dance Film Festival, including reviews of 21 films shown there.

"Dance Films, Folk and Ethnic," Sightlines, Service Supplement, Sept./Oct. 1968, from EFLA (see details in Appendix A).

Macmillan special Dance catalog, includes Multimedia Dance Films "From Sculpture to Video Dance," by Doris Chase, from Macmillan Films Inc., 34 MacQuestern P'way So., Mt. Vernon, N.Y. 10550.

"One with Dance," Film News, vol. 31, no. 3, 1974.

DEAF

Films for the Deaf. Captioned, from BFA, send for catalog (see Appendix F for address).

Send for catalogs of other major distributors, specify special needs.

DEATH

"Films on Death and Dying," Sightlines, Service Supplement, vol. 7, no. 2, 1973/74, from EFLA (see details in Appendix A).

DRUGS

Drug Addiction and Narcotics, from National Audiovisual Center, Washington, D.C. 20409.

EFLA. "99+ Films on Drugs," from EFLA (see details in Appendix A).

EARLY CHILDHOOD/CHILD DEVELOPMENT

Child Day Care Association of St. Louis, Mo. Child Development and Early Childhood--An Annotated Film Biography, from Child Day Care Assn., 915 Olive Street, St. Louis, Mo. 63101.

As of this writing there were a few copies left of their 1974 list. No new lists are anticipated.

Winnick, Mariann Pezella. Films for Early Childhood--A Selected Annotated Bibliography, from Early Childhood Education Council of New York City (ECEC), 196 Bleeker Street, New York, N.Y. 10012. 1973.

ENERGY

Science of Energy, series of 10 films, from Stuart Finley, 4328 Mansfield Rd., Falls Church, Va. 22041.

Send for catalog. Check catalogs of other major distributors (see Appendix F).

ENVIRONMENT

Conservation Education Association. A Selected List of Filmstrips on Conservation of Natural Resources, from Interstate Printers and Publishers Inc., Danville, Ill. 61832.

"Environmental Crisis Media," English Journal, April, 1973.

William, Hannah (ed.). Critical Index on Man and His Environment, written for Conservation Education Assn., from Interstate Printers and Publishing Co. (See address above).

William, Hannah. "Man and His Environment," Sightlines, Service Supplement, Nov. 1972, from EFLA (see details in Appendix A).

Check catalogs of major distributor for more lists.

ETHNIC STUDIES

Artel, Linda. "Ethnic America," Sightlines, vol. 9, no. 3, Spring 1976, pp. 13-16.

Black Americans, Chinese Americans, Italian Americans, Japanese Americans, Jewish Americans, Mexican Americans, Native Americans, Puerto Rican Americans, and other films on immigrants.

Johnson, Harry A. Ethnic American Minorities: A Guide to Media and Materials, New York: R. R. Bowker, 1976, $15.95.

Kotzin, Miriam, and the staff of Media & Methods. "Your Life? Ethnic Experience on Film," Media & Methods, Dec. 1973, pp. 33-35.

Ledevich, Laurel and Thomas Swiss. "Resources for the Study of Native Americans," Media & Methods, May/June 1977, pp. 52-54.

Walden, Daniel. "American Ethnic Studies and Film," Sightlines, Fall 1977, pp. 18-19.

Filmography on Blacks and Jews, including historical and contemporary films.

FAMILY LIFE

Mason, Edward, M.D. "The Children of Separation and Divorce," Sightlines, Spring 1978, pp. 15-17, annotated, extensive filmography "Separation and Divorce," pp. 18-19.

Sightlines, vol. 11, no. 3, Spring 1978, pp. 9-12+, an annotated list by Catherine Egan, "From Kitchen to Camera: Feminism and the Family Film."

FEATURE FILMS ON 16mm

Limbacher, James. "Feature Films in Public Libraries," Previews, Sept. 1975, pp. 5-7.

James Limbacher has also written a book on the subject for R. R. Bowker, and Sightlines carries supplemental lists from time to time.

Mallery, David, Jane Gaines and Ralph Ameli. "Feature Film Feast--New Releases and Sleepers," Media & Methods, Dec. 1976, pp. 22-29.

FILM STUDY, FILM MAKING, FILM USE

English Journal. "Annotated Bibliography of Materials Available to Teachers of Film Study, Film Usage, and Filmmaking," Sept. 1971, pp. 831-8.

Isaaczon, David. "Film Study in the High School English Curriculum," English Journal, April 1973, pp. 651-8.
A bibliography of curriculum guides and materials useful in film study courses.

Limbacher, James. "More Movies About Movies," Sightlines, Service Supplement, March 1971, from EFLA (see details in Appendix A).

Limbacher, James. "More Movies About Movies," Sightlines, Service Supplement, Nov./Dec. 1968, from EFLA.

Miller, Hannah. "$65 Buys a Film Library," K-eight, Sept. 1973, p. 47.
Annotated bibliography of films on film making.

Parker, David L. A Filmography of Films About Movies and Movie Making, Rochester, N.Y.: Eastman Kodak Co., 1971.
Contains 233 titles of 16mm films on aspects of motion picture production, history of cinema, general facts about movies, and the nature of film medium. Gives brief description, date of film release, and distributor.

Schillaci, Dr. Peter. Contemporary Films: Mini-Course on Film Study--A Teacher Guide, from McGraw-Hill Films, 1221 Ave. of the Americas, New York, N.Y. 10020, 1973.

Trojan, Judith. "Film on Film: A Checklist," Take One, vol. 5, no. 8, March 1977, p. 30.
Annotated list of twenty-five 16mm documentaries on film and film making. List continued in May 1977 issue of Take One.

FUTURISTIC

Greene, Edward. "Teaching Futuristics in the Classroom--Today," _Previews_, Feb. 1976, p. 7-9.
Bibliography of 16mm films, filmstrips, slides and kits, and audio cassettes.

Check catalogs of major distributors for more films.

Martin, Marie. _Films on the Future_, 1977, from World Future Society, Washington, D.C.
Annotated list, uncritical.

GUIDANCE

Bennett, Janet. "Films for Human Survival," _Media & Methods_, March, 1976, pp. 38-40.
Uses films about famous older people (e.g., Einstein, I. F. Stone, Kurt Vonnegut, Jr., Koestler) to discuss "Time and Lifetime," "The Chance Factor," "School, Education, Intelligence," "Obstacles, Handicaps, Conflicts, Success," "Personal Success and Failure," "Success and Human Survival," "Enthusiasm, Work, and Discipline." Filmography.

Miller, Hannah. "A Little Bit of Sugar Helps the Medicine Go Down," _K-eight_, May/June 1972, pp. 40-41 (write to North American Publishing Co., 134 N. 13th Street, Philadelphia, Pa. 19107).

Miller, Hannah. "Unusual Guidance Films," _Spectator_ (published by National Association of Elementary School Principals, 1801 North Moore Street, Arlington, Va. 22209), Spring 1975. p. 13.

Check catalogs of major distributors.

HEALTH

Educational International Guide to Free and Lost Cost Audio-Visual Teaching Aids, published by Pharmaceutical Communications Inc., 42-15 Crescent Street, L.I. City, N.Y. 11101, 1977, $10.
For professionals and college students.

National Audiovisual Center, Catalog, Washington, D.C. 10409.

Films and filmstrips covering drug addiction, narcotics, rehabilitation, safety and geriatrics.

HISTORY AND SOCIAL STUDIES

Kislia, T. A. "Around the World in Sponsored Films," Previews, March 1975, pp. 5-6.

National Audiovisual Center, General Services Administration, USIA Film Collection, Washington, D.C. 20409.
For U.S. Information Agency films.

Check the catalogs of commercial distributors.

University Film Libraries are an excellent source in this area.

JEWISH MEDIA SERVICE

Lown Building, 415 South Street, Waltham, Mass.
Catalog of films on topics of interest to Jewish Groups. Yiddish Feature Collection.

KRISHNAMURTI FOUNDATION

Krishnamurti Foundation of America, P. O. Box 216, Ojas, Cal. 93123.
Catalog lists films, tapes, phonograph records and videotapes. Gives sources if they cannot be purchased from the Foundation. Publishes Bulletin.

LATIN AMERICA

Hawkins, John. Latin American Studies, from Latin American Center, University of California, Los Angeles, Cal. 90007. 1975.
List arranged according to grade levels.

MASCULINITY

Eppel, Ron. "Films By/About Men," Media & Methods, October 1975, pp. 36-37.
Reviews short films on the masculine image.

Wagner, Bonnie. "The Masculine Image: A Film Centered Approach," Media & Methods, Sept. 1976, pp. 50-52.
Describes how to start a course, and how to use films. Includes bibliography and filmography.

MUSIC

Miller, Hannah. "Films to Learn Music By," K-eight, Jan./Feb. 1973, pp. 102-105.

MYSTICISM, PSYCHICS, MEDITATION

Hartley Film Foundation, Cat Rock Road, Cos Cob, Conn. 06807.

Trojan, Judith. "The Cosmic Drama," Sightlines, vol. 9, no. 1, Fall 1975, pp. 7-9.
Films on psychic phenomena, the occult, and ancient mysteries.

NEAR EAST

Hawkins, John and Jon Maksik. Teacher's Resource Handbook for Near Eastern Studies, published by Gustave E. von Grunebaum Center for Near Eastern Studies, University of California, Los Angeles, Cal. 90007.

NON-NARRATIVE FILMS

Parlato, Salvatore, Jr. Films Too Good for Words, New York: R. R. Bowker Co., 1972, $12.50 (order from R. R. Bowker Order Dept., P. O. Box 1807, Ann Arbor, Mich. 48106).
Covers wide range of subjects. Entries are annotated, give distributors, running time, date, etc. Book includes information on equipment.

SIM Presents Adventures in Education Through Non-Verbal Films. Commercial, free catalog, from SIM, Weston Woods, Weston, Conn. 06880.

PHYSICS

American Physical Society Lectures, from State University Film Service, 1400 Washington Ave., Albany, N.Y. 12203.
Thirteen lectures on 16mm film.

POETRY

Emmens, Carol A. "Poets and Poetry on Film," Media & Methods, May/June 1977, pp. 42-46.

A list of films depicting poems by blending films and poetry successfully.

Scattergood, Sara P. "A Sense of Poetry," Film News, Jan./Feb. 1976, March/April 1976, pp. 22-24.
Based on seven films, 5-13 minutes, distributed by Learning Corp. of America. Films are 1974 releases.

POPULATION

Film News, "Films About the Population Problem," Oct. 1974, p. 24.

Check catalogs of Commercial distributors and University libraries.

RELIGION

Audiovisual Resource Guide for Peace and Justice, Merten Center, 1213 E. Carson Street, Pittsburgh, Pa. 15203 (some film rentals are limited to Western Pa.). $21.
Lists free and inexpensive resources, films, filmstrips and slides on ecology, minorities, the elderly and war and peace.

McClure, William. "Secular Films in Church," Sightlines, vol. 9, no. 1, Fall 1975, pp. 5-6.
Lists films used in churches throughout the U.S.

National Council of Churches. Audiovisual Resource Guide. New York: Friendship Press, 19th ed. $8.95.
Contains summary of plots of films, filmstrips, slides, records, tapes and other audiovisual evaluations.

RUSSIA AND EASTERN EUROPE

Hawkins, John and Jon Maksik. Teacher's Resource Handbook for Russian and East European Studies, UCLA Center for Russian and Eastern European Studies Publication, Curriculum Inquiry Center, Graduate School of Education, 1976.
Lists print and non-print media, including price and source. Arranged according to grade levels.

SCIENCE

Kislia, J. A. "Free and Fabulous Science Films in the

Classroom," <u>Previews</u>, April 1974, pp. 21-23.
Annotated list of 14 films, with student ratings.

SENIOR CITIZENS

<u>Booklist</u>, "Film Programs for Senior Citizens," May 15, 1976, pp. 1344-46.
Annotated list, with subject headings.

SEX EDUCATION

Burelson, Derek and Gary Barbash. <u>Film Resources for Sex Education</u>. New York: Human Science Press, 1976.
Evaluation of sex education films. Subject and audience level index.

SMOKING

U.S. Department of Health, Education and Welfare. "What's New on Smoking in Print and on Film," Public Health Service, National Clearinghouse for Smoking and Health, Rockville, Md. 20852. Free.

SPECIAL EDUCATION

Miller, Hannah. "Films About Learning Disabilities," <u>Spectator</u>, National Assn. of Elementary Principals (1801 N. Moore Street, Arlington, Va. 22209), Fall 1974, pp. 14-15.

National Center on Educational Media and Materials for the Handicapped (NCEMMH), 221 W. 12 Street, Columbus, Ohio 43210.
Write for available information.

Pre-School Workshops (38 Old Country R., Garden City, N.Y. 11530).
Two films on learning disabilities, available through New York University Film Library.

<u>Journal of Learning Disabilities</u> (see Appendix C).

STUDENT-MADE FILMS

Anderson, Yvonne. <u>Yellow Ball Workshop</u> (72 Tarbell Street, Lexington, Mass. 02173).
Send for catalog (see Bibliography in Chapter 8).

Budget Films Inc., 4590 Santa Monica Blvd., Los Angeles, Cal. 90029.
Free catalog. Small collection.

TEACHER TRAINING

Miller, Hannah. "Selected Films for Teacher Training, In-Service Programs and Workshops," National Elementary Principal, April 1971, pp. 68-72.

Winnick, Mariann Pezella. Films for Early Childhood (see EARLY CHILDHOOD in this appendix).

THIRD WORLD

Ackerman, Jean Marie. Films of a Changing World/Critical International Guide, vol. II, Society for International Development (1346 Conn. Ave., N.W., Washington, D.C. 20036), $4.
(Ms. Ackerman is media editor for International Development Review, see Appendix C.) Covers 1972-1976, reviews of films, filmstrips and other media, filmographies, references, articles on films and Third World countries.

Cyr, Helen. A Filmography of the Third World. Metuchen, N.J.: Scarecrow Press, 1976, $11.
An annotated list of 16mm films.

UNITED NATIONS

U.N. Radio and Visual Services. U.N. Secretariat, New York, N.Y. 10017.
Send for free 16mm catalog.

UNICEF Films, Public Information Division, UNICEF, United Nations, New York, N.Y. 10017.

UNICEF Film Distribution. Adm. Offices, 331 East 38 Street, New York, N.Y. 10016.
Send for free lists. Lists are distributed by states. Catalog includes sources, such as university libraries, public libraries and commercial distributors.

VIDEO

Brown, Mary A. "Video and Cable Bibliography," Sightlines,

Service Supplement, Jan. 1973, from EFLA (see details in Appendix A).

Lee, Rohama and Jeff Laffel. "Made-for-TV Movies, A Whole New Ball Game," Film News, Sept. 1974, pp. 16-20.
A list of 16mm films, originally seen on TV, now available to non-theatrical audiences.

Films Inc., a commercial distributor, has many videocassettes available. See Appendix F for list of other commercial distributors.

WOMEN AND FILMS†

Betancourt, Jeanne. Women in Focus. Dayton, Ohio: Pflaum/Standard Publ., 1974. $7.50.
Films by and about women.

Emmens, Carol A. "International Women on Film," Sightlines, vol. 10, no. 1. Fall 1976, pp. 13-15.
Selected filmography of roles of women in developing and underdeveloped countries, and in various economic and sociological classes, including two primitive tribes.

Films By and About Women 1972, a directory of film makers, films and distributors. Women's History Research Center Inc., 2325 Oak Street, Berkeley, Cal. 94708.

Film Library Quarterly. Winter 1971-72, entire issue on Women and Films.

Grilikkes, Alexandra. "Films by Women, 1928-71," Film Library Quarterly, Winter 1972-73.

Lester, Eleanore. "At Last: A Festival of Women's Films," Ms. October 1972.
About the first International Women's Film Festival in New York.

National Film Board of Canada. "Working Mothers," a series of 10 films; send for catalog, NFBC, 16th floor, 1251 Ave. of the Americas, New York, N.Y. 10020.

†Check frequently for new films and new distributors of films about women and related subjects.

Non-Sexist Films for Young People. Booklegger Press, $5.
By San Francisco collective of women's information specialists.

Rosen, Marjorie. "Women--Their Films and Their Festivals," Saturday Review, August 12, 1972.

Schrank, Louise Welsh. "When the Shoe No Longer Fits: Selected Films on Working Women," Media & Methods, April 1977, pp. 48-49.

Take One, Spring 1972, entire issue on Women and Films.

Wheeler, Helen. Womanhood Media. Metuchen, N.J.: Scarecrow Press, 1972, $8.50.
Films about the feminist movement.

Women and Film, a new journal devoted to women and film. 2812 Arizona Ave., Santa Monica, Cal.

Women and Films: A Resource Handbook. From projects on the status and education of women, Association of American Colleges, 1818 R. Street, N.W., Washington, D.C. 20009.

Women's Film Co-op, 20 Main St., Northampton, Mass. 01600.
Catalog of films for and about women.

Women's Films, A Critical Guide, Indiana University AV Center, $5.95 (see Appendix F).

APPENDIX E

Sources of Free and Inexpensive Films

According to J. A. Kislia, in "Free and Fabulous" (Previews, April 1974), free films "run the entertainment scale from 'outstanding' to 'deadly.' In reliability they rank from 'inspired' to 'honest' to 'self-serving,' down to a very few films filled with half-truths that were little better than outright lies. Their variety seems almost infinite." (The article is about science films, and the quotes are from student ratings.)

Free films are democratic. They are available to the richest and the poorest schools, libraries and individuals. One need only write for them and pay the return postage. Like all films you intend to show your class, preview first since there is no substitute for this.

Less and less material comes absolutely free. Distribution costs have risen over the past few years, and some sources are no longer available for this reason. Others have handed over their film distribution to professionally run companies. Because of this, there have been, and will continue to be, changes in the reliability of obtaining materials. It is no longer possible to guarantee any one source, and this includes commercial distributors. You will have to try them and make your own appraisals.

Aubrey, Ruth H. Selected Free Materials for Classroom Teachers. 5th ed., $2.75. From Fearon Publications Inc., 6 Davis Drive, Belmont, Cal. 94002.

Free and Inexpensive Learning Materials, 18th ed., $3.50. From George Peabody College for Teachers, Nashville, Tenn. 37203.

Guide to Government-Loan Films (16mm)- Volumes I & II, $9.95. From Serina Press, 70 Kennedy St., Alexandria, Va. 22305.

Vol. I--The Civilian Agencies; Vol. II--The Defense Agencies. Contains synopses of free-loan films, subject index and list of sources.

Guide to Free Loan Films About Foreign Lands, 1975, $9.95. From Serina Press (see address above).

Films dealing with 76 countries; synopses and sources listed.

Guide to Free Loan Films on the Urban Condition, 1976, $7.95. From Serina Press (see address above).

Synopses of over 500 films on a free-loan basis, from 88 sources for public, non-profit showing. We tried to get several films from these lists in 1977, and were not altogether successful. Many sources were not available.

Kislia, J. A. "Sponsored Films," *Previews*, March 1975, pp. 5-6.

Information about rent free travel films.

Kislia, J. A. *Let's See It Again: Free Films for Elementary Schools*, Dayton, Ohio: Pflaum Pub., 1975.

Educator's Guide to Free Films, published annually since 1941 by the Educator's Progress Service, 214 Center Street, Randolph, Wisc. 53956.

It is well organized: A Table of Contents gives a general outline; a Film Listing by curriculum areas gives short synopses of the films, dates of publication, sound or silent, running time, and source; a Title Index, arranged alphabetically, lists all titles and the page they appear on; an alphabetically arranged Subject Index lists subject headings; and a Source and Availability Index gives source addresses, terms and conditions of loans, probable availability of films, and page references to cited films.

Among the many sources to be found in the *Guide* are individual business concerns, local, state and federal government agencies, foreign government embassies and consulates, religious organizations, newspapers, universities and a few Canadian sources. By far the largest contributors of free films are business concerns, and many of their films are surprisingly free of advertisement. Often the only reference to the industrial sponsor is the

Educator's Guide to Free Films (cont.)

company name in the title. Foreign government embassies and consulates are another excellent source. Here is a complete list of available Audiovisual Guides from Educators Progress Service, Inc., Randolph, Wisc. 53956:

1) Educator's Guide to Free Films, 37th edition, $12.75. 745 listings of 4,377 titles.

2) Educator's Guide to Free Filmstrips, 29th edition, $10. 559 titles, including 19 which may be retained permanently.

3) Educator's Guide to Free Audio and Video Material, 24th edition, $10.50. 983 audio tapes, 169 videotapes, 13 scripts and 316 audiodiscs.

Multimedia Guides:

1) Educator's Guide to Free Guidance Materials, 17th edition, $10.75. Includes 970 films, 108 filmstrips, 68 sets of slides, 475 audiotapes, 61 videotapes, 196 audiodiscs, and 432 other materials.

2) Educator's Guide to Free Social Studies Materials, 17th edition, $11.75. 1,636 films, 144 filmstrips, 160 sets of slides, 823 audiotapes, 74 videotapes, 308 audiodiscs, and 706 other materials.

3) Educator's Guide to Free Science Materials, 18th edition, $11.25. 1,066 films, 28 filmstrips, 35 slides, 162 audiotapes, 37 videotapes, 631 charts and other materials.

4) Educator's Guide to Free Health, Physical Education and Recreation Materials, 10th edition, $11. 1,360 films, 104 filmstrips, 97 sets of slides, 76 audiotapes, 62 videotapes and other materials.

Printed Materials Guide:

Elementary Teachers Guide to Free Materials, 34th edition, $11.50.

Some sources listed in these Guides may not be available, and, unfortunately, some private companies, and foreign consulates are using Modern Talking Pictures and Association Films to distribute their films. We have not always found them to be as reliable as we would wish.

Some Foreign Embassies and Consulates (from Educator's Guide):

1) Australian Information Services, Australian

Educator's Guide to Free Films (cont.)

Consulate-General, 636 5th Ave., New York, N. Y. 10020.

2) Embassy of Cypress, 2211 R. Street, N.W., Washington, D.C.

3) Royal Danish Consulate General (write to nearest office): 360 N. Michigan Ave., Chicago, Ill. 60601; 3440 Wilshire Blvd., Los Angeles, Cal. 90010; Danish Information Office, 280 Park Ave., New York, N. Y. 10017.

4) Consulate General of Finland--all requests for films should go to Films of the Nations, 7820 20th Ave., Brooklyn, N.Y. 11214.

5) German Information Center, c/o Association Films, 866 3rd Ave., New York, N.Y. 10022.

6) Consulate General of Iceland, 370 Lexington Ave., New York, N.Y. 10017.

7) No entry.

8) Consulate General of Ireland, 400 N. Michigan Ave., Chicago, Ill. 60611; or 580 5th Ave., New York, N.Y. 10036.

9) Consulate General of Israel, c/o Alden Films, 7820 20th Ave., Brooklyn, N.Y. 11214.

10) Consulate General of Japan, c/o Association Films, 600 Grand Ave., Ridgefield, N.J. 07657.

11) Embassy of Malaysia, Information, 2401 Massachusetts Ave., N.W., Washington, D.C. 20008.

12) Royal Netherland Embassy, 4200 Linnean Ave., N.W., Consulate General Office, Washington, D.C. 20008. There are offices in New York City, San Francisco, Los Angeles, Houston, and Chicago.

13) New Zealand Films, c/o Association Films, 866 3rd Ave., New York, N.Y. 10022.

14) Embassy of Poland, Press Office, 2640 16th Street, N.W., Washington, D.C. 20009.

15) Embassy of Switzerland, 2900 Cathedral Ave., N.W., Washington, D.C. 20008. For college level and above only.

All of the above have some very beautiful films about their countries, their crafts, their sports, their scenery. Not all have catalogs, but most of them will reply if one requests a list of films they distribute. Again, those embassies no longer handling their own distribution may be more difficult to contact.

Tourist Offices--Foreign. Many governments maintain tourist offices in some of the larger cities in the U.S. These are not necessarily part of the Consulates, but they are good P.R., and are good for the tourist business. Look in your local phone book, or write to the nearest Consulate, or Embassy in Washington, D.C. for information and addresses.

Tourist Offices--U.S. Try the Chamber of Commerce of any state or town you wish to study, and learn more about. The following are a few examples:

1) Florida Department of Commerce, Division of Tourism, Film Library, 107 West Gaines Street, Tallahassee, Fla. 32304.

2) Maine Department of Agriculture, Motion Picture Service, State Office Building, Augusta, Me. 04333.

3) Tennessee Department of Conservation Educational Services, 2611 West End Ave., Nashville, Tenn. 37203.

Government Departments. Many U.S. Government Departments have excellent films:

1) Bureau of Mines, U.S. Department of the Interior, Motion Pictures, 4800 Forbes Ave., Pittsburgh, Pa. 15213.

2) Department of the Air Force, Air Force Central Audiovisual Library, Aerospace Audiovisual Services, Norton Air Force Base, Cal. 92409. Try them for subjects like propaganda, and attitudes towards war and the military.

3) Department of the Army. Many different installations serve different sections of the country. Contact any army base near your home. Their anti-communist films are very useful in English and Social Studies classes.

4) Coast Guard. Write to Public Information Division, Washington, D.C. 20226 for address nearest you.

5) U.S. Geological Survey, Branch of Visual Services, 303 National Center, Reston, Va. 22092.

6) NASA has films available from many offices. Write to National Audiovisual Center, General Services Administration, Washington, D.C. 20409 for address of nearest office.

7) Department of the Navy, Naval Education and Training Support Center, Commanding Officer, Atlantic Naval Station, Building Z-86, Norfolk, Va. 23511 (for states east of the Mississippi). Commanding Officer, Pacific Fleet Station Post Office Building, San Diego, Cal. 93132 (for states west of the Mississippi).

8) Dept. of H. E. W., Public Health Service, 5600 Fishers Lane, Rockville, Md. 20852.

Commercial Companies--Industry. Some of the films produced by industrial companies are amazingly free from advertisement, and are often good classroom material. "How Industry and Education Can Put It All Together" (*Audiovisual Instruction*, September 1971), tells of several films that were sponsored by industry and made available to schools. The author of the article, Donna Dee, tells of one such, "The Story of Menstruation," sponsored by Kimberly Clark, and produced by the Disney Studio. She also mentions the Bell Telephone Co., the Population Council and Upjohn as other companies that have made such projects.

1) The American Cancer Society (777 3rd Ave., New York, N.Y. 10017) has brief anti-smoking films. Check your local telephone directory for the office nearest you.

2) The Bell Telephone Company will send a free film catalog. Call your local telephone business office for a copy. Films range from telephone science and research to music. Also try A.T.&T., 195 B'way, R. 07-1106, New York, N.Y. 10007.

3) International Telephone and Telegraph (ITT) is currently showing the first worldwide children's television series "The Big Blue Marble." Write to Big Blue Marble Information Center (866 3rd Ave., Room 2000, New York, N.Y. 10022) for information. The program is free to educators upon request. Each program deals with several countries, states in the U.S., and other items of interest to young viewers: segments on "How-to," "If Children Ruled the World," etc. Each segment is complete. There is a detailed catalog for the first eight shows. The films are authentic, and excellent.

4) Consolidated Edison Co. of N.Y., 4 Irving Place, New York, N.Y. 10003.

5) Try your local advertising companies and local TV stations for free films.

6) Two companies that distribute films for commercial companies, foreign consulates, business and industrial films, etc. are:

a. Association Films Inc., 866 3rd Ave., New York, N.Y. 10022. There are several other offices in other parts of the country from which to order their films. Atlanta, Ga.; Dallas, Texas; Dublin, Cal.; LaGrange, Ill.; Littleton, Mass.; Minneapolis, Minn.; Oakmont, Pa.; Portland, Ore.; Ridgefield,

N. J.; Sun Valley, Cal. Unfortunately, they have not been as reliable recently as we would like.

b. Modern Talking Pictures, Park Road, New Hyde Park, N. Y. 11040. This clearinghouse for many commercial films issues separate catalogs on "Elementary Films," "Adult," "Church Groups," Business and Industry," and lends 3/4 inch videotapes. You are asked to order from the office nearest you: Atlanta, Ga.; Boston, Mass.; Buffalo, N. Y.; Cedar Rapids, Iowa; Charlotte, N. C.; Chicago, Ill.; Dallas, Texas; Cincinnati, Ohio; Denver, Colo.; Cleveland, Ohio; Detroit, Mich.; Harrisburg, Pa.; Honolulu, Hawaii; Houston, Texas; Indianapolis, Ind.; Los Angeles, Cal.; Milwaukee, Wisc.; Minneapolis, Minn.; Philadelphia, Pa.; Pittsburgh, Pa.; St. Louis, Mo.; San Francisco, Cal.; Seattle, Wash.; Summit, N. J.; Washington, D. C. Recently this company has not been too reliable. Some of their sources no longer exist.

Film Library Circuits. In 1949 Virginia Beard started the first film library circuit in Ohio. Called the Ohio Regional Film Circuit, there were 10 member libraries, sponsored by a grant from the Carnegie Corporation. This circuit helped to set the pattern for many library circuits that service the public throughout the country today. Check your own public library to see if they have films they lend, and/or belong to a circuit, for these films are usually more carefully selected than other free sources.

Unfortunately some communities do not have this service, and where schools have money allocated for films, there may be a charge for a school or teachers to borrow films. (Your PTA may be willing to pay this fee for your school.) Much depends on local branches, whether they choose to belong to a circuit. Many smaller libraries lack funds to buy and replace films, even when this is shared by many members of the circuit. Smaller branches also lack staff to coordinate such a circuit. Circuits may be statewide, as in Pennsylvania (since 1966), which has two regional centers. It may be made up of towns within a county, or districts within a large city. Catalogs are often free to those requesting to have their names placed on the mailing list. Some libraries have projectors that can be rented for a small fee.

Many states have state library bulletins, kept in the reference department of local branches. Check with your local library about local, and/or regional circuits. The Film Library Quarterly carried these items of interest in their Winter 1969-70 issue: Kansas Film Service, designated Wichita as the Film Center for 14 counties of South Central Kansas in 1970; The Suburban Audio Visual Service now covers the suburban area of Chicago; and the Public Library Commission and Lincoln City Branch, Nebraska have combined their Audiovisual Departments to serve the entire state of Nebraska.

See also: The Directory of Film Libraries in North America, from EFLA, 43 West 61 Street, New York, N.Y. 10023. $5. This lists over 1300 libraries that carry films in their collection.

The following is a partial list of some of the larger city libraries that provide film services, and have extensive collections:

1) Brooklyn Public Library, Audio-Visual Department, Grand Army Plaza, Brooklyn, N.Y. 11238.

2) Cleveland Public Library, Film Bureau, 325 Superior Ave., Cleveland, Ohio 44114.

3) Dallas Public Library, 1954 Commerce Street, Dallas, Texas 75201.

4) Enoch Pratt Free Library, 400 Cathedral Street, Baltimore, Md. 21201

5) Kansas City Public Library, 311 East 12 Street, Kansas City, Mo. 64006

6) Los Angeles Public Library, 630 West 5th Street, Los Angeles, Cal. 90017

7) Nassau Library System, Roosevelt Field Shopping Center, Garden City, N.Y. 11530

8) New York Public Library, Film Library, 20 West 53 Street, New York, N.Y. 10019

9) Queensborough Public Library, Audio-Visual Department, 89-11 Merrick Boulevard, Jamaica, N.Y. 11432

Other Ways to Get "Free" Films

"Free" films may not always be entirely free. Aside from paying return postage, there are the phone calls one has to make to make sure the film will be where you want it, when you want it. There are also innumerable letters to be written. However, try Museums, Universities and Film Societies in your area for free showings. Some Film Festivals may also be free, or charge only a small admission fee.

Inviting local film makers to visit your school or library to talk about their films can make for interesting encounters. Some film makers are happy to have young audiences on whom to test their films.

State Education Department Film Libraries

In a survey we conducted in 1974, and again in 1977, we found that there have been severe budget cuts by many state legislatures that have been applied directly to film collections. Some have eliminated film libraries entirely. Others cut staff, which crippled their ability to maintain circulation.

To the best of our ability, the following information is accurate, as of November 1977. (Those states marked with a star (*) only replied to the 1974 questionnaire.) Information is quoted as given on the questionnaires.

We suggest that you check with your own State Department of Education, as well as one of the many state universities (see Appendix F). We have found that university film collections are often the best sources for less expensive film rentals. Charges vary from state to state, and from university to university. Catalogs may be free, or there may be a small charge. Whatever the fees, they will be less than those of commercial distributors.

ALABAMA STATE DEPARTMENT OF EDUCATION. No information available.

ALASKA STATE LIBRARY, Southeast IMC, Pouch G, Juneau, Alaska 99801. State owns approximately 8,000 titles. Also distributes cassettes, tapes and videocassettes. All Alaskans may borrow these through their local library or school.

ARIZONA STATE DEPARTMENT OF EDUCATION, Film Library, Phoenix, Ariz. Films are loaned by four regionally funded libraries to any Arizona educator.

ARKANSAS STATE FILM LIBRARY, Audio-Visual Services, Department of Education, Arch Foret Bldg., Little Rock, Ark. 72201. State owns 1,585 titles. Any public school or institute of higher learning within the state may borrow. Pay return postage.

CALIFORNIA STATE DEPARTMENT OF EDUCATION, Film Library, Sacramento, Cal. 95800. State owns approximately 1,000 films. There are 49 film libraries operated by offices of Superintendents of Schools through the state, and 25 film libraries operated by large city school systems.

COLORADO STATE LIBRARY, Colorado Department of Education, 1362 Lincoln Street, Denver, Colo. 80203. State owns approximately 900-1,000 films. Other sources are the Denver Public Library, and the University of Colorado, Bureau of Audiovisual Instruction. A severe budget cut in 1977 has cut the staff of the state library, and they are unable to book all film requests.

CONNECTICUT DEPARTMENT OF EDUCATION, Box 2219, Hartford, Conn. 06115. Films are distributed by six regional educational facilities. The state does not own any films for circulation.

*DELAWARE STATE DEPARTMENT OF EDUCATION, Film Library, Dover, Del. 19901. State owns 2,000 titles, some filmstrips, tapes, cassettes and slides. Lends to public and private schools within the state. Three school districts maintain a library of films for their own use.

FLORIDA STATE DEPARTMENT OF EDUCATION, School Library Media Service, Tallahassee, Fla. 32304. State owns mostly videotapes. These are stored in the State Department of Education's curriculum library. There is an Instructional Media Center (Florida State University, Tallahassee, Florida 32304), that lends films.

GEORGIA STATE DEPARTMENT OF EDUCATION, Audiovisual Services, 1066 Sylvan Road, S.W., Atlanta, Ga. 30310. State owns approximately 4,300 films and reel-to-reel and audio tapes which are lent to Public and Private Schools. Each school pays $70/year, which entitles the school to four films a year.

HAWAII STATE DEPARTMENT OF EDUCATION, Audiovisual Services, 641 18th Ave., Honolulu, Hawaii 96816. State Library owns 1,525 titles, 1,725 prints. The Department of Education owns 5,375 titles. All public schools and state university can borrow these films. Address of Hawaii State Library: Audio-Visual Unit, 4785 King Street, Honolulu, Hawaii 96813.

IDAHO PROFESSIONAL LIBRARY, State Department of Education, Boise, Idaho 83700. Films are lent by the University of Idaho at Moscow, Idaho State University at Pocatello, and Boise State University at Boise. The State Department of Education has films on Traffic Safety, which are lent to anyone in the state.

ILLINOIS OFFICE OF EDUCATION, Media Resource Center, 100 North First Street, Springfield, Ill. 62777. The state owns 900 films, 800 filmstrips, 50 tapes and cassettes, 50 kits and 500 videotapes. These can be borrowed for in-service courses and for classroom use. When ordering videotapes include viewing format.

INDIANA PROFESSIONAL LIBRARY, Department of Professional Instruction, Division of Instructional Media, 120 West Market Street, 10th floor, Indianapolis, Ind. 46204. State owns 275 films, sound filmstrips, super 8 films, slides, videotapes, tapes and kits. School administrators, supervisors, college professors in teacher's education in the state of Indiana may borrow media. The Indianapolis Marion County Library, and Indiana University at Bloomington also have collections.

IOWA EDUCATIONAL MEDIA SECTION, Department of Public Instruction, Crimes Office Bldg., Des Moines, Iowa 50319. Sixteen regional Educational Media Centers each lend films to schools in their own geographic area. University of Iowa, c/o Audio-Visual Center, Media Library C-5, East Hall, Iowa City, Iowa 52242, and Iowa State University, Media Resource Center, 121 Pearson Hall, Ames, Iowa 50001, both lend films.

KANSAS STATE DEPARTMENT OF EDUCATION, Film Library, Topeka, Kan. 40601. Some sections of the state have films that are available to teachers in Kansas. The University of Kansas has the Lawrence Film Library.

KENTUCKY STATE DEPARTMENT OF EDUCATION, Materials Center, Capital Plaza Tower, Frankfort, Ky. 40601. Library has about 45 films, available to anyone in state. They are mainly used by educators. The University of Kentucky also has a film library.

LOUISIANA AUDIO VISUAL EDUCATION, P. O. Box 44064, Baton Rouge, La. 70804. The Center holds 1,300 titles, produced after 1960, that can be borrowed from nine regional film libraries by all public, and approved private schools.

MAINE STATE LIBRARY, Film Coordinator, Cultural Building, Augusta, Me. 70804. The Maine State Library belongs to a cooperative with Vermont and New Hampshire. Use of the films for in-school classrooms is prohibited. Free loans are made to community groups, churches, day care centers, Nursing Homes, Hospitals and private libraries in Maine. The State Departments of Transportation, Agriculture, Human Services, Fish and Game, Civil Preparedness and Fire Service Training have some films they loan. The State library has some videocassettes that are available to teachers.

MARYLAND STATE MEDIA CENTER, P. O. Box 8718, Friendship International Airport, Baltimore, Md. 21240. Holds 574 films that are loaned to the staff of the State Department of Education, teachers in 24 counties and private and parochial school educators.

*MASSACHUSETTS STATE DEPARTMENT OF EDUCATION, 182 Tremont Street, Boston, Mass. 02111. As of June 1974 the State Department terminated its film service. Schools are now served by Fitchburg State College, Fitchburg, Mass.

MICHIGAN STATE LIBRARY SERVICE, Box 30007, Lansing, Mich. 48909. Holds 700 films, available to all Michigan State residents. There are four public library film regions, but they do not loan to schools. Schools may borrow from: University of Michigan at Ann Arbor, Michigan State at East Lansing, Wayne State University at Detroit, and Western Michigan University at Kalamazoo.

MINNESOTA LIBRARY SERVICE, University of Minnesota, 3300 University Ave., S.E., Minneapolis, Minn. 55414. Its 8,375 titles, 1,405 reels, 3,000 audio tapes, videotapes, filmstrips and slides are loaned to colleges and public schools in Minnesota. There is a service fee of $2.50-$10, catalogs are available, topical bibliographies on request.

MISSISSIPPI EDUCATIONAL MEDIA SERVICE, Division of Instructions, Department of Education, Jackson, Miss. 39205. Send for catalog. Films are available to all educators within the state from: University of Mississippi, Media Center at above address, and University of Southern Mississippi, Southern Station, Hattisburg, Miss.

MISSOURI STATE DEPARTMENT OF EDUCATION, Film Library, Jefferson City, Mo. 65101. The film library holds special titles only. These are available to public schools on request. All branches of the State University loan films, as does the Department of Health Film Library, 1407 Southwest Blvd., Jefferson City, Mo. 65101.

MONTANA STATE AUDIO-VISUAL LIBRARY, State Department of Education, Helena, Mont. 59601. Its 5,000 films are available to educational groups in the state.

*NEBRASKA STATE EDUCATION DEPARTMENT, Film Library, Lincoln, Neb. 68500. One hundred films are available to professionals for in-service use. Films may also be borrowed from: University Film Library, Instructional Media Center, 421 Nebraska Hall, University of Nebraska, Lincoln, Neb. 68505.

NEW HAMPSHIRE DEPARTMENT OF INSTRUCTIONAL MEDIA, Department of Education, 64 North Main Street, Concord, N.H. 03301. Films are lent to libraries, organizations, and individuals by the Film Consultant, Inter-State Film Collection, State Library, Concord, N.H. 03301. Films are lent to anyone, but mainly to schools by the University of New Hampshire, Department of Media Service, Durham, N.H. 03824. Send for free catalog.

NEW JERSEY STATE LIBRARY, Department of Education, 185 West State Street, P. O. Box 1898, Trenton, N.J. 08625. Several thousand films can be borrowed by any library in the state, and individuals affiliated with state institutions. Films may also be borrowed from: New Jersey Film Circuit (for libraries only), Garden State Film Circuit (there are five regional film centers), and for school loans, County Audio-Visual Commission, New Jersey State Museum, West State Street, Trenton, N.J. 08625.

NEW MEXICO LIBRARIES AND LEARNING RESOURCES, State Department of Education, Educational Building, Santa Fe, N.M. 87503. Films may be borrowed by libraries from: The N.M. State Library, 300 Don Gaspar,

Santa Fe, N. M. 87503. There are several district and regional school film libraries in the state which serve their own areas.

NEW YORK STATE DEPARTMENT OF EDUCATION, State Library, Albany, N. Y. 12230. Its 900 films are loaned to New York State residents through local public libraries.

*NORTH CAROLINA STATE DEPARTMENT OF EDUCATION, Raleigh, N. C. 27500. The state does not maintain a film library.

NORTH DAKOTA, DIVISION OF GUIDANCE SERVICE, Department of Public Instruction, Capitol, Bismarck, N.D. 58505. Fifty films, all in the Guidance Division, can be borrowed by all North Dakota schools. The State Film Library is located in Fargo, N.D.

OHIO SCHOOL MEDIA PROGRAMS, State of Ohio, Department of Education, Columbus, Ohio 43215. Nine regional centers, each autonomous, lend films within their own regions. School districts pay a per pupil fee, or $3 per film for this service. Kent State University has a 9,000-film collection for rent from their Audio-Visual Service. Send for catalog. Several commercial rental sources in Ohio, and the following governmental sources lend films: Lewis Research Center in Cleveland, Ohio Department of Mental Health and Mental Retardation, and the Ohio Department of Health in Columbus.

OKLAHOMA VOCATIONAL TELEVISION & INSTRUCTIONAL MEDIA DEPARTMENT, State Department of Education, Oklahoma City, Okla. 73125. Films are rented by the Oklahoma State University, at Stillwater, Okla. 74074. There is a small rental fee for teachers and department personnel in Oklahoma.

OREGON DEPARTMENT OF EDUCATION, 942 Lancaster Drive N.E., Salem, Ore. 97302. Send for free catalog listing some 7,287 films that are loaned to Oregon and surrounding states.

PENNSYLVANIA AUDIOVISUAL SERVICES, 17 Willard Bldg., University Park, Pa. This is located at Penn State University. Send for free catalog of "Films for the Elementary Classroom." "Audiovisual Services Newsletter" lists new acquisitions.

*RHODE ISLAND DEPARTMENT OF EDUCATION, Film Library, Providence, R. I. 02900. There is a film library for use by all public and private schools within state.

SOUTH CAROLINA STATE DEPARTMENT OF EDUCATION, Audio-Visual Library, 1513 Gervais Street, Columbia, S. C. 29201. Approximately 4,000 films may be borrowed by public schools, K-12 only. Other sources of films within the state are: University of South Carolina, Audio-Visual Aids, Carolina Coliseum, Columbus, S. C.; South Carolina Department of Mental Health, Film Library, 2414 Bull Street, Columbus, S. C.; and South Carolina State Board of Health, Bureau of Audio-Visuals, 2600 Bull Street, Columbus, S. C.

SOUTH DAKOTA STATE DEPARTMENT OF EDUCATION, Film Library, Pierre, S. D. 57100. Public School teachers may borrow some 1,000 titles from Public Schools, Sioux Falls, S. D. 57100.

TENNESSEE DEPARTMENT OF EDUCATION, Educational Media Center, Bldg. 308 11th Ave., Smyrna, Tenn. 37167. Its 1,425 films may be borrowed by public school educators, "approved" private schools and members of educational organizations within the state.

*TEXAS STATE DEPARTMENT OF EDUCATION, Media Center, Austin, Tex. 78700. There is a small collection of films for use by Texas educators. There are twenty regional Education Service Centers that lend to member schools in their region.

*UTAH STATE DEPARTMENT OF EDUCATION, Film Library, Salt Lake City, Utah 84100. Small collection loaned to staff as needed.

*VERMONT STATE DEPARTMENT OF EDUCATION, Film Library, Montpelier, Vt. 05602. Small collection is loaned to school teachers, librarians, college faculty and department staff members.

VIRGINIA STATE DEPARTMENT OF EDUCATION, Film Library, Richmond, Va. 23200. Its 18,000 prints are loaned to Virginia supported schools and institutions within the counties and cities of the state.

WASHINGTON STATE AUDIOVISUAL SERVICES, Olympia,

Wash. 98504. From 700-26,000 films are loaned to all schools. School districts may borrow from state library. Other film collections in state are: University of Washington, Central Washington State University, Washington State University, State Libraries, Educational Service Districts (9), and large city libraries.

WEST VIRGINIA EDUCATIONAL MEDIA SERVICE, Department of Education, Charleston, W. Va. 25305. Six hundred films and other non-print media may be borrowed by the West Virginia educational community.

WISCONSIN, University of Wisconsin Extension, Bureau of Audio-Visual Instruction, Box 2093, 1321 University Ave., Madison, Wisc. 53701. Its 7,200 films are loaned without restriction in the U.S. Users pay rental fees and return postage.

WYOMING STATE DEPARTMENT OF EDUCATION, Instructional Resource Center, Hathaway Bldg., Cheyenne, Wyo. 82002. The department has only a few films. University of Wyoming has larger collection.

If still available, Annotated Film Bibliography, from Child Day Care Association of St. Louis, 915 Oliver Street, St. Louis, Mo. 63103, Section III-B lists state offices and university film libraries by state.

Also: North American Film and Video Directory. New York: R. R. Bowker, 1976. Lists libraries and media centers that loan films and video materials in the U.S. and Canada.

APPENDIX F

Distributors

The 1977 EFLA Film Festival Guide (see Appendix A) lists 227 distributors of 16mm non-theatrical films. Some of these are University Film Libraries (see p. 274), others are societies, but the majority are commercial companies. Although all of the latter are in business for financial gain, we have found them to be sincere, and often totally dedicated people, who truly want to help film makers and film users. You may come across some who do not fit this description. The simplest way of dealing with these is to take your business elsewhere, particularly since many films are distributed by more than one company.

It is because our experience has been a positive one that we would like to give our readers some idea of who these distributors are, and which ones have been instrumental in bringing more creative films into the schools and libraries. As the personnel of some of these companies have changed, so have their film acquisitions, therefore knowing something about these key people is valuable.

Our apologies to those distributors whose names have been omitted, for reasons of brevity, because they are new and/or unknown to us. A good source of a list of 137 distributors of 16mm films, containing information on the type of films handled, method of distribution and preview policies is Carol Emmens' "Non-Theatrical Film Distributors: Sales Service Policies," published by EFLA, 43 West 61 Street, New York, N.Y. 10023. 1974.

Commercial Distributors

ACI FILMS. Now distributed by Paramount Communications,

Inc., 545 Marathon St., Hollywood, Cal. 90038. Stelios Roccos, president of ACI, was the director of one of the first non-narrative films (THE PURPLE TURTLE, 1958) to be filmed in the U.S. The successful "Rediscovery: Art Media Series" followed soon. Paramount distributes films on Arts and Crafts from many countries and ethnic groups, as well as films in the area of social studies, language arts, etc. All are done creatively for grades K-12.

AIMS INSTRUCTIONAL MEDIA SERVICE, 626 Justin Ave., Glendale, Cal. 91201. Aims distributes films and filmstrips for primary grades through college level. They carry films on special education.

YVONNE ANDERSEN see YELLOW BALL WORKSHOP

ATLANTIS PRODUCTION INC., 850 Thousand Oaks Blvd., Thousand Oakes, Cal. 91260.

BARR FILMS, P. O. Box 5667, Pasadena, Cal. 91107. Primarily distribute Arthur Barr productions.

BENCHMARK FILMS INC., 145 Scarborough Rd., Briarcliff Manor, N.Y. 10510.

BFA EDUCATIONAL MEDIA, 2211 Michigan Ave., Santa Monica, Cal. 90406. BFA is the educational media division of CBS, formed in 1966 when they purchased two small, independent companies. In January 1971, the CBS Educational Publishing group consolidated its media activities and merged with the media department of Holt. They are especially strong in the areas of social studies, and distribute series on dance and music. The majority of their films are curriculum oriented. Teacher's guides are available.

STEPHEN BOSUSTOW PRODUCTIONS, 1649 11th Street, Santa Monica, Cal. 90404. Founded in 1968 by Stephen Bosustow of UPA fame, the company is now run by Nick Bosustow. They distribute their own films, and produce films for other distributors. Particularly strong in animated films.

BRAVURA FILMS INC., 680 Beach Street, # 360, San Francisco, Cal. 94109.

WILLIAM BROSE PRODUCTION INC., 3168 Oakshire Blvd., Hollywood, Cal. 90068.

BUDGET FILMS, 4590 Santa Monica Blvd., Los Angeles, Cal. 90020. Carries a limited selection of youth made films.

CAROUSEL FILMS INC., 1501 Broadway, New York, N.Y. 10036. Carousel distributes a variety of films on many topics. They also distribute many television programs on 16mm, such as SANTIAGO'S ARK, HUNGER IN AMERICA, and THE FORGOTTEN AMERICAN, as well as some excellent films on ecology.

CENTER FOR MASS COMMUNICATION, Columbia University Press, 562 West 113 Street, New York, N.Y. 10025.

CENTRON FILMS, 1621 West 9 Street, Lawrence, Kan. 66044.

CHURCHILL FILMS, 662 N. Robertson Blvd., Los Angeles, Cal. 90069. Robert Churchill has been one of the most active producers of films for children for many years. The company has rental agreements with university libraries all over the U.S. Their guidance films for different age levels are well known. We have found this a most cooperative company to deal with. They also distribute Dimension films.

CONNECTICUT FILMS INC., 6 Cobble Hill Rd., Westport, Conn. 06880. This company has produced films related to children's books, libraries and story-telling. They also distribute the delightful SWIMMY and FREDERICK, both by the Italian team of Leo Lionni and Guilio Gianini.

CORONET INSTRUCTIONAL MEDIA, 65 East South Water Street, Chicago, Ill. 60601. David Smart returned from Europe in 1938 greatly impressed by the impact of the propaganda films in Hitler's Germany. Thus motivated, he began making educational films in his studio in Glenview, Illinois, in 1939 with the help of the AV department of the University of Wisconsin and Indiana University. At first they produced "instructional" films for schools, each one averaging 11 minutes to fit into the 45-minute classroom periods. In the last eight years they have added filmstrips and other non-print media. Coronet is today the largest producer of educational films.

THERE'S SOMETHING ABOUT A STORY, from Connecticut Films, Inc.

CRYSTAL PRODUCTION, Airport Business Center, Aspen, Colo. 81611. Multi-media materials on arts and crafts for teaching.

DOCUMENTARY EDUCATIONAL RESOURCES, 24 Dane St., Somerville, Mass. 02143. Unusual documentaries on Eskimo life, as well as other developing countries.

ECCENTRIC CIRCLE, P. O. Box 1481, Evanston, Ill. 60204.

ENCYCLOPAEDIA BRITANNICA EDUCATIONAL CORPORATION, 425 N. Michigan Ave., Chicago, Ill. 60611. EBEC began making educational films in 1929 when they were still known as the Electric Research Products Inc., then a subsidiary of Western Electric. Their first films were based on courses offered at the University of Chicago. They celebrated their 50th anniversary in 1978. EBEC produces instructional films as well as multi-media programs.

FAMILY FILMS, 14622 Lanark Street, Panorama City, Cal. 91402.

FILMS FOR THE HUMANITIES INC., P. O. Box 2053, Princeton, N. J. 08540.

FILMS INCORPORATED, 1144 Wilmette Ave., Wilmette, Ill. 60091. Founded in 1927 by Orton Hicks, Films Inc. today distributes films from such sources as the British Film Institute (experimental films), the Arts Council of Great Britain (major artists and their works), prints of the National Geographic TV specials, the American Federation of Arts series "The Art of Seeing," National Film Board of Canada Films, films from the Japanese Broadcasting System, Films from Eastern European countries (many of these are children's films), Metro-Media production, etc. Many experimental films from international producers and independent sources can be found in their catalog. Films Inc. is the oldest distributor of feature films to the non-theatrical field. They also distribute videocassettes.

STUART FINLEY INC., 3428 Mansfield Rd., Falls Church, Va. 22041.

FRANCISCAN COMMUNICATION CENTER, 1229 S. Santee Street, Los Angeles, Cal. 90015.

GROVE PRESS INC., 53 East 11 Street, New York, N. Y. 10003. Grove Press began their collection the "Cinema 16" films. Today they have an extensive library of American and European feature shorts, avant-garde films, most of Godard's works, and some animated shorts.

HOLT RINEHART & WINSTON MEDIA, 383 Madison Ave., New York, N. Y. 10017. In 1972 this company bought the 16mm library of KING SCREEN releases. Their own catalog shows curriculum films, whereas King Screen films are short, imaginative films on contemporary and environmental issues.

HUBLEY STUDIOS, 165 East 72nd St., New York, N. Y. Distribute some of their own films.

INTERNATIONAL FILM BUREAU INC., 332 South Michigan Ave., Chicago, Ill. 60604. The IFB was incorporated by Hammond Greene in 1937. Greene left his company for three years (1942-45) to become chief of world distribution for NFBC. He helped to initiate many film programs in the Chicago area that are still active today, as well as the Chicago Film Festival in 1947, which was the forerunner of many of our current film festivals. He initiated the production of foreign language films, and the student guidebooks that accompany them. The company distributes foreign language series from other countries, as well as producing their own. GUTEN TAG, first seen on NET, is distributed by IFB. There is a separate list of 30 films from the National Mental Health Board in their catalog.

INTERNATIONAL FILM FOUNDATION, 475 5th Ave., New York, N.Y. 10017. In 1945 the Davella Mills Foundation, on the advice of the U.S. Department of State, made a grant to establish the IFF as the first nonprofit organization to promote better world understanding through films. Julien Bryan became its executive director, assuming the dual role of producer and distributor. In 1947 he produced some of the first educational films dealing with racial prejudice, and later introduced non-narrative films in this area to "promote better understanding between people of different nations, races, and religions through the production of motion pictures." In 1948 a second gift placed the IFF on an independent operation basis. IFF has produced over 50 documentaries on life in countries all over the world.

Bryan began his motion picture career in 1939 while traveling in Russia. He was then the only foreign correspondent to record the siege of Warsaw. His films were shown at the White House during the Roosevelt administration. During W.W. II, the U.S. Government asked Bryan to create a series of films explaining South America to U.S. audiences. He was also asked to do a series of films on small town life in the U.S. that were translated into 40 languages for international distribution. Some of the films in their collection contain live footage of present day conditions in the country the film is about. Historical passages are done in animation by well known animators. The IFF catalog contains quotes from reviews written by children. Mr. Bryan died in 1974, and his son is now heading the business.

JANUS FILMS, 745 5th Ave., New York, N.Y. 10022. Distribute films from the Children's Film Foundation of England, and classic film programs.

KAROL MEDIA, East 36A Midland Ave., Paramus, N.J. 07652. A new company whose catalog shows National Geographic films and science films.

THE PLEASURE IS MUTUAL, from Connecticut Films, Inc.

LAWREN PRODUCTION, P. O. Bx. 666, Mendocino, Cal. 95460. Current topical films.

LEARNING CORPORATION OF AMERICA, 1350 Ave. of the Americas, New York, N.Y. 10019. Established in 1969, LCA was a subsidiary of Columbia Pictures for 5 years before they were bought by W. F. Hall Printing Co. in 1974. Some of the series listed in their catalog use excerpts from feature films. Their "Many American" series, about children of different nationalities living in the U.S. has won many awards, and some of the films have been shown on television. Their excellent public relations department has promoted their films in schools and libraries. They distribute a series of award-winning television programs on 16mm. All their films come with study guides.

LUCERNE FILMS INC., 7 Bahama Road, Morris Plains, N.J. 17450. Distribute films from the Children's Film Foundation of England.

MACMILLAN FILMS INC., 34 MacQueston Parkway South, Mt. Vernon, N.Y. 10550. Brandon Films, formed in 1940, and Audio/Fleetwood, founded in 1946, were both bought by Crowell, Colliers and Macmillan in 1969. Brandon Films was most important in the field of non-theatrical films in the U.S. Thomas Brandon helped to start the Film Society movement back in 1934. It is generally conceded that he was the first distributor to go to Europe for 16mm films. He was also the first to give synopses of stories of films, as well as other pertinent information in his catalogs, and the first to provide program notes. Brandon's 35mm, non-theatrical Film Festival featured French, Russian, German and Japanese films years before foreign films became popular in the U.S. Probably the best known children's film of all times, THE RED BALLOON, is distributed by this company. WHITE MANE, another classic, is still in the catalog, which lists 50 selected films. Many people active in film distribution today, received their early training with Brandon. Macmillan is carrying on the tradition of Brandon, and their films, and customer relations are excellent.

MASS COMMUNICATIONS INC., 25 Sylvan Rd., Westport, Conn. 06880. Sumner Glimcher has long been known for the documentaries he produces (e.g., ALBERT GIACOMETTI). He now distributes his own films, as well as making films for other distributors.

McGRAW-HILL FILMS, 1221 Ave. of the Americas, New York, N.Y. 10020. McGraw-Hill Films is known for their curriculum materials. In 1968, Contemporary film joined McGraw, which made the company the largest distributor of every type of non-theatrical films. Leo Dratfield of Contemporary Films brought in many creative short films from Eastern European countries. Contemporary Films no longer exists, and today McGraw-Hill has largely gone back to the curriculum material as started by Albert Rosenberg in 1945. Their early projects were devoted to the high school and college levels. The company was the first to distribute films from sources other than their own productions. In 1957 they began distributing films for the elementary grades as well.

J. GARY MITCHELL FILM CO., 2000 Bridgeway, Sausalito, Cal. 94965.

MODERN TALKING PICTURE SERVICE (see Appendix E), 2323 New Hyde Park Rd., New Hyde Park, N.Y. 11040.

ARTHUR MOKIN PRODUCTION INC., 17 West 60 Street, New York, N.Y. 10023. Distributes films produced by Arthur Mokin.

NATIONAL AUDIOVISUAL CENTER, Information Branch, Washington, D.C. 20499. Rents, lends and sells audio-visual material produced by governmental agencies.

NATIONAL FILM BOARD OF CANADA, 1251 Ave. of the Americas, 16th floor, New York, N.Y. 10020. The NFBC makes some of their films available to American audiences free of charge through the Canadian Consulate. The majority of their films are available for purchase through the Canadian and American offices of the NFBC, and for loan from commercial distributors and university libraries in the U.S. The NFBC is a government agency which was established in 1939 to review government film activities and to advise the Governor of Canada. Their function is to promote the production and distribution of films of national interest, and to be the official film maker and distributor of Canadian films related to the common interest of Canadians, and interests they can share with people in countries around the world. Recognized as one of the leading producers of short films, NFBC has been able to do experimentation with this medium, partially because of government support, but mostly because of their enlightened leadership. The quality of their films is outstanding, and they produced experimental films long before others had the funds to do so, or the encouragement needed. Both the McClaren films and the many other experimental films listed in their catalog have won many awards.

NATIONAL GEOGRAPHIC SOCIETY, 17th & M Street, Washington, D.C. 20036.

NBC-TV, 30 Rockefeller Plaza, New York, N.Y. 10020. Established to bring NBC documentaries and network specials to the educational community shortly after broadcast, their catalog includes complete individual programs, segments of "First Tuesday" and documentaries and specials. Their catalog goes back to the 1968-69 season, and their films are available through many of the university libraries.

NET FILM SERVICE, Audiovisual Center, Indiana University, Bloomington, Ind. 47401.

NEW YORKER FILMS, 43 West 61 Street, New York, N.Y. 10023.

ODEON, 1619 B'way, New York, N.Y. 10019.

PARAMOUNT COMMUNICATIONS see ACI FILMS

PARENTING PICTURES, R. D. One, Box 355B, Columbia, N.Y. 07832.

PERENNIAL EDUCATION, 1825 Willow, Northfield, Ill. 60093.

PERSPECTIVE FILMS, 369 W. Erie Street, Chicago, Ill. 60610. Art of film series for high school and college.

PHOENIX FILMS INC., 470 Park Ave. South, New York, N.Y. 10011. Barbara Bryant, Leo Dratfield and Heinz Geller formed this company in 1973 after being active in the film distribution world for many years. Leo Dratfield, one of the original principals of Contemporary Films, was in charge of acquisitions until he joined Films Inc. in 1975. Films from many award winning producers, Jiri Trnka films, films from NFBC, and a group of films by Robin Lehman are included in their catalog.

PICTURE FILMS, 111 8th Ave., New York, N.Y. 10011.

PYRAMID FILMS, P. O. Box 1048, Santa Monica, Cal. 90406. Founded about 16 years ago by David and Eileen Adams, this leading west coast distributor now sells and rents films of which approximately 25 percent are produced by the company itself. The remainder come from independent film makers and producers, including Saul Bass, Reader's Digest, CBS, Charles Braverman, ABC Media Concepts and NFBC. Pyramid specializes in short films, and distributes the Kemp Niver series, "The First Twenty Years." Their film study collections are excellent, and they list many films on film making, including the Academy Award winner FRANK FILM, and films on current topics. Pyramid runs workshops for teachers, and is one of the very active company in the U.S.

SCREENSCOPE INC., 1022 Wilson Blvd., Arlington, Va. 22209.

SIM see WESTON WOODS STUDIOS INC.

STERLING EDUCATIONAL FILMS, 241 East 34 Street, New York, N.Y. 10016. The company goes back some 31 years, but its real growth started with the acquisition of the Walter Read Organization in 1963. Len Feldman spearheaded the expansion. They distribute MGM films, the post 1950 Paramount library, a number of 20th Century-Fox films, RKO, Disney and Republic films. They are interested in the film study movement.

TEXTURE FILMS, 1600 Broadway, New York, N.Y. 10019. Texture Films began by distributing the films of their two principals, Sonya Friedman and Herman Engel. Herman Engel is the producer of the 1973 award winning film ABOUT SEX. Today the company distributes such films as ANANSI THE SPIDER and ARROW TO THE SUN by Gerald McDermott, BIG TOWN by Eliot Noyes Jr., THE ITALIAN IN ALGIERS by Luzzati and Gianini, and films on topics of current concern. Texture has helped many young film makers.

TIME-LIFE MULTIMEDIA, 1271 Ave. of the Americas, New York, N.Y. 10020. Their catalog lists the BBC 13-part series "Of Man and Science," THE ASCENT OF MAN seen on NET in 1975, "Vision On" a new children's series that originated in England and others.

TRICONTINENTAL FILM CENTER, 333 Ave. of the Americas, New York, N.Y. 10014.

TWYMAN FILMS INC., 329 Salem Ave., Dayton, Ohio 45401. A distribution of all types of films, old and new, at competitive prices. Now in their 41st year.

WARD'S NATURAL SCIENCESTAB, Modern Learning Aids Div., P. O. Box 1712, Rochester, N.Y. 14603.

WESTON WOODS STUDIOS INC., Weston, Conn. 06880. In 1956 Morton Schindel founded the Weston Woods Studio,

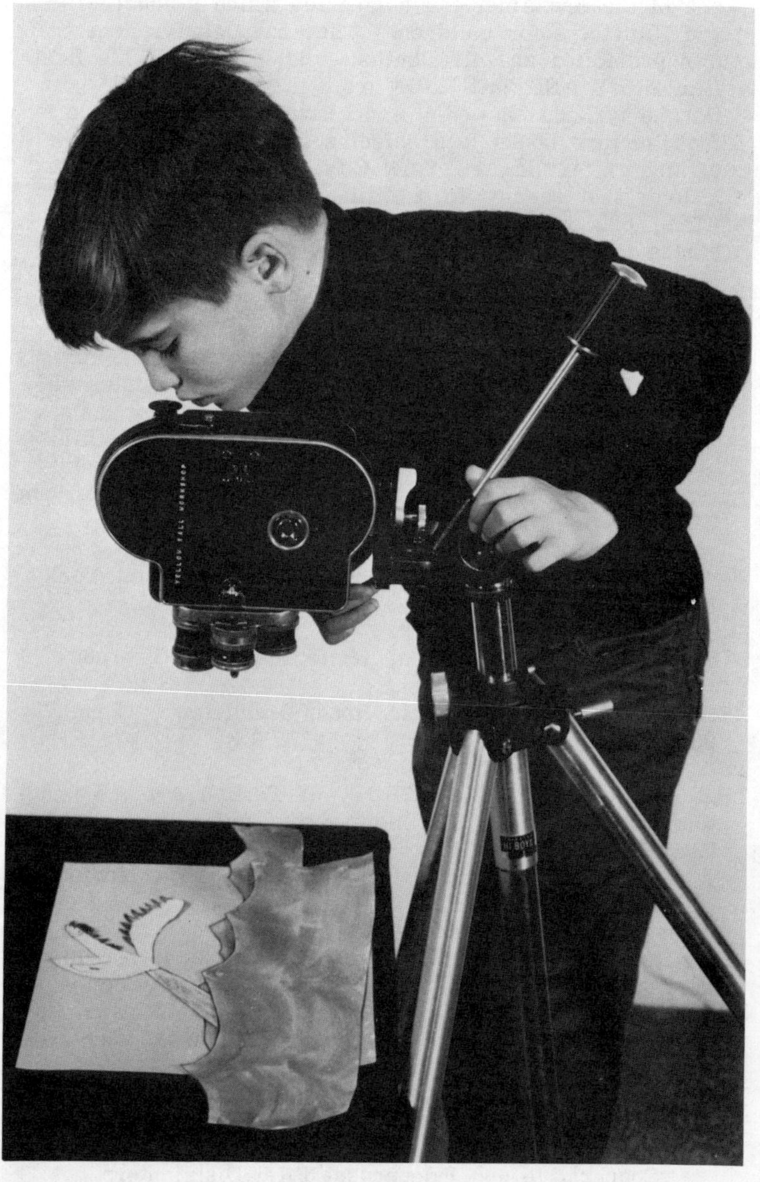

Paul Falcone working on his UNDERWATER CREATURES, from Yellow Ball Workshop.

one of the few American companies which produced films and filmstrips for children. They have always done their own promotion and distribution. Schindel made his first film ANDY AND THE LION from the book by Jack Daugherty, and showed it, with five other films made from picture books to a select audience at the Museum of Modern Art in New York City. Despite the negative attitude that seemed to prevail concerning the use of films, 600 educators and librarians, as well as many others interested in films attended the showing. The studio has been the leader in the production of films, filmstrips and other media based on children's books for many years. Schindel's main technique at first was iconographic, which is still being used, but more and more of his newer films are animated, or a mixture of the two.

SIM is a subsidiary of Weston Woods. Their films are more provocative than those of the parent organization. MR. KOUMAL, a series of one minute shorts, and GIANTS are excellent discussion starters.

WNET/13 MEDIA SERVICES, 356 W. 58th St., New York, N.Y. 10019.

WOMBAT, 77 Tarrytown Rd., White Plains, N.Y. 10607.

XEROX FILMS, 245 Long Hill Road, Middletown, Conn. 06457.

THE YELLOW BALL WORKSHOP, 62 Tarbell Ave., Lexington, Mass. 02173. The most active studio in the production of youth-made films, Yvonne Andersen has been a leader in this field since the late 1960s. The studio now distributes 21 reels of prize-winning films. There are classes for children and adults in Lexington, and at other institutions throughout the country. Ms. Andersen is currently the animation instructor at the Rhode Island School of Design. See Audio-Visual Communications (Sept. 1977) for a write up of a recent class project.

YOUNG FILM MAKERS WORKSHOP, New York, N.Y.

Cooperative and Independent Film Distributors

CANYON CINEMA COOP, Independent Center Bldg. Room 220, Sausalito, Cal. 94965. A nonprofit cooperative

UNDERWATER CREATURES, from "Yellow Ball Cache," a product of Yellow Ball Workshop.

distribution center for independent film makers. Catalog $2.

FILM-MAKER'S COOP, 175 Lexington Ave., New York, N.Y. 10016.

IMPACT FILMS, 144 Bleeker Street, New York, N.Y. 10012.

PHILADELPHIA FILMMAKERS COOP, 2226 Frameford, Philadelphia, Pa. 19103. Films on current topics.

POLYMORPH FILMS, 331 Newburry Street, Boston, Mass. 02115. Films on current topics.

SERIOUS BUSINESS CO., 1609 Jayne Street, Berkeley, Cal. 94703.

THIRD WORLD NEWSREEL, 160 5th Ave., R. 911, New York, N.Y. 10010.

WOMEN'S FILM COOP, 200 Main Street, Northhampton, Mass. 01060.

Religious Film Distributors

THE BROADCASTING AND FILM COMMISSION, National Council of Churches, 475 Riverside Dr. R. 860, New York, N.Y. 10027.

JEWISH MEDIA SERVICE, on the campus of Brandeis University, Lown Judaic Center, 415 S Street, Waltham, Mass. 02154.

MASS MEDIA MINISTRIES, 2116 North Charles Street, Baltimore, Md. 21218.

Reference. The Film Bandit Strikes Again, or Copyright Law and the Non-Theatrical Film User. From Non-Theatrical Film Distribution Assn., 40 West 57 Street, New York, N.Y. 10019. Clarifies copyright laws as they relate to non-theatrical film exhibitors.

Sources of Videocassettes

Many non-theatrical distributors are issuing more and more 16mm films on videocassettes. Videodisc player units sell for as little as $500. With features like 10 speeds, freeze-frame settings, and counters to locate frames, the units are hard to compete with.

The following companies handle videocassettes, but send preview prints only on 16mm (see previous listings for missing addresses):

AMERICAN EDUCATIONAL FILMS, 132 Nasky Dr., Beverly Hills, Cal. 90212.
FILM FAIR COMMUNICATIONS, P. O. Box 1728, Studio City, Cal. 91604.
FILMS FOR THE HUMANITIES, P. O. Box 2053, Princeton, N.J. 08540.
FILMS INC.
INDIANA UNIVERSITY A/V CENTER, Bloomington, Ind. 47401.
INTERNATIONAL FILM BUREAU
McGRAW-HILL
MEDIA FIVE, 3211 Cahuenga Blvd., West Hollywood, Cal. 90068.
NATIONAL AUDIOVISUAL CENTER
PHOENIX FILMS

POLYMORPH FILMS, 331 Newburry St., Boston, Mass. 02115.
PYRAMID FILMS
ROUNDTABLE FILMS, 113 North San Vincente Blvd., Beverly Hills, Cal. 90211.

Major Distributors for Educational Television Networks

PBS PUBLIC TELEVISION LIBRARY, 475 L'Enfant Plaza, S.W., Washington, D.C. 20024.
GREAT PLAINS NATIONAL INSTRUCTIONAL TV LIBRARY, P. O. Box 80669, Lincoln, Neb. 68500.
AUDIOVISUAL CENTER, University of Indiana.
UNIVERSITY OF CALIFORNIA EXTENSION MEDIA CENTER, 2223 Fulton St., Berkeley, Cal. 94720. Newsletter EMC-ONE, and EMC-TWO, published twice a year.
PENN STATE UNIVERSITY AUDIOVISUAL CENTER, Willard Bldg., University Park, Pa. 16802.
EFLA, 43 West 61 Street, New York, N.Y. 10023.
AMERICAN ASSOCIATION FOR THE ADVANCEMENT OF SCIENCE, 1515 Mass. Ave., N.W., Washington, D.C. 20023.
MEDCOME INC., 2 Hammarskjold Plaza, New York, N.Y. 10001.
WNET/13 MEDIA SERVICES, 356 W. 58 St., New York, N.Y. 10019. Free catalog.

Distributors Using Both Videocassettes and 16mm Format
(Some of these sell videocassettes cheaper than 16mm films. Others charge the same rates.)

AGENCY FOR INSTRUCTIONAL TELEVISION, Box A, Bloomington, Ind. 47401.
PERENNIAL EDUCATION
TIME-LIFE MULTI-MEDIA

References

Trojan, Judith, "Film and Video: Film Distributors Comment on the Impact of the Videocassette and Videodisc on 16mm Usage," Media & Methods, May/June 1977, pp. 48+.

Media & Methods, October 1977. Special video issue.

Additional Sources of Educational Videotapes (from Sightlines, Winter 1977/78, p. 7)

Castelli-Sonnabend Tapes and Films, 420 West B'way, New York, N.Y. 10012.
Electronic Arts Internis Inc., 84 5th Ave., New York, N.Y. 10011.
Great Plains National Instructional Television Library, Box 80669, Lincoln, Neb. 68501.
Heritage Visual Sales, 508 Church St., Toronto, Ontario; New York Office: Ann Selt-Petrach, 368 Clinton St., New York, N.Y. 11231.
KCET-TV, 4400 Sunset Dr., Los Angeles, Cal. 90027.
Maryland Center for Public Broadcasting, 11767 Bonita Ave., Owing Mills, Md. 21117.
University Community Video, Studio A, Rarig Center, University of Minnesota, Minneapolis, MN 55455
University of Southern California, Division of Public Broadcasting, University Park, Los Angeles, Cal. 90007.
Video Tape Network, 115 E. 62 St., New York, N.Y. 10021.
WGBH Educational Foundation, 125 Western Ave., Boston, Mass. 02134.
Western Instructional Television, 1549 N. Vine St., Los Angeles, Cal. 90028.

University Film Libraries

As a rule, University Film Libraries serve as rental and purchase agents for films produced by independent film makers, television programs produced by educational TV, films made by organizations and schools who want to see their films distributed commercially, and in general, as a less expensive source of films than commercial distributors. Some of the larger libraries issue several catalogs on special topics, and some publish newsletters, listing their latest acquisitions.

The following list contains information as of November 1977. Except where so stated, the libraries listed will rent films anywhere in the U.S. Some sell films as well as rent them, and some produce their own films. Write to the library nearest you for pertinent information:

1. Boston University, School of Education, Krasker Memorial Library, 765 Commonwealth Ave., Boston, Mass. 02215. Free catalog; 9000 prints.

2. Brigham Young University, Media Selection, 290HRCB, Provo, Utah 84601. Free catalog to customers,

charge to others; videotapes and films. Distributes some of their own films on special education, and special topics. Has 6,800 prints; double rental charge outside the six intermountain states.

3. University of California, Extension Media Center, 2223 Fulton Street, Berkeley, Cal. 94720. Free catalog; 13,000+ prints.

4. University of Southern California, Film Distribution Center, Division of Cinema, University Park, Los Angeles, Cal. 90007. Catalog $1; many special lists, from many departments; 4,500 prints.

5. University of Colorado, Educational Media Center, Film Library, Boulder, Colo. 80309. Some videotapes; free catalog; 5,200 prints.

6. Hawaii State Library, Audiovisual Unit, 478 S. King Street, Honolulu, Hawaii 96813. Free loans to state of Hawaii residents only. Catalog $2; 1,525 titles, 1,725 prints.

7. University of Connecticut, Film Library, Storrs, Conn. 06268. Rents to Eastern U.S. only; free catalog; 7,000 prints.

8. University of Illinois, Visual Aids Service, 1325 Oak Street, Champaign, Ill. 61820. Free catalog to customers, $5 to others; 33,000 prints. The Lens and the Speaker, published 4/year, featuring special topics (e.g., in Fall 1976 issue, articles and selected bibliography on sports films; in Spring 1977 issue, and BBC filmography).

9. Indiana State Audiovisual Center, Terre Haute, Ind. 47809. For Indiana and surrounding states only. Free catalog.

10. Indiana University Audiovisual Center, Bloomington, Ind. 47401. Free catalog to schools and libraries, $5 to others. One of the most active film libraries in the country; 12,000 titles; 38,000 prints.

11. Kent State University, Audiovisual Services, Kent, Ohio 44242. Free catalog to libraries, media centers, resource centers, A/V departments, $5 to individuals; 8,100 titles; 9,700 prints.

12. University of Michigan Audiovisual Center, 416 4th Street, Ann Arbor, Mich. 48103.

13. Michigan State University, Learning Resource Division, Instructional Media Center, East Lansing, Mich. 48823. Catalog, first copy free, $3 additional copies; 4,000 titles.

14. New York University, Film Library, 26 Washington Plaza, New York, N.Y. 10003. Catalog $1; 2,000 prints.

15. University of Minnesota, Audiovisual Library Service, 3300 University Ave., Minneapolis, Minn. 55414. Catalog $6; 5,500 titles.

16. University of New Hampshire, Audiovisual Center, Durham, N.H. 03820. Free catalog; 3,006 titles.

17. University of Northern Illinois, Media Distribution, Altgeld 114, Division of Communications Services, De Kalb, Ill. 60115. Free catalog (publ. 2/year); 4,000 titles; 4,500 prints.

18. Oklahoma State University, Audiovisual Center, Stillwater, Okla. 74074. Free catalog; 5,000 titles.

19. Penn State University, Audiovisual Services, Special Services Bldg., University Park, Pa. 16802. Also rents videotapes and videocassettes. Free catalog; 14,000 titles.

20. Syracuse University, Film Rental Center, 1455 East Colvin Street, Syracuse, N.Y. 13210. Free catalog to customers in the Eastern U.S.; 16,000 prints.

21. University of Utah, Educational Media Center, 207 Milton Bennion Hall, Salt Lake City, Utah 84112. Free catalog; 5,000 prints.

22. University of Wisconsin, Bureau of Audiovisual Instruction, 1327 University Ave., P. O. Box 2093, Madison, Wisc. 53701. Free catalog; 15,000 titles.

For information on centers in specific areas write to:
James Buterbaught, CUFC President, Instructional Media

Center, 431 Nebraska Hall, University of Nebraska, Lincoln, Neb. 68588.

Film Festivals (partial list)

1. American Film Festival, EFLA, 43 West 61 Street, New York, N.Y. 10023 (since 1958). May

2. Ann Arbor 8mm Film Festival, Ann Arbor Film Cooperative, Box 529, Ann Arbor, Mich. 48107 (since 1969). February

3. Athens International Film/Video Festival, F. F. Chairman, Ohio University, Box 388, Athens, Ohio 45701.

4. Birmingham International Educational Film Festival, Craig Battles, c/o Alabama Power Co., P. O. Box 2641, Birmingham, Ala. 35291 (since 1973). March

5. Chicago International Film Festival, Michael J. Kutza Director, CIFF, 415 N. Dearborn, Chicago, Ill. 60611 (since 1954). November

6. CINE, Council for International Non-Theatrical Events, 1201 16th Street, N.W., Washington, D.C. 20036 (since 1957). November

7. Columbus (Ohio) International Film Festival, Film Council of Greater Columbus, E. Broad Street, Columbus, Ohio (since 1952). October

8. Congress and Festival International Scientific Film Association, Mrs. Ann Seltz, American Association for the Advancement of Science, 1776 Massachusetts Ave., N.W., Washington, D.C. 20005 (since 1946). August

9. Dance Film Festival, Miss Susan Braun, Pres., Dance Film Assn., 250 West 57 Street, New York, N.Y. 10019 (since 1972). June

10. International Animated Film Festival, ASIFA [worldwide organization of animated film makers], affiliated with UNESCO, only held in North America once--Ottowa, Canada, 1976 (since 1957). August

11. International Children's Film Festival, c/o Richard Harmetz, Division of Cinema, University of Southern California, University Park, Los Angeles, Cal. 90007 (since 1969).

12. International Crafts Film Festival, sponsored by New York State Craftsmen Inc., c/o New School for Social Research, 66 West 12 Street, New York, N.Y. 10016 (since 1976).

13. International Ski Festival, Jerry Simon Assn., STE 201, Ruffert Towers, 1619 3rd Ave., New York, N.Y. 10028 (since 1974). October

14. Iranian Children's Film Festival, the one festival featuring entries from countries all over the world, many of which do not get distributed in the U.S.

15. Midwestern Film Conference, 2550 Green Bay Rd., Evanston, Ill. 60201 (since 1969).

16. National Educational Festival, William Pogetto, Chairman. NEFF, 5555 Ascot Drive, Oakland, Cal. 94611 (since 1970). April

17. Northwest Film and Video Festival, (for residents of Oregon, Washington, Idaho, Montana, and British Columbia,) Northwest Film Study Center, Portland Art Museum, S.W. Park & Madison, Portland, Ore. 97205 (since 1969).

18. San Francisco International Film Festival, S.F. Film Festival, 1406 Bush Street, San Francisco, Cal. 94109 (since 1956). October

19. Teenage Film Awards, originally sponsored by the Kodak Corp., now jointly sponsored by the University Film Assn., The University Film Foundation, and CINE, c/o CINE, 1201 16th Street, N.W., Washington, D.C. 20036.

20. U.S.A. Film Festival, U.S.A. Film Festival, Box 3105, Dallas, Tex. 75275. Experimental and documentary films (since 1970).

21. Virgin Island International Film Festival (originally held in Atlanta, Ga.), J. Hunter Todd, Director,

P. O. Box V. I. F. F., St. Thomas, U. S. Virgin Is. 00802 (since 1967). November

22. Visual Anthropology Conference, Temple University, Philadelphia, Pa. 19122. Motion pictures and videotapes, noncompetitive. Alternate years, even numbered (since 1964). March

HOW TO MAKE MOVIES YOUR FRIENDS WILL WANT TO SEE TWICE, from Benchmark Films.

INDEX